BLACK HAMMER '45™

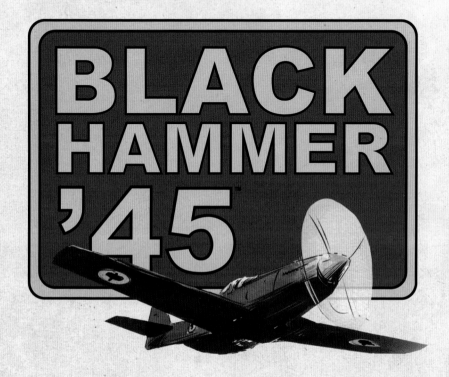

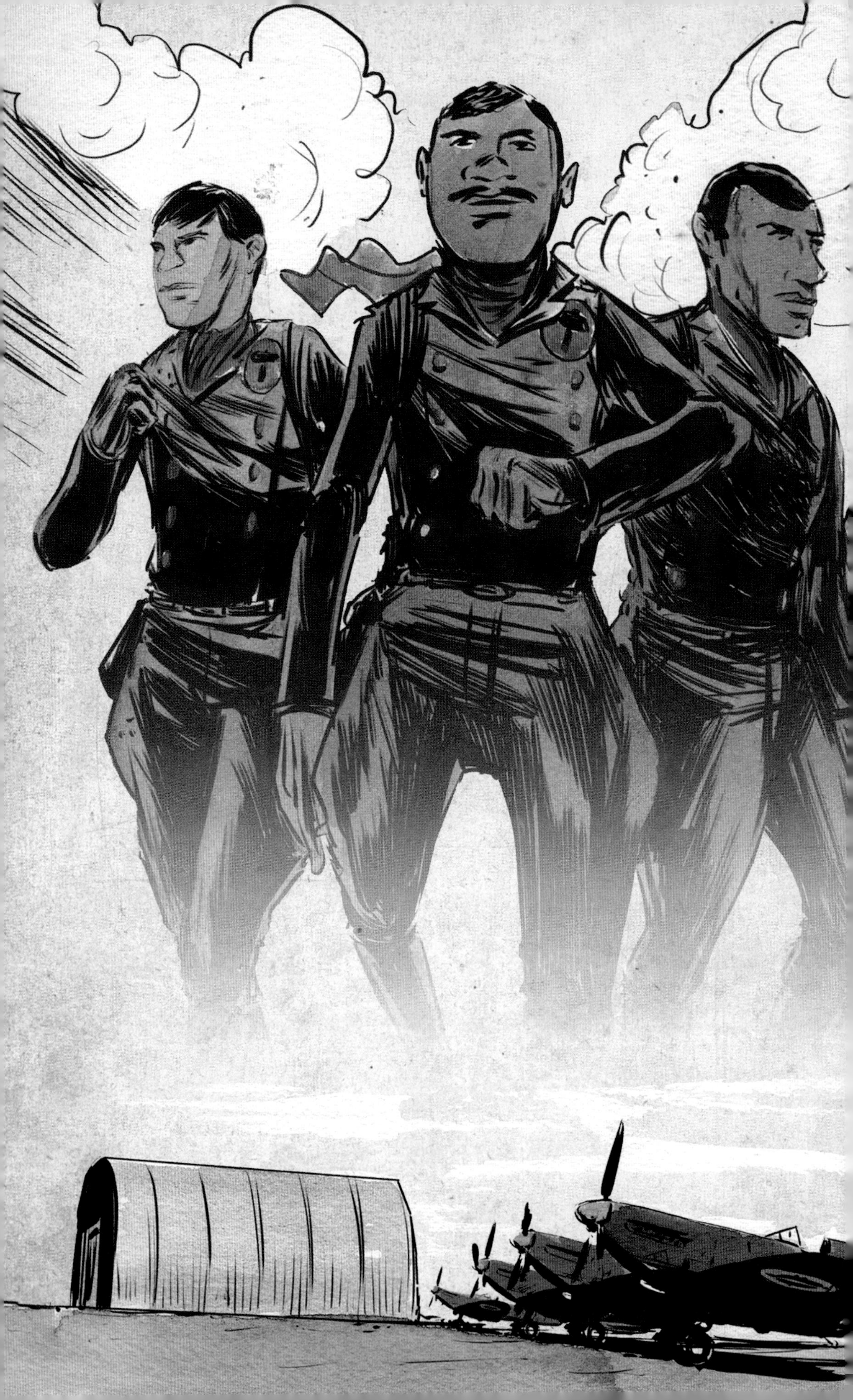

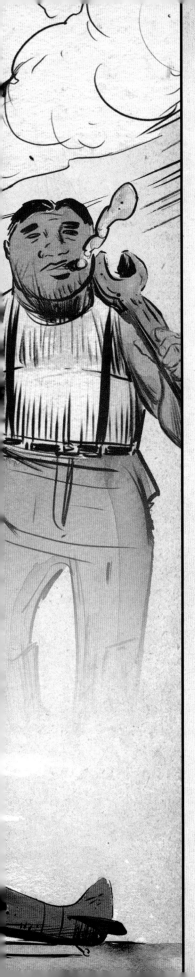

BLACK HAMMER '45

Story by
JEFF LEMIRE AND
RAY FAWKES

Script by
RAY FAWKES

Artist
MATT KINDT

Colorist
SHARLENE KINDT

Letterer
MARIE ENGER

Chapter breaks by
VERONICA FISH, GLENN FABRY WITH **ADAM BROWN,
DENYS COWAN** AND **DON HUDSON** WITH **NOELLE GIDDINGS,**
AND **SANFORD GREENE**

DARK HORSE BOOKS

President & Publisher
MIKE RICHARDSON

Editor
DANIEL CHABON

Assistant Editors
CHUCK HOWITT AND BRETT ISRAEL

Designer
ETHAN KIMBERLING

Digital Art Technician
JOSIE CHRISTENSEN

BLACK HAMMER '45

Collects issues #1–#4 of the Dark Horse Comics series *Black Hammer '45.*

Published by
Dark Horse Books
A division of Dark Horse Comics LLC
10956 SE Main Street
Milwaukie, OR 97222

DarkHorse.com
To find a comics shop in your area, visit comicshoplocator.com

First edition: October 2019
ISBN 978-1-50670-850-8
Digital ISBN: 978-1-50670-872-0

1 3 5 7 9 10 8 6 4 2
Printed in China

Neil Hankerson, Executive Vice President · Tom Weddle, Chief Financial Officer · Randy Stradley, Vice President of Publishing · Nick McWhorter, Chief Business Development Officer · Dale LaFountain, Chief Information Officer · Matt Parkinson, Vice President of Marketing · Cara Niece, Vice President of Production and Scheduling · Mark Bernardi, Vice President of Book Trade and Digital Sales · Ken Lizzi, General Counsel Dave Marshall, Editor in Chief · Davey Estrada, Editorial Director · Chris Warner, Senior Books Editor · Cary Grazzini, Director of Specialty Projects · Lia Ribacchi, Art Director · Vanessa Todd-Holmes, Director of Print Purchasing · Matt Dryer, Director of Digital Art and Prepress · Michael Gombos, Senior Director of Licensed Publications · Kari Yadro, Director of Custom Programs · Kari Torson, Director of International Licensing Sean Brice, Director of Trade Sales

Library of Congress Cataloging-in-Publication Data

Names: Lemire, Jeff, author. | Fawkes, Ray, author. | Kindt, Matt, artist. |
  Kindt, Sharlene, colourist. | Enger, Marie, letterer.
Title: Black Hammer '45 : from the world of Black Hammer / story by Jeff
  Lemire and Ray Fawkes ; script by Ray Fawkes ; artist, Matt Kindt ;
  colorist, Sharlene Kindt ; letterer, Marie Enger.
Description: First edition. | Milwaukie, OR : Dark Horse Books, 2019. |
  "Collects issues #1–#4 of the Dark Horse Comics series Black Hammer '45."
Identifiers: LCCN 2019016374 | ISBN 9781506708508 (paperback)
Subjects: LCSH: Comic books, strips, etc. | BISAC: COMICS & GRAPHIC NOVELS /
  Superheroes. | COMICS & GRAPHIC NOVELS / Fantasy.
Classification: LCC PN6728.B51926 L38 2019 | DDC 741.5/973--dc23
LC record available at https://lccn.loc.gov/2019016374

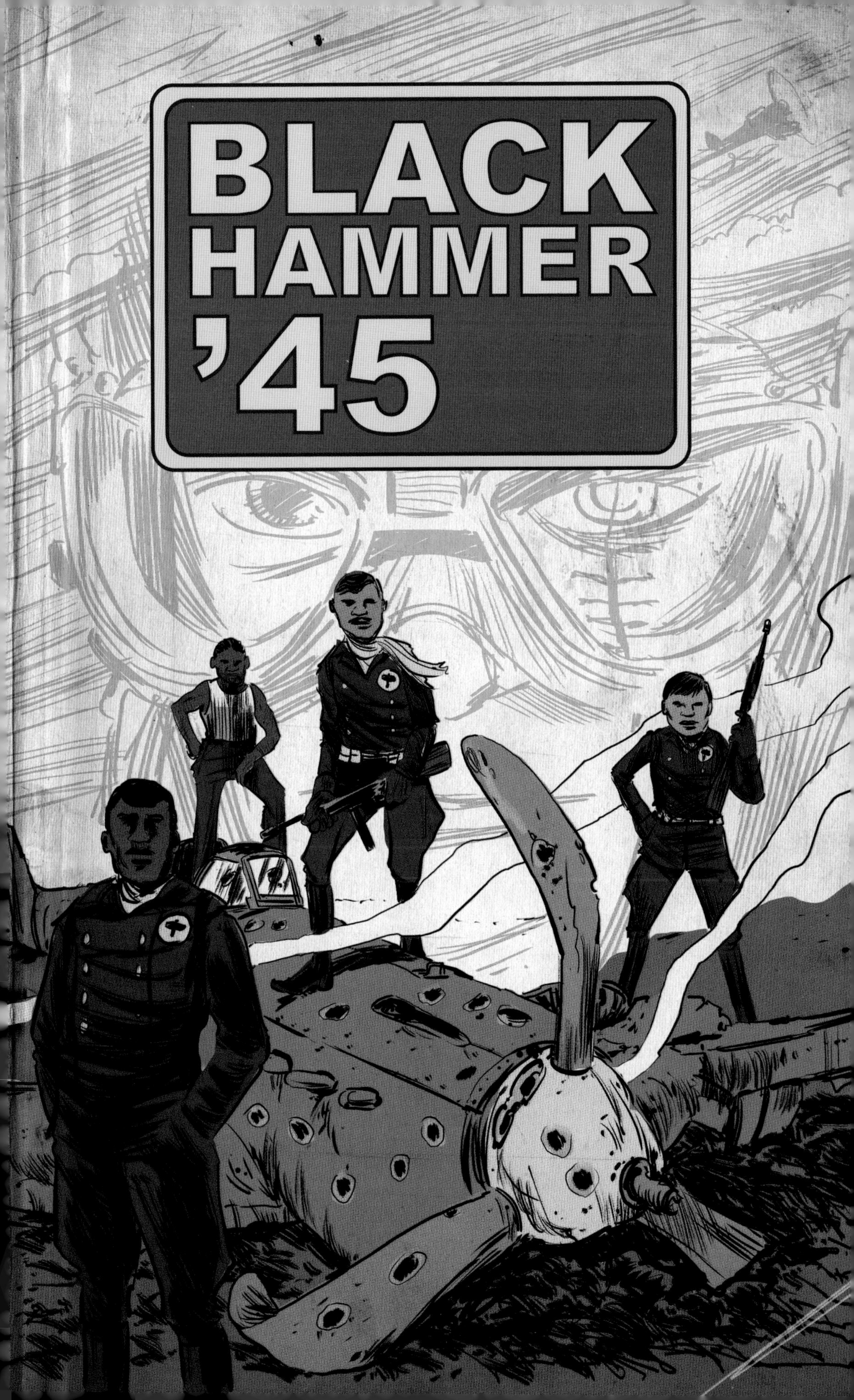
BLACK
HAMMER
'45

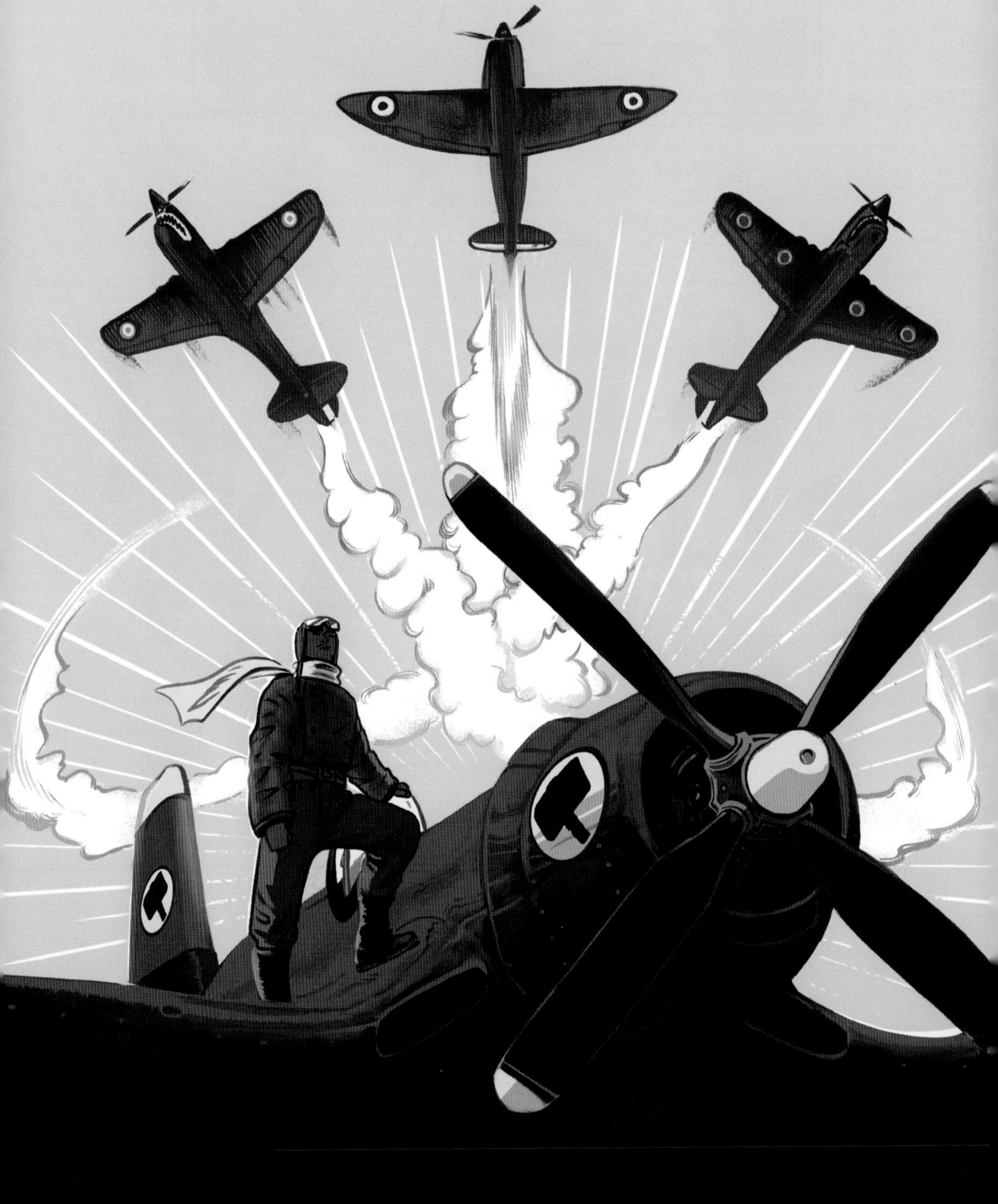

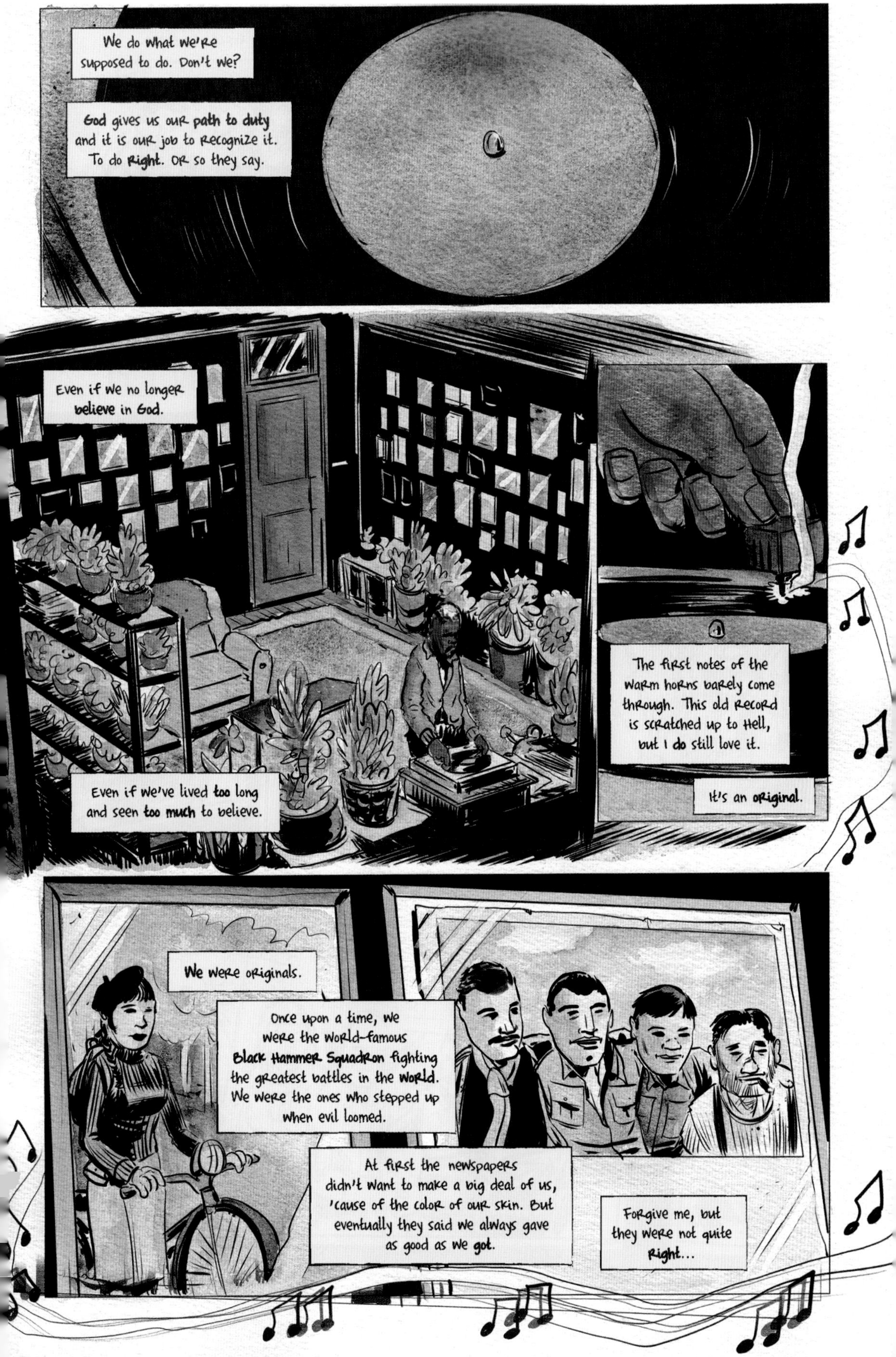
We do what we're supposed to do. Don't we?
God gives us our path to duty and it is our job to recognize it. To do right. Or so they say.
Even if we no longer believe in God.
Even if we've lived too long and seen too much to believe.
The first notes of the warm horns barely come through. This old record is scratched up to Hell, but I do still love it.
It's an original.
We were originals.
Once upon a time, we were the world-famous Black Hammer Squadron fighting the greatest battles in the world. We were the ones who stepped up when evil loomed.
At first the newspapers didn't want to make a big deal of us, 'cause of the color of our skin. But eventually they said we always gave as good as we got.
Forgive me, but they were not quite right...

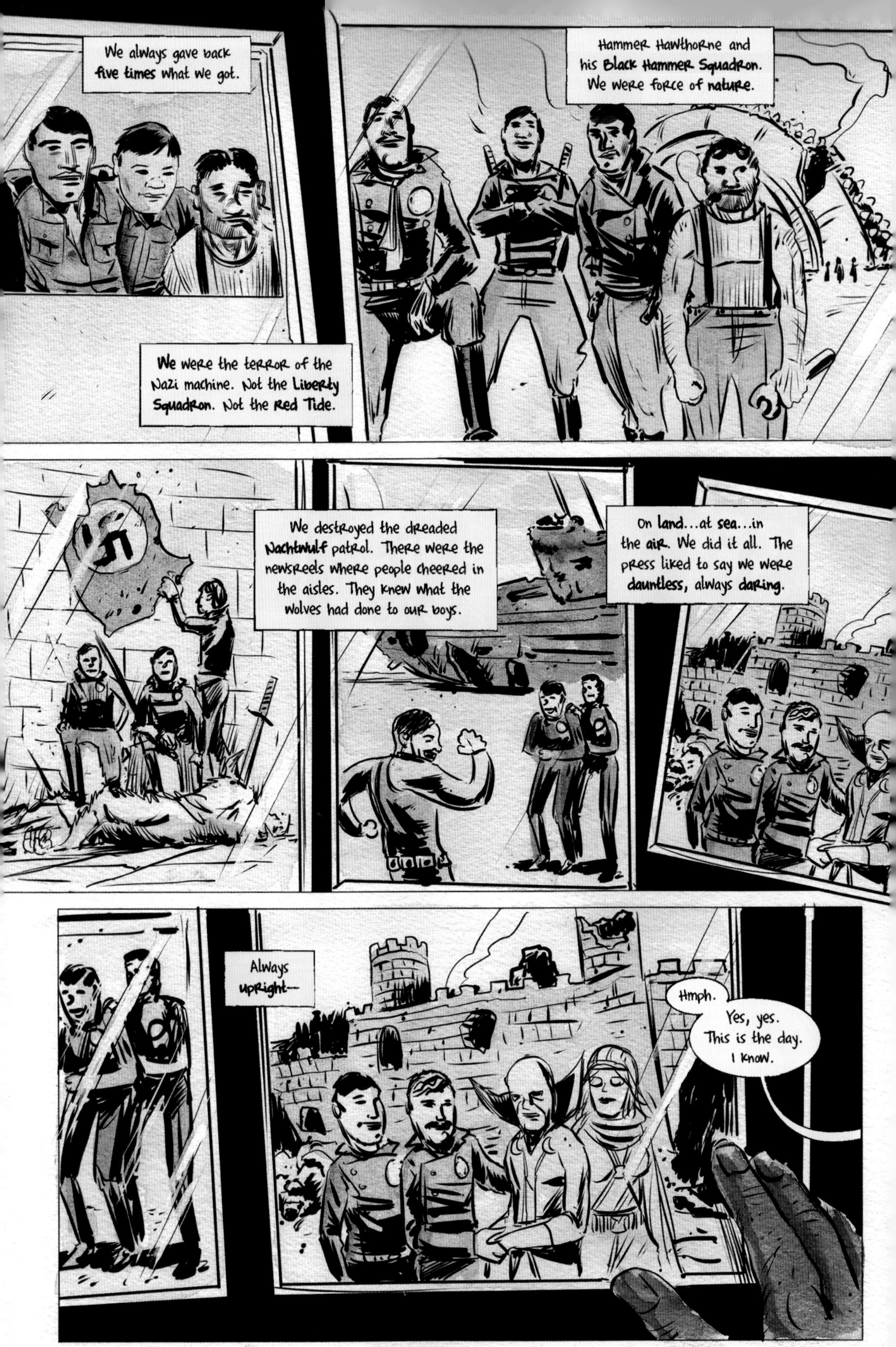

We always gave back five times what we got.
Hammer Hawthorne and his Black Hammer Squadron. We were force of nature.
We were the terror of the Nazi machine. Not the Liberty Squadron. Not the Red Tide.
We destroyed the dreaded Nachtwulf patrol. There were the newsreels where people cheered in the aisles. They knew what the wolves had done to our boys.
On land...at sea...in the air. We did it all. The press liked to say we were dauntless, always daring.
Always upright--
Hmph.
Yes, yes. This is the day. I know.

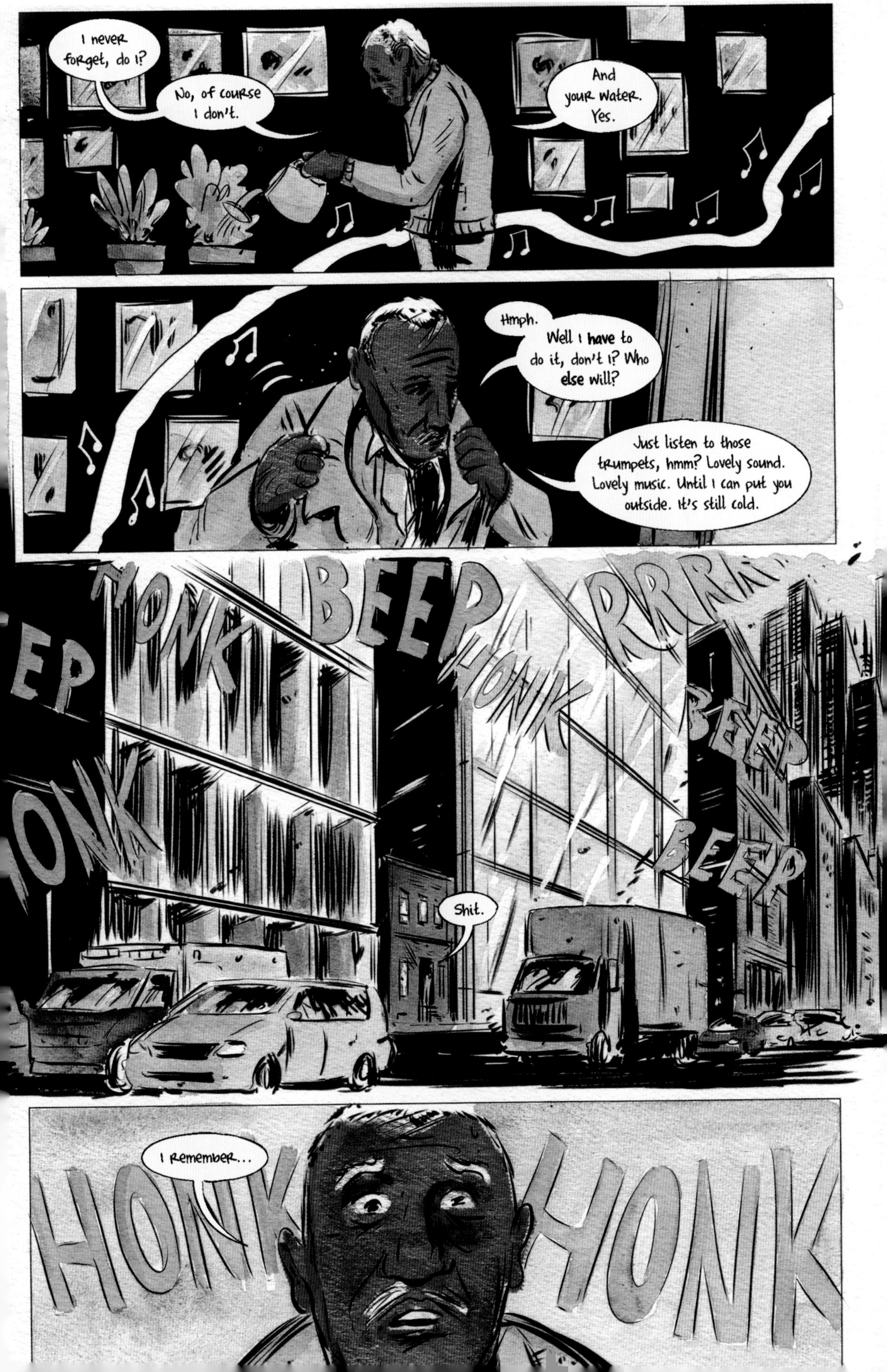
I never forget, do I?
No, of course I don't.
And your water. Yes.
Hmph.
Well I have to do it, don't I? Who else will?
Just listen to those trumpets, hmm? Lovely sound. Lovely music. Until I can put you outside. It's still cold.
HONK
BEEP
RRR
EP
HONK
BEEP
ONK
BEEP
Shit.
I remember...
HONK
HONK

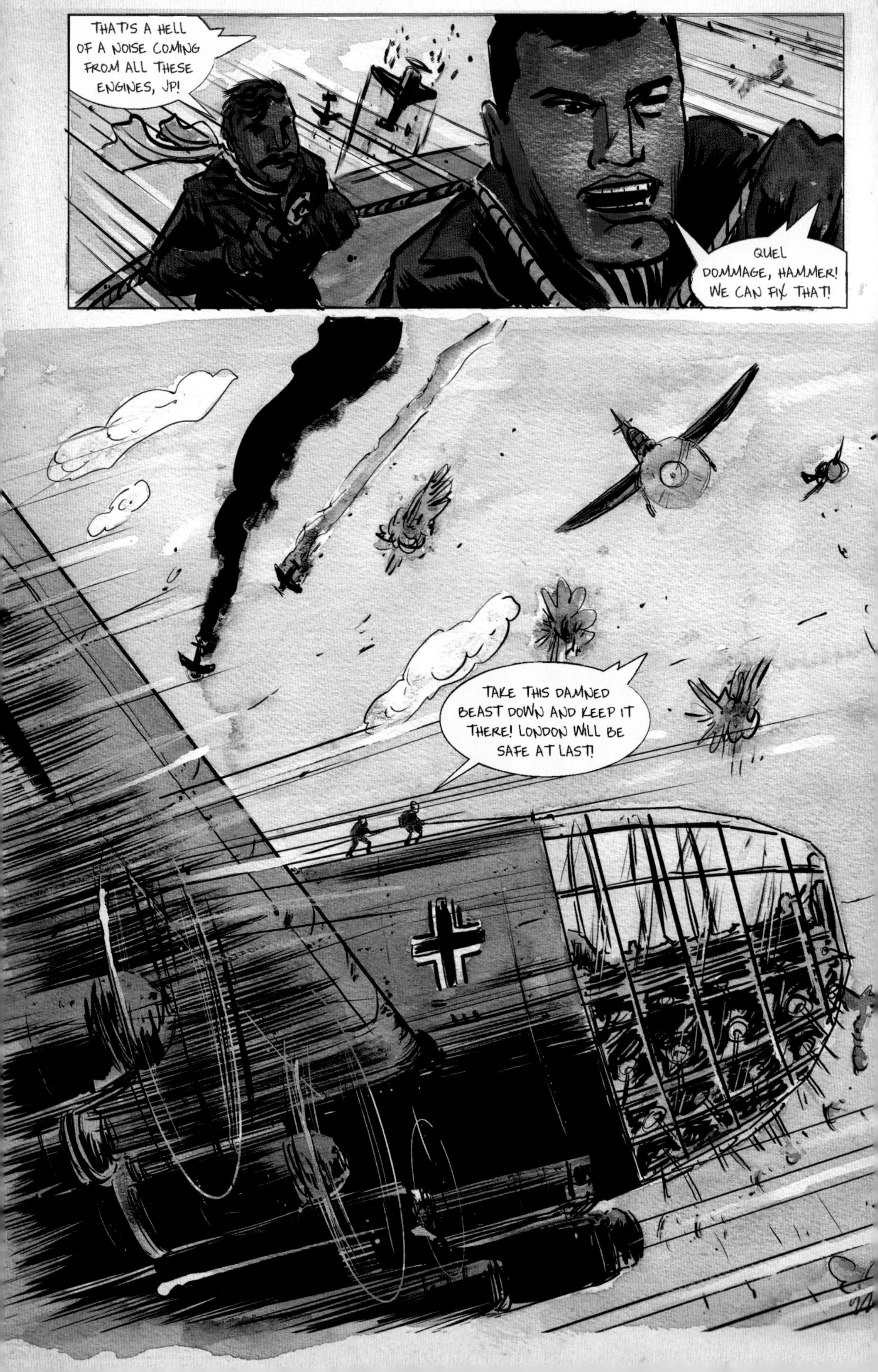
THAT'S A HELL OF A NOISE COMING FROM ALL THESE ENGINES, JP!
QUEL DOMMAGE, HAMMER! WE CAN FIX THAT!
TAKE THIS DAMNED BEAST DOWN AND KEEP IT THERE! LONDON WILL BE SAFE AT LAST!

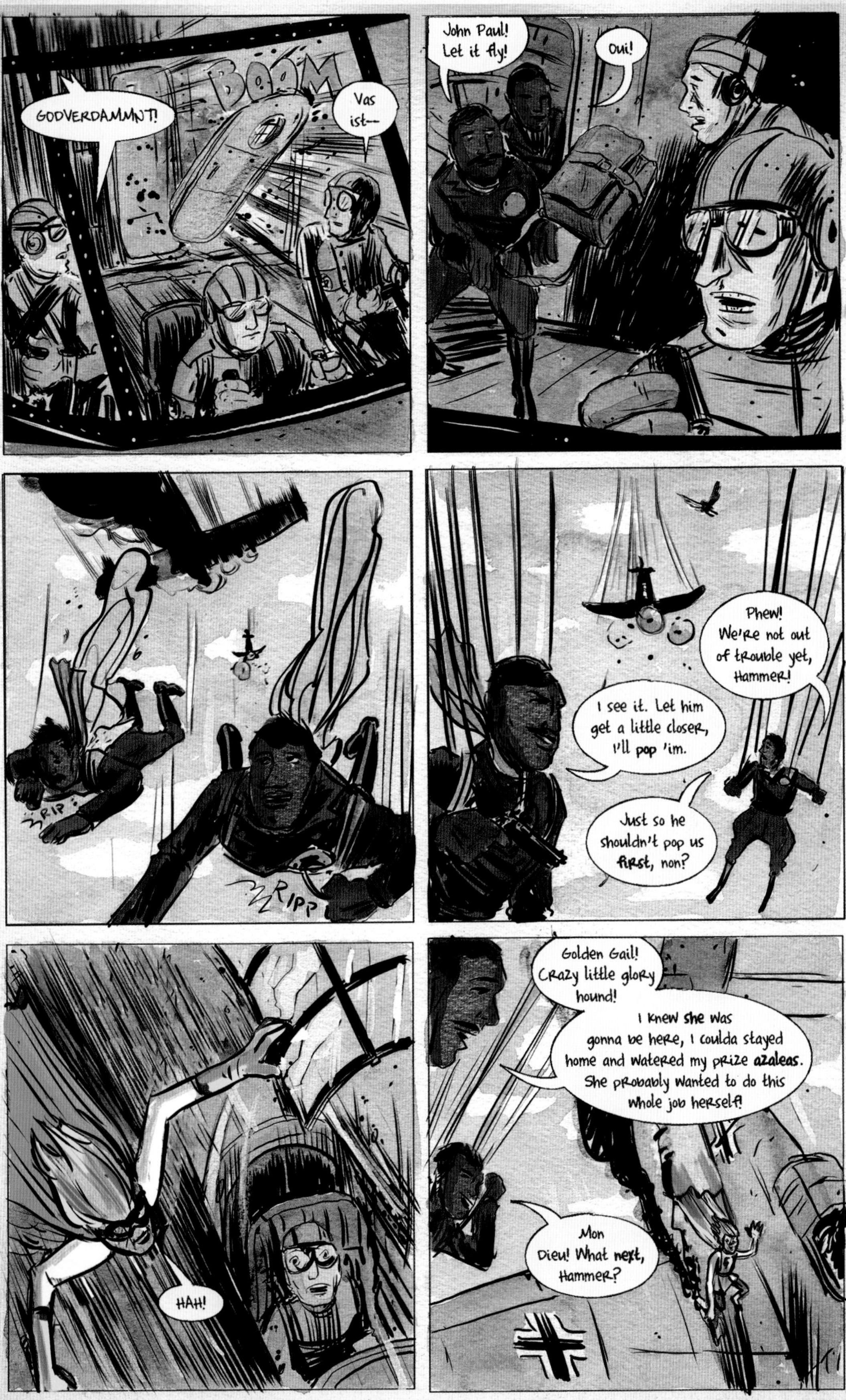
BOOM
GODVERDAMMNT!
Vas ist--
John Paul! Let it fly!
Oui!
RIP
RIPP
Phew! We're not out of trouble yet, Hammer!
I see it. Let him get a little closer, I'll pop 'im.
Just so he shouldn't pop us first, non?
HAH!
Golden Gail! Crazy little glory hound!
I knew she was gonna be here, I coulda stayed home and watered my prize azaleas. She probably wanted to do this whole job herself!
Mon Dieu! What next, Hammer?

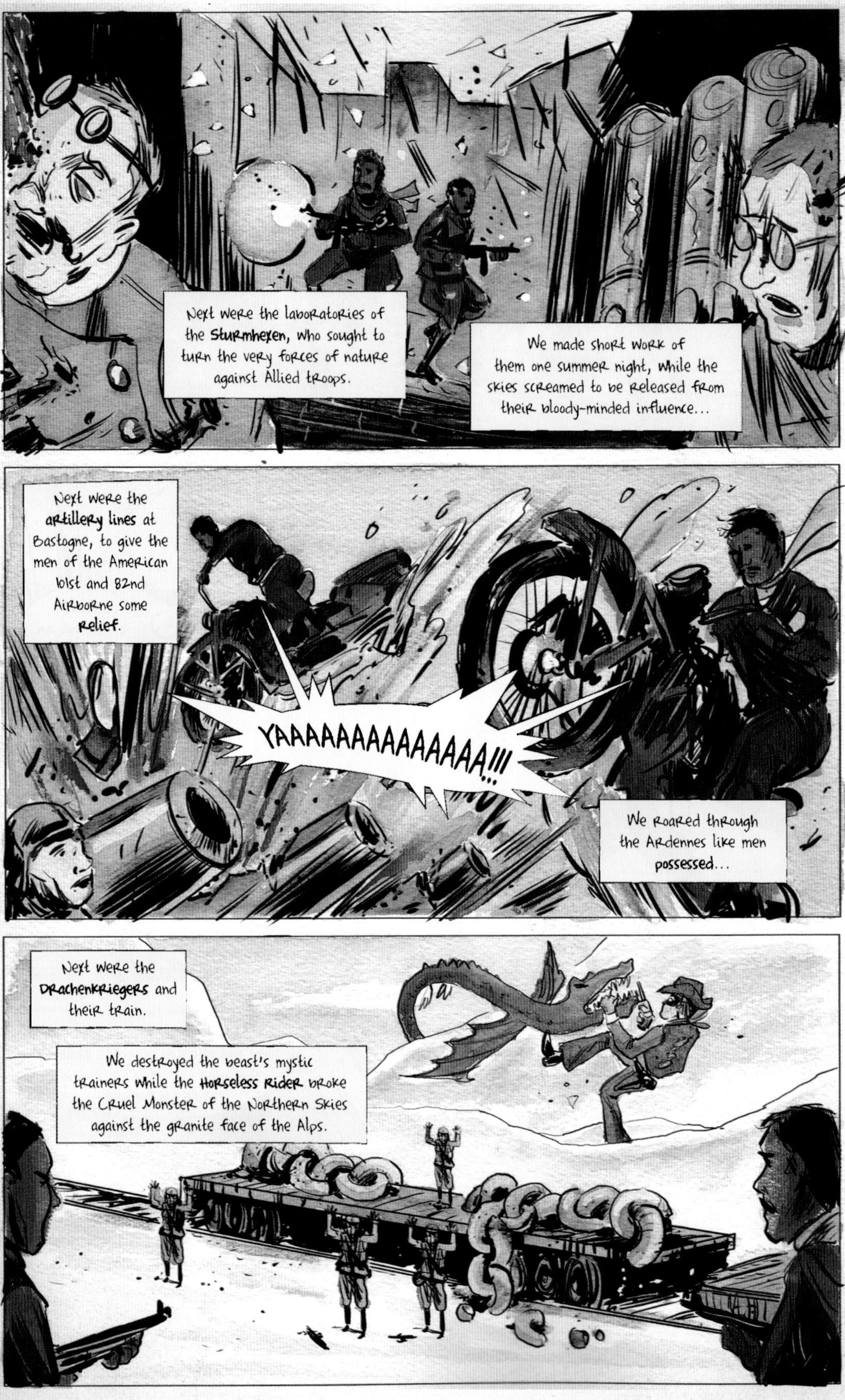
Next were the laboratories of the Sturmhexen, who sought to turn the very forces of nature against Allied troops.
We made short work of them one summer night, while the skies screamed to be released from their bloody-minded influence...
Next were the artillery lines at Bastogne, to give the men of the American 101st and 82nd Airborne some relief.
YAAAAAAAAAAAAAA!!!
We roared through the Ardennes like men possessed...
Next were the Drachenkriegers and their train.
We destroyed the beast's mystic trainers while the Horseless Rider broke the Cruel Monster of the Northern Skies against the granite face of the Alps.

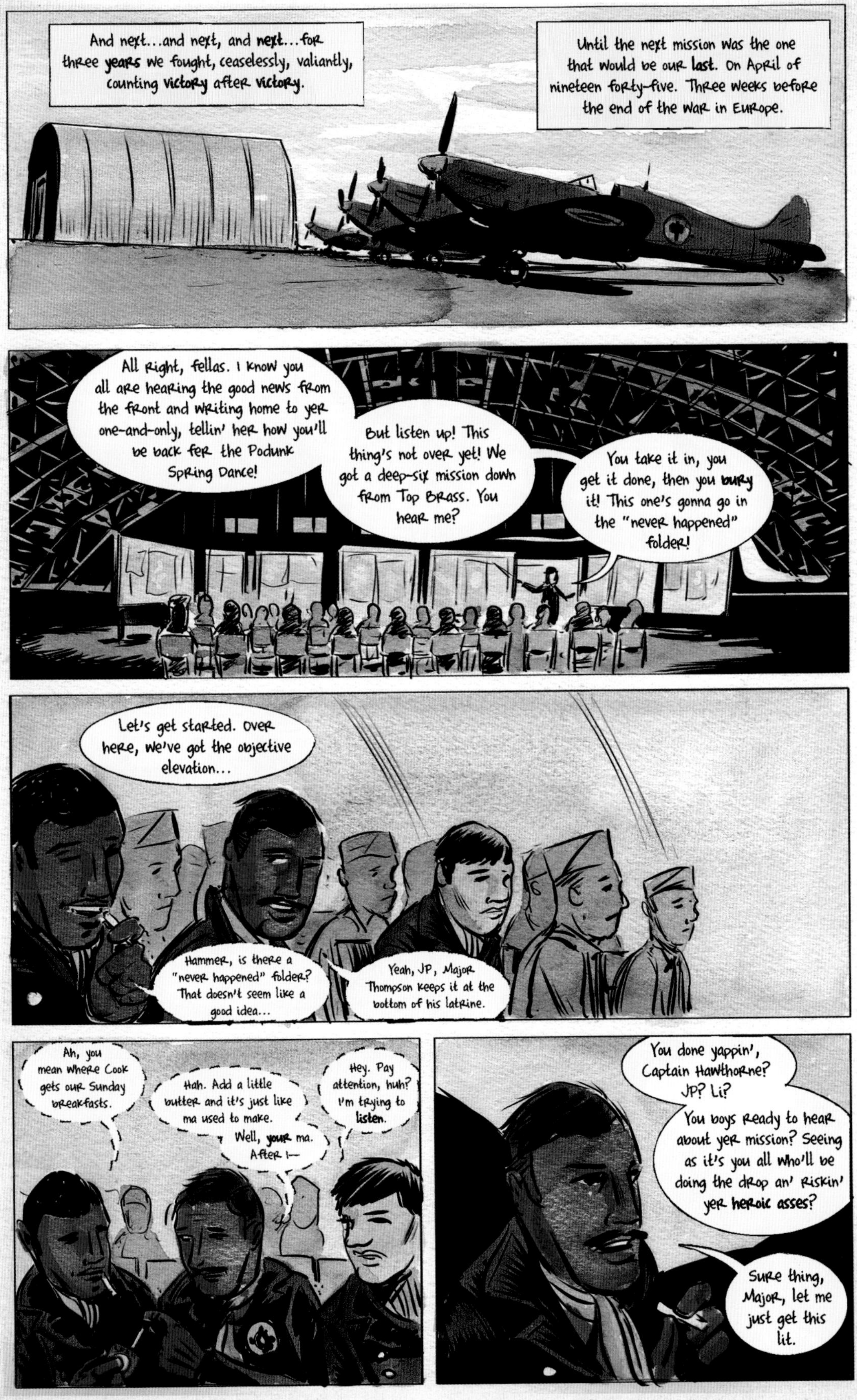
And next...and next, and next...for three years we fought, ceaselessly, valiantly, counting victory after victory.
Until the next mission was the one that would be our last. On April of nineteen forty-five. Three weeks before the end of the war in Europe.
All right, fellas. I know you all are hearing the good news from the front and writing home to yer one-and-only, tellin' her how you'll be back fer the Podunk Spring Dance!
But listen up! This thing's not over yet! We got a deep-six mission down from Top Brass. You hear me?
You take it in, you get it done, then you bury it! This one's gonna go in the "never happened" folder!
Let's get started. Over here, we've got the objective elevation...
Hammer, is there a "never happened" folder? That doesn't seem like a good idea...
Yeah, JP, Major Thompson keeps it at the bottom of his latrine.
Ah, you mean where Cook gets our Sunday breakfasts.
Hah. Add a little butter and it's just like ma used to make.
Well, your ma. After I—
Hey. Pay attention, huh? I'm trying to listen.
You done yappin', Captain Hawthorne? JP? Li?
You boys ready to hear about yer mission? Seeing as it's you all who'll be doing the drop an' riskin' yer heroic asses?
Sure thing, Major, let me just get this lit.

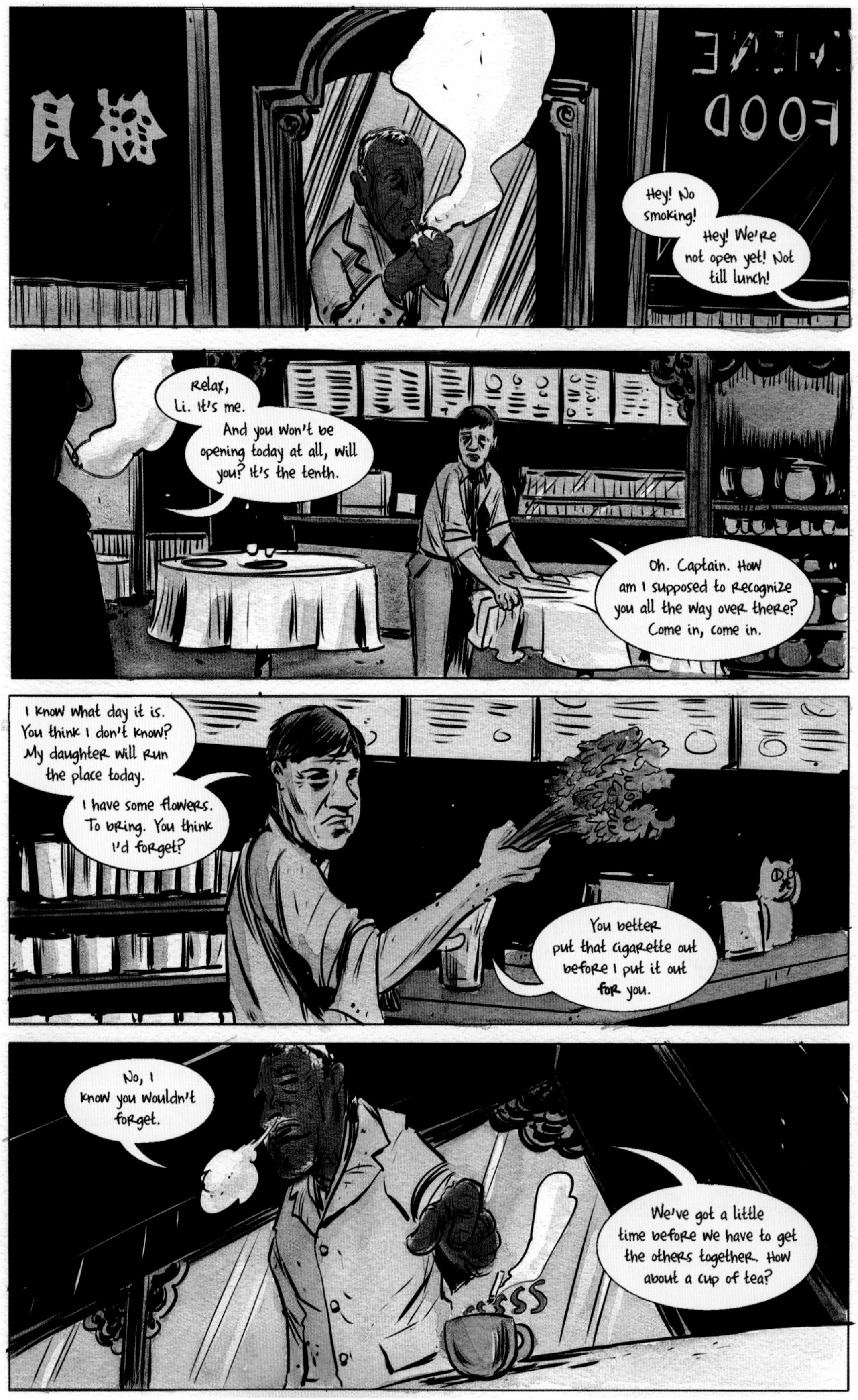
Hey! No smoking!
Hey! We're not open yet! Not till lunch!
Relax, Li. It's me.
And you won't be opening today at all, will you? It's the tenth.
Oh. Captain. How am I supposed to recognize you all the way over there? Come in, come in.
I know what day it is. You think I don't know? My daughter will run the place today.
I have some flowers. To bring. You think I'd forget?
You better put that cigarette out before I put it out for you.
No, I know you wouldn't forget.
We've got a little time before we have to get the others together. How about a cup of tea?

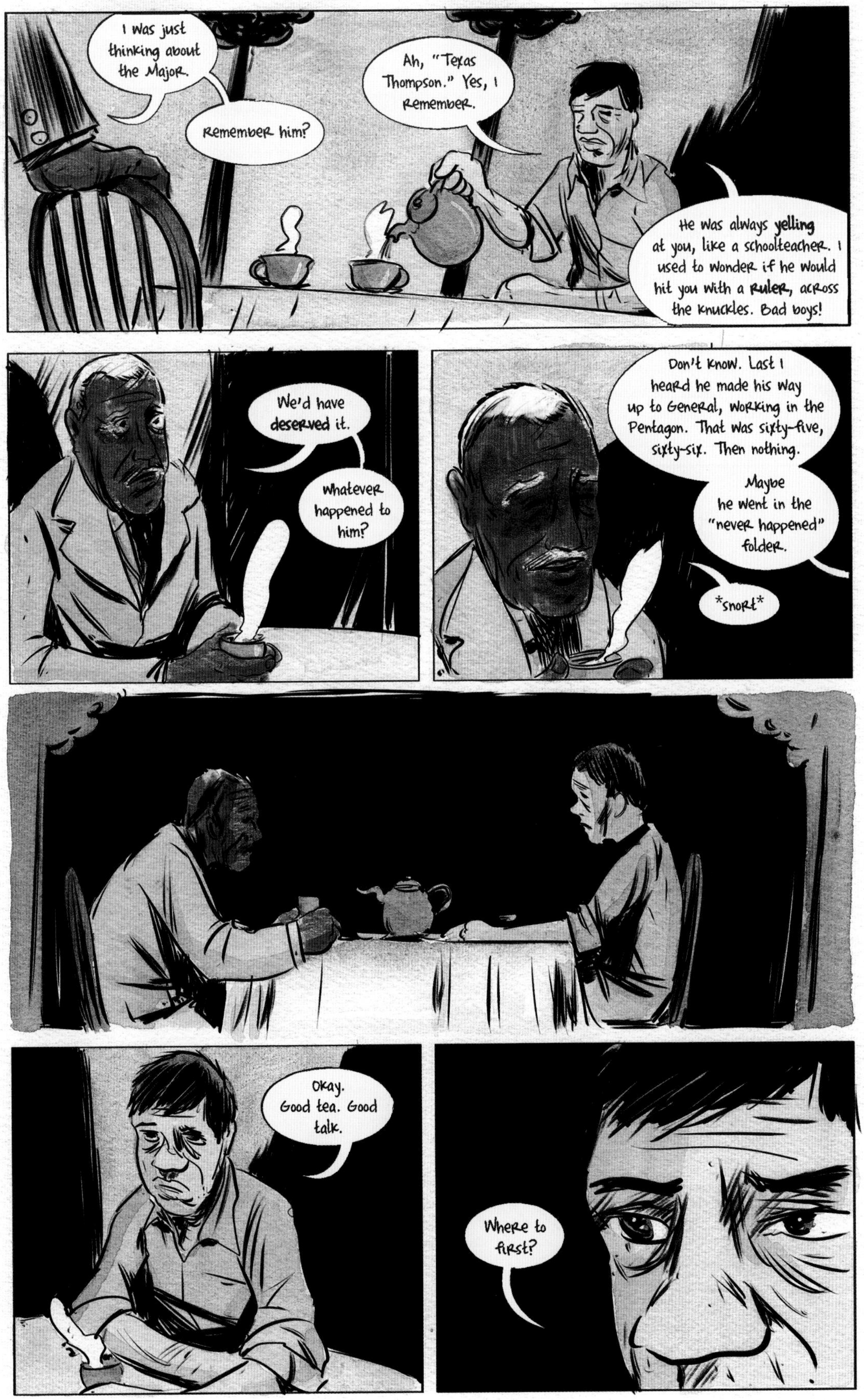
I was just thinking about the Major.
Remember him?
Ah, "Texas Thompson." Yes, I remember.
He was always yelling at you, like a schoolteacher. I used to wonder if he would hit you with a ruler, across the knuckles. Bad boys!
We'd have deserved it.
Whatever happened to him?
Don't know. Last I heard he made his way up to General, working in the Pentagon. That was sixty-five, sixty-six. Then nothing.
Maybe he went in the "never happened" folder.
snort
Okay. Good tea. Good talk.
Where to first?

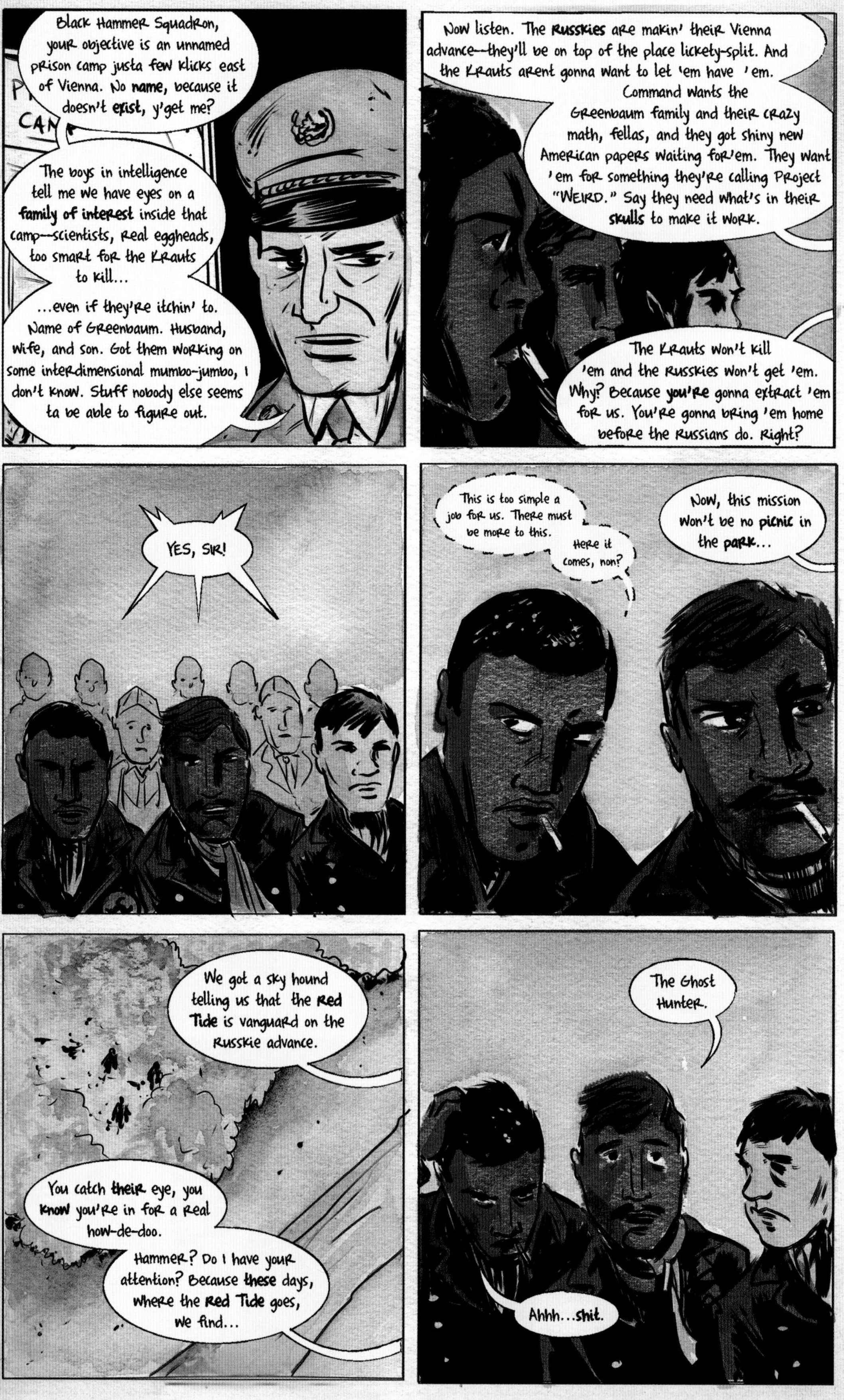

Black Hammer Squadron, your objective is an unnamed prison camp justa few klicks east of Vienna. No name, because it doesn't exist, y'get me?
The boys in intelligence tell me we have eyes on a family of interest inside that camp--scientists, real eggheads, too smart for the Krauts to kill...
...even if they're itchin' to. Name of Greenbaum. Husband, wife, and son. Got them working on some interdimensional mumbo-jumbo, I don't know. Stuff nobody else seems ta be able to figure out.
Now listen. The Russkies are makin' their Vienna advance--they'll be on top of the place lickety-split. And the Krauts arent gonna want to let 'em have 'em.
Command wants the Greenbaum family and their crazy math, fellas, and they got shiny new American papers waiting for 'em. They want 'em for something they're calling Project "WEIRD." Say they need what's in their skulls to make it work.
The Krauts won't kill 'em and the Russkies won't get 'em. Why? Because you're gonna extract 'em for us. You're gonna bring 'em home before the Russians do. Right?
YES, SIR!
This is too simple a job for us. There must be more to this.
Here it comes, non?
Now, this mission won't be no picnic in the park...
We got a sky hound telling us that the Red Tide is vanguard on the Russkie advance.
You catch their eye, you know you're in for a real how-de-doo.
Hammer? Do I have your attention? Because these days, where the Red Tide goes, we find...
The Ghost Hunter.
Ahhh...shit.

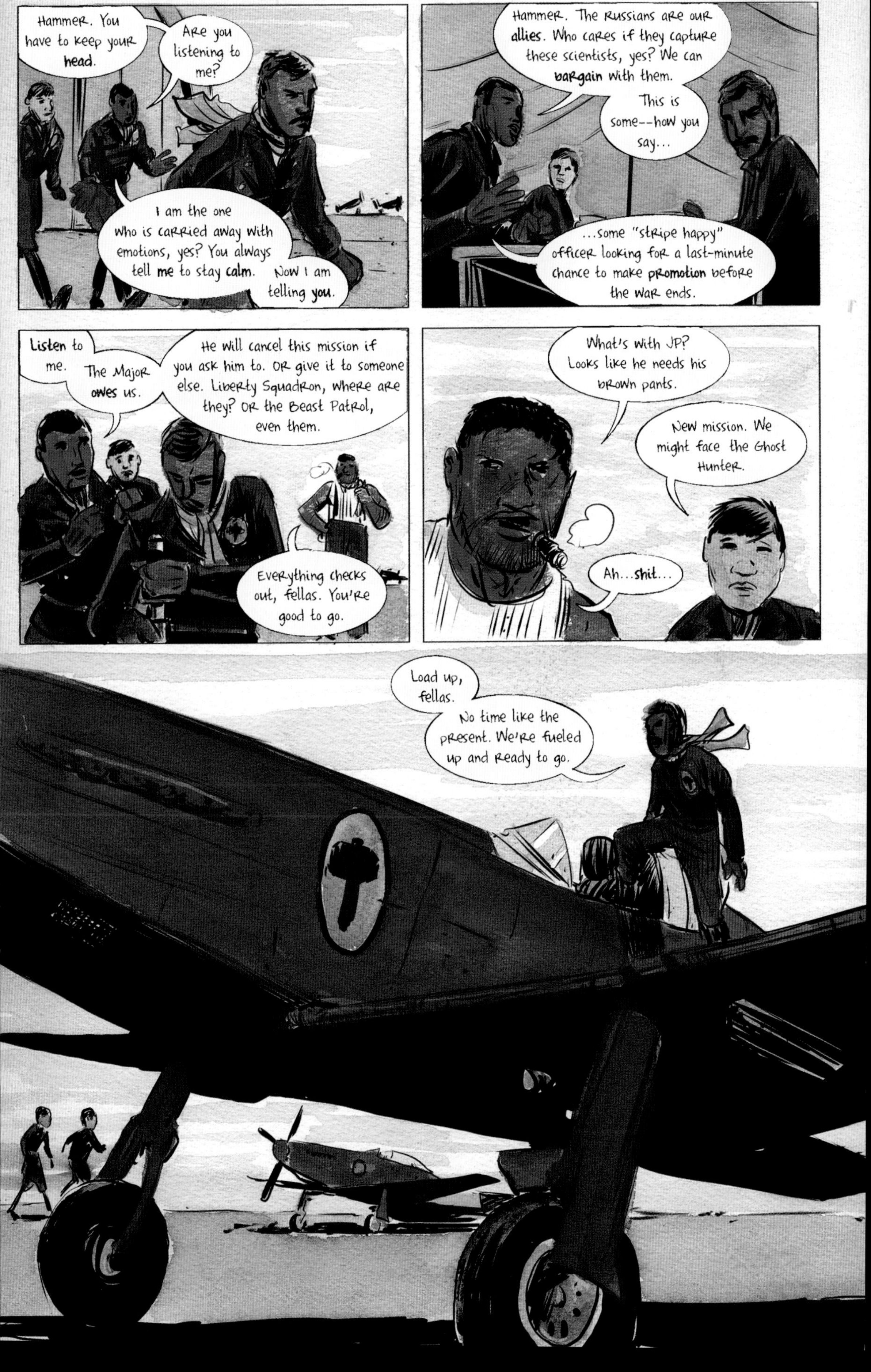

Hammer. You have to keep your head.
Are you listening to me?
I am the one who is carried away with emotions, yes? You always tell me to stay calm.
Now I am telling you.
Hammer. The Russians are our allies. Who cares if they capture these scientists, yes? We can bargain with them.
This is some--how you say...
...some "stripe happy" officer looking for a last-minute chance to make promotion before the war ends.
Listen to me.
The Major owes us.
He will cancel this mission if you ask him to. Or give it to someone else. Liberty Squadron, where are they? Or the Beast Patrol, even them.
Everything checks out, fellas. You're good to go.
What's with JP? Looks like he needs his brown pants.
New mission. We might face the Ghost Hunter.
Ah...shit...
Load up, fellas.
No time like the present. We're fueled up and ready to go.

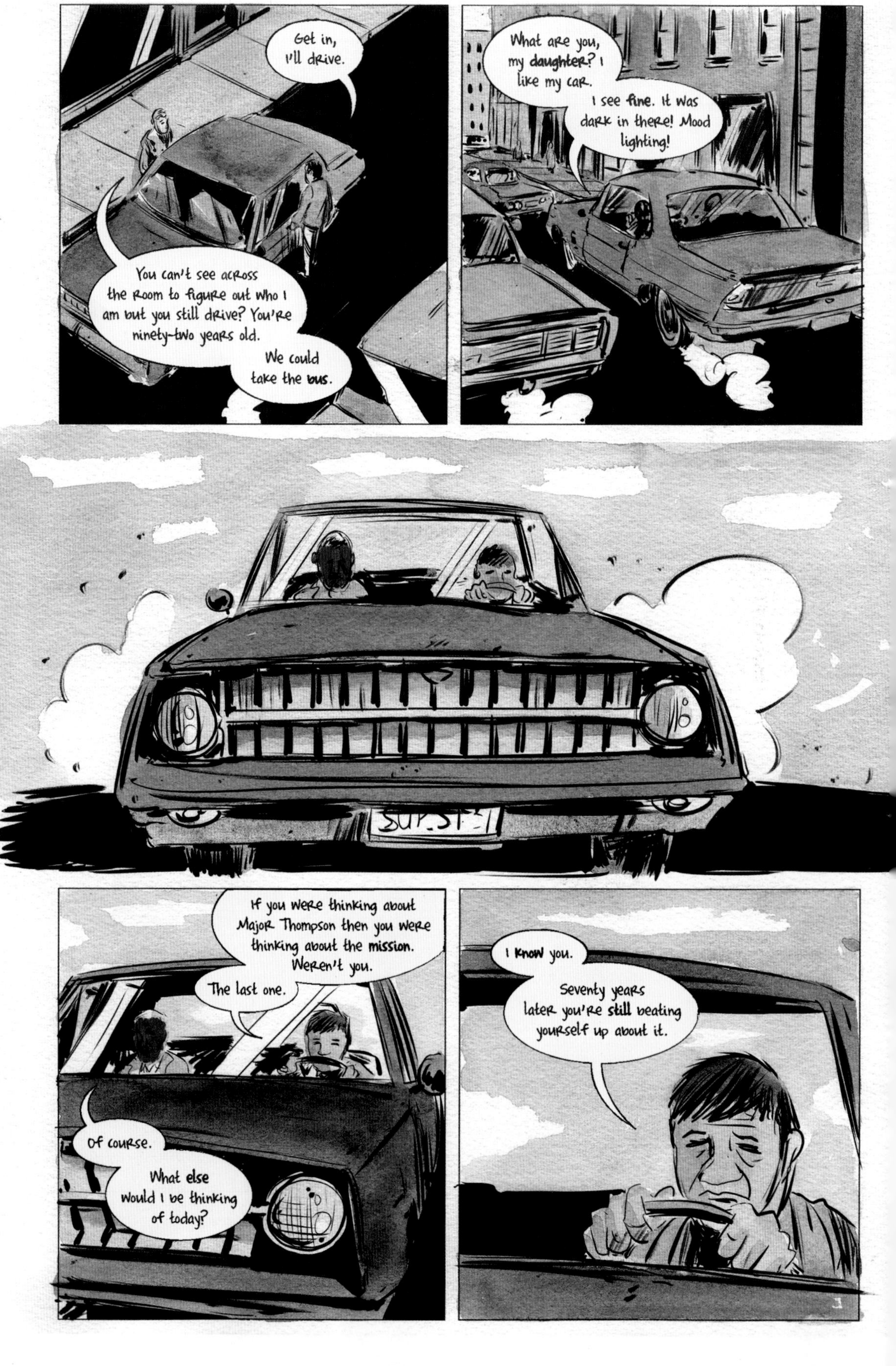
Get in, I'll drive.
You can't see across the room to figure out who I am but you still drive? You're ninety-two years old.
We could take the bus.
What are you, my daughter? I like my car.
I see fine. It was dark in there! Mood lighting!
SUP.ST
If you were thinking about Major Thompson then you were thinking about the mission. Weren't you.
The last one.
Of course.
What else would I be thinking of today?
I know you.
Seventy years later you're still beating yourself up about it.

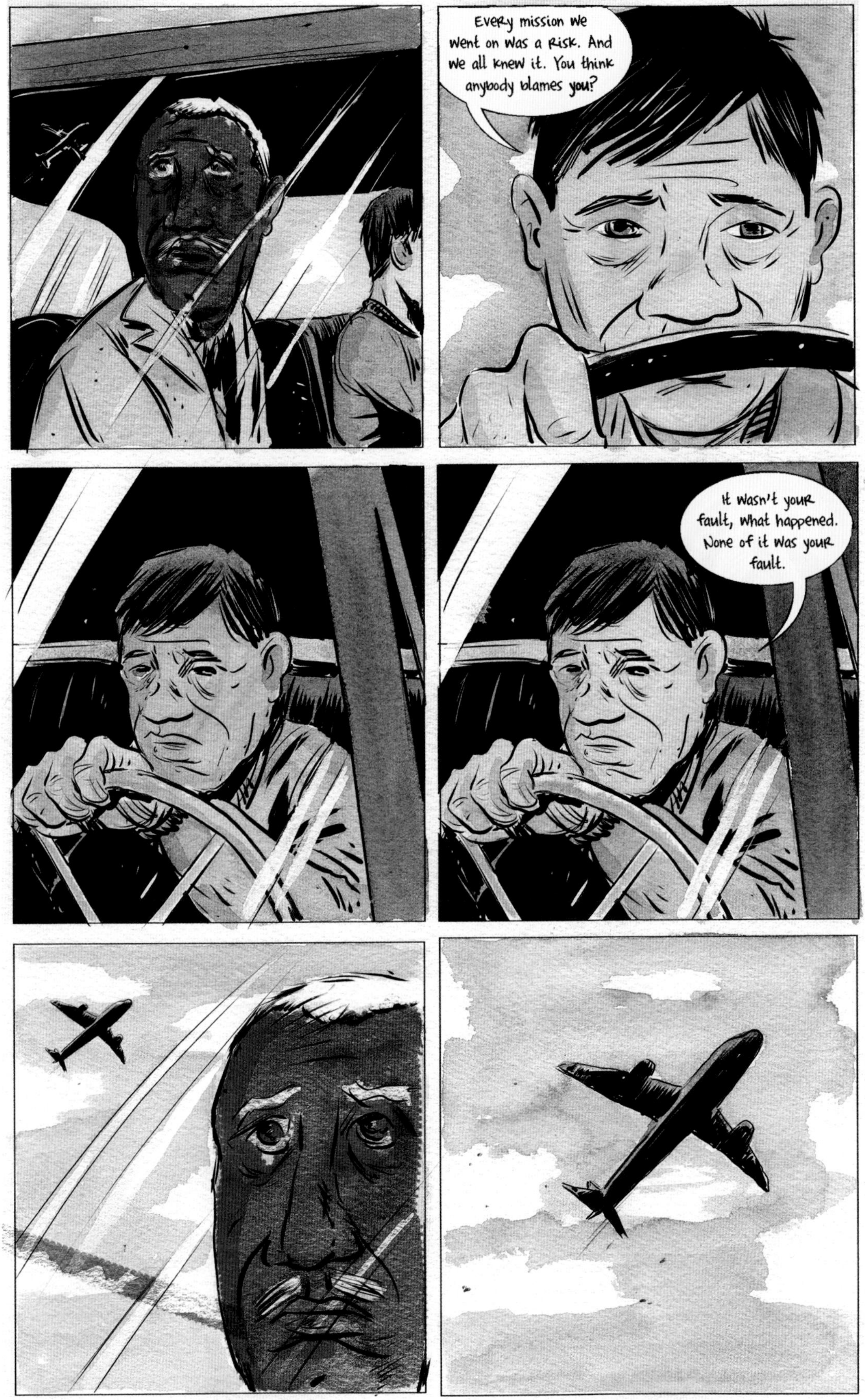
Every mission we went on was a risk. And we all knew it. You think anybody blames you?
It wasn't your fault, what happened. None of it was your fault.

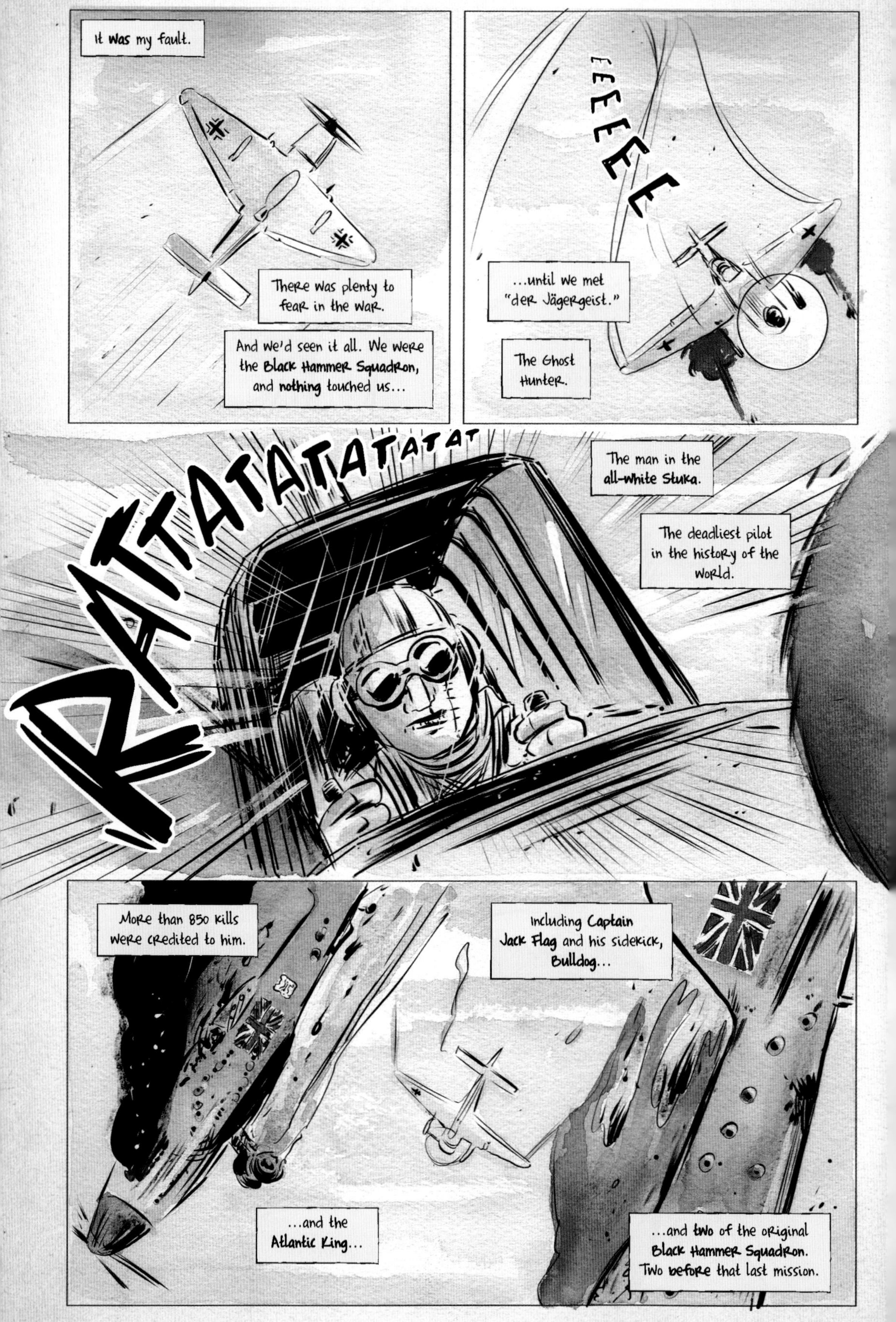
It was my fault.
There was plenty to fear in the war.
And we'd seen it all. We were the Black Hammer Squadron, and nothing touched us...
EEEEEE
...until we met "der Jägergeist."
The Ghost Hunter.
RATATATATATAT
The man in the all-white Stuka.
The deadliest pilot in the history of the world.
More than 850 kills were credited to him.
Including Captain Jack Flag and his sidekick, Bulldog...
...and the Atlantic King...
...and two of the original Black Hammer Squadron. Two before that last mission.

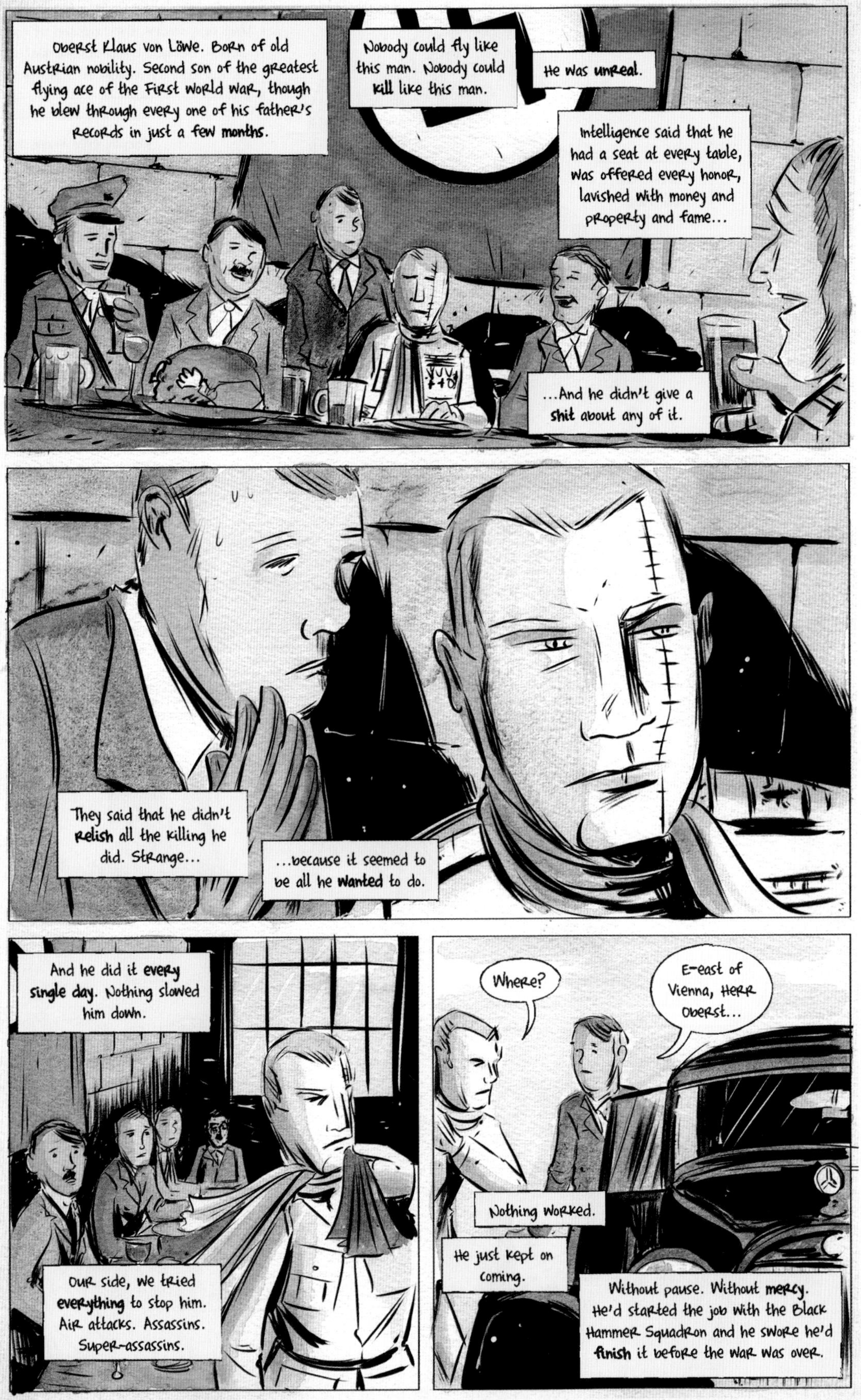
Oberst Klaus von Löwe. Born of old Austrian nobility. Second son of the greatest flying ace of the First World War, though he blew through every one of his father's records in just a few months.
Nobody could fly like this man. Nobody could kill like this man.
He was unreal.
Intelligence said that he had a seat at every table, was offered every honor, lavished with money and property and fame...
...And he didn't give a shit about any of it.
They said that he didn't relish all the killing he did. Strange...
...because it seemed to be all he wanted to do.
And he did it every single day. Nothing slowed him down.
Our side, we tried everything to stop him. Air attacks. Assassins. Super-assassins.
Where?
E-east of Vienna, Herr Oberst...
Nothing worked.
He just kept on coming.
Without pause. Without mercy. He'd started the job with the Black Hammer Squadron and he swore he'd finish it before the war was over.

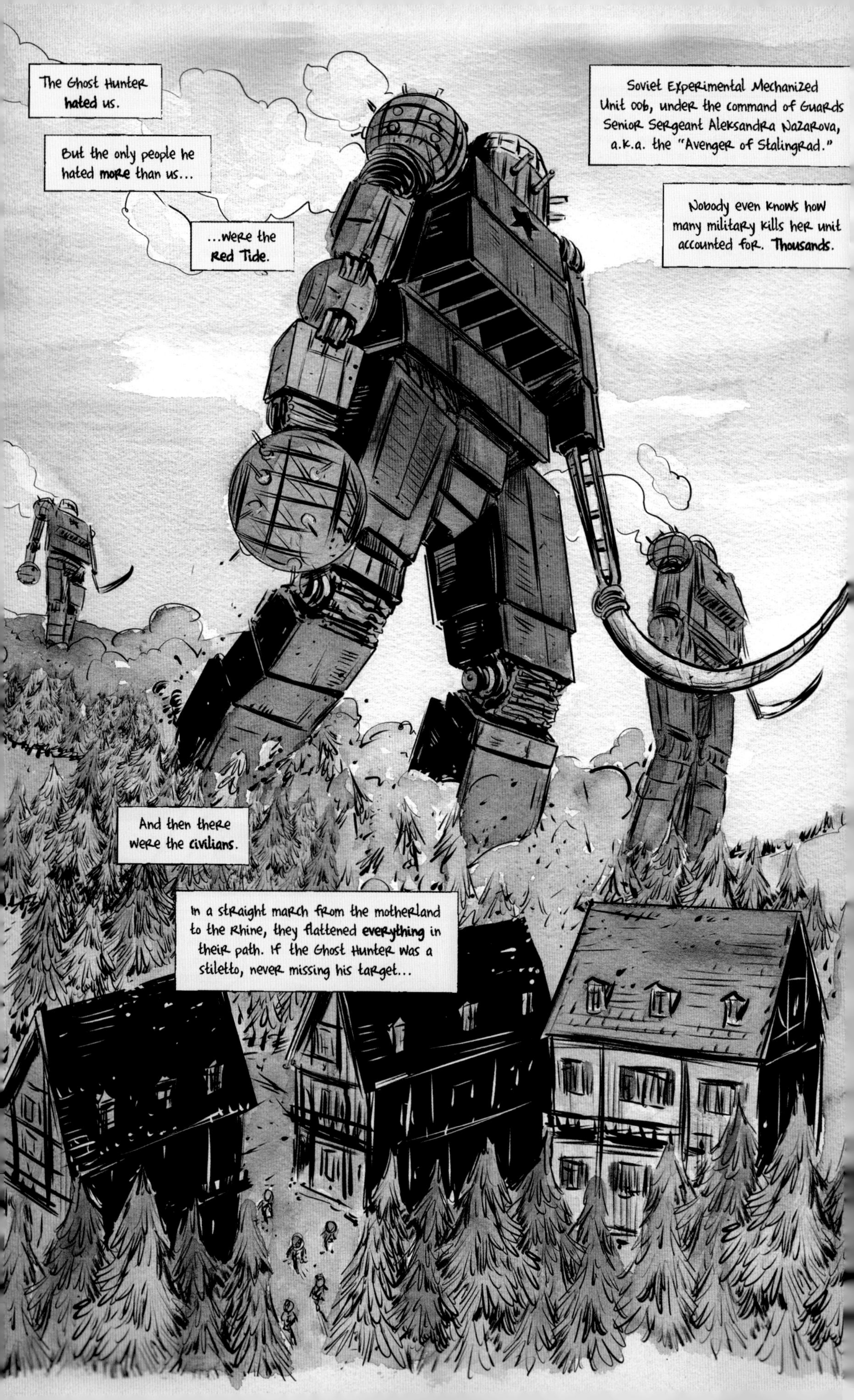
The Ghost Hunter hated us.
But the only people he hated more than us...
...were the Red Tide.
Soviet Experimental Mechanized Unit 006, under the command of Guards Senior Sergeant Aleksandra Nazarova, a.k.a. the "Avenger of Stalingrad."
Nobody even knows how many military kills her unit accounted for. Thousands.
And then there were the civilians.
In a straight march from the motherland to the Rhine, they flattened everything in their path. If the Ghost Hunter was a stiletto, never missing his target...

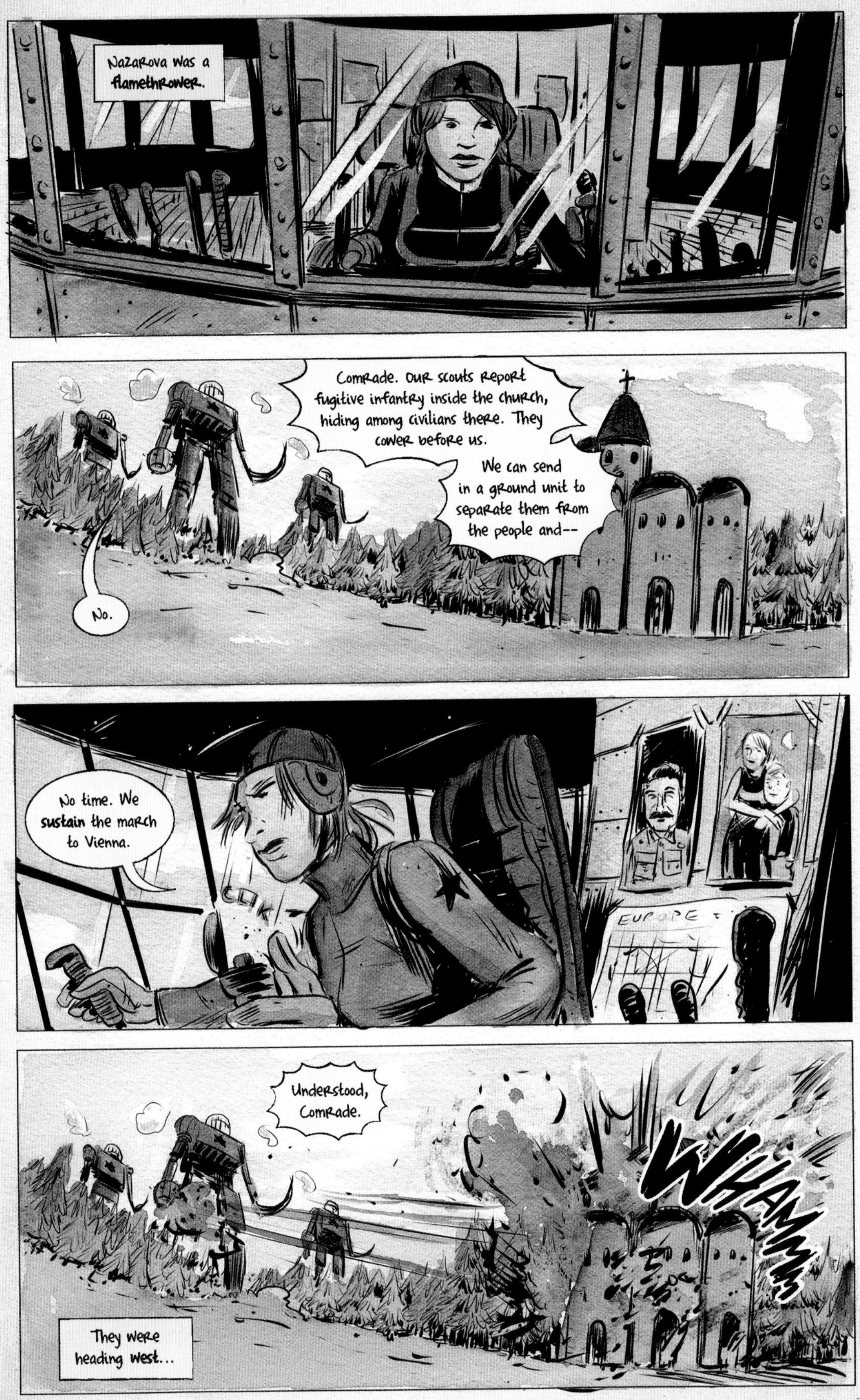

Nazarova was a flamethrower.
Comrade. Our scouts report fugitive infantry inside the church, hiding among civilians there. They cower before us.
We can send in a ground unit to separate them from the people and--
No.
No time. We sustain the march to Vienna.
CLIK
EUROPE
Understood, Comrade.
WHAMM
They were heading west...

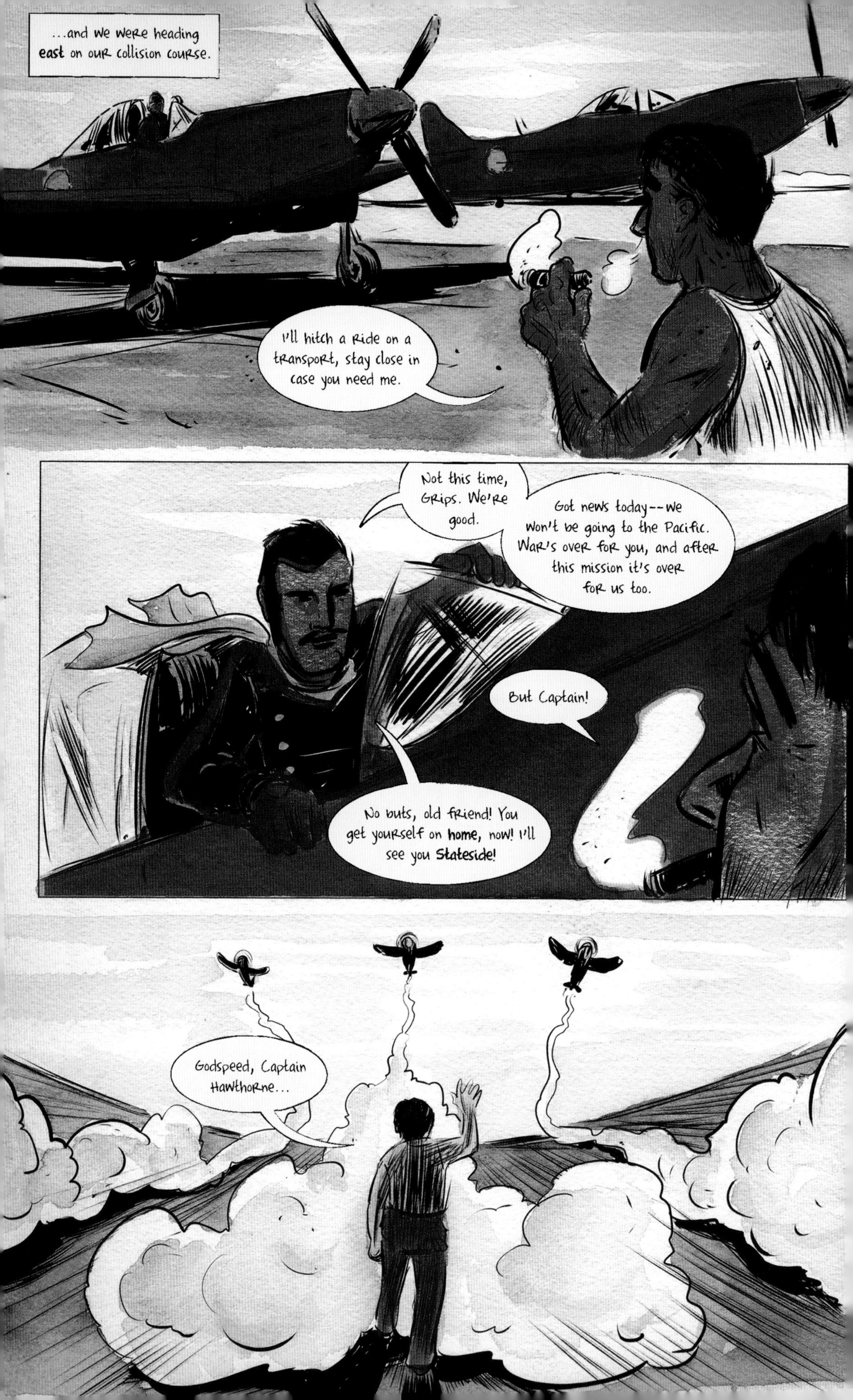
...and we were heading east on our collision course.
I'll hitch a ride on a transport, stay close in case you need me.
Not this time, Grips. We're good.
Got news today--we won't be going to the Pacific. War's over for you, and after this mission it's over for us too.
But Captain!
No buts, old friend! You get yourself on home, now! I'll see you Stateside!
Godspeed, Captain Hawthorne...

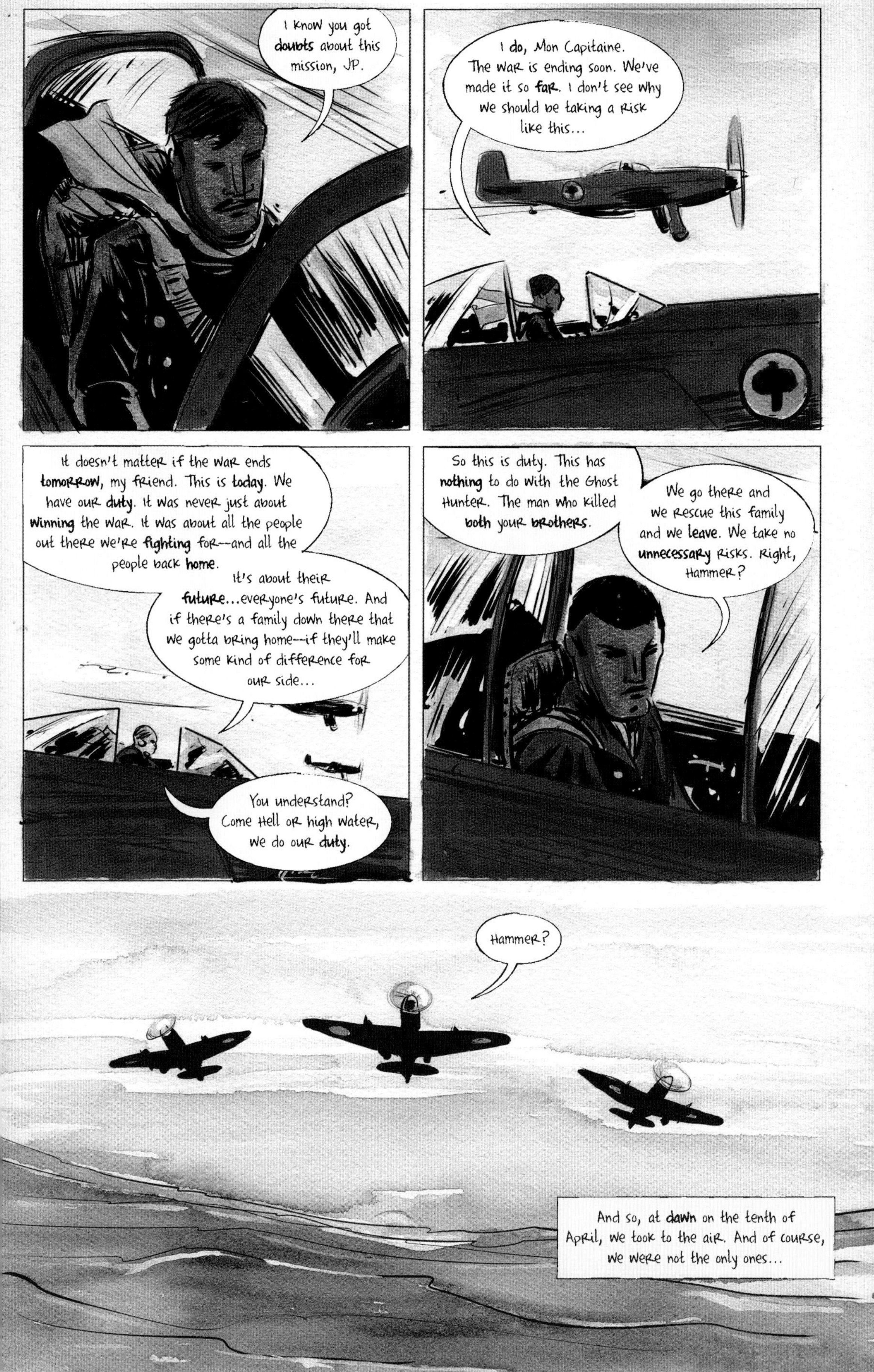

I know you got doubts about this mission, JP.
I do, Mon Capitaine. The war is ending soon. We've made it so far. I don't see why we should be taking a risk like this...
It doesn't matter if the war ends tomorrow, my friend. This is today. We have our duty. It was never just about winning the war. It was about all the people out there we're fighting for--and all the people back home.
It's about their future...everyone's future. And if there's a family down there that we gotta bring home--if they'll make some kind of difference for our side...
You understand? Come Hell or high water, we do our duty.
So this is duty. This has nothing to do with the Ghost Hunter. The man who killed both your brothers.
We go there and we rescue this family and we leave. We take no unnecessary risks. Right, Hammer?
Hammer?
And so, at dawn on the tenth of April, we took to the air. And of course, we were not the only ones...

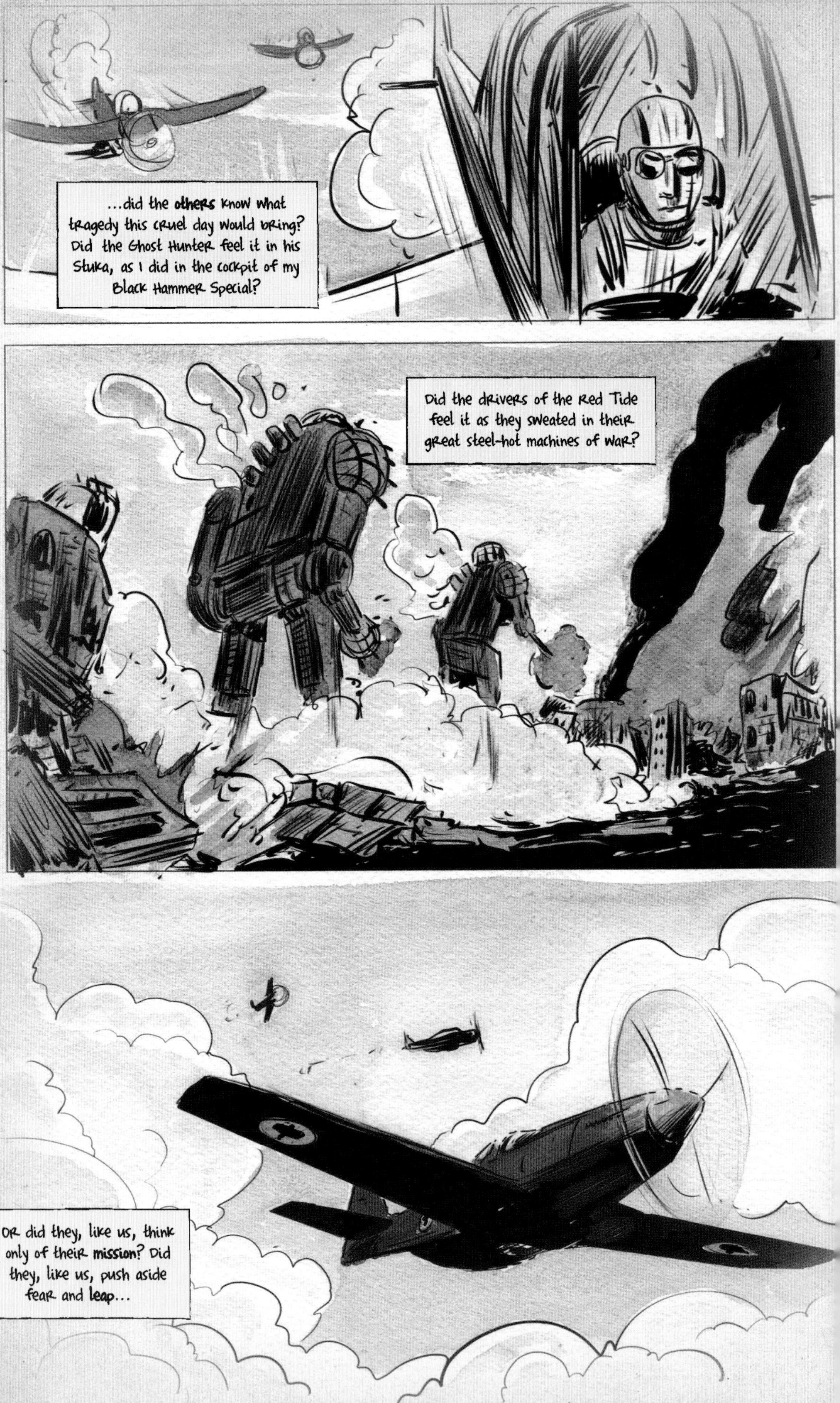
...did the others know what tragedy this cruel day would bring? Did the Ghost Hunter feel it in his Stuka, as I did in the cockpit of my Black Hammer Special?
Did the drivers of the Red Tide feel it as they sweated in their great steel-hot machines of war?
Or did they, like us, think only of their mission? Did they, like us, push aside fear and leap...

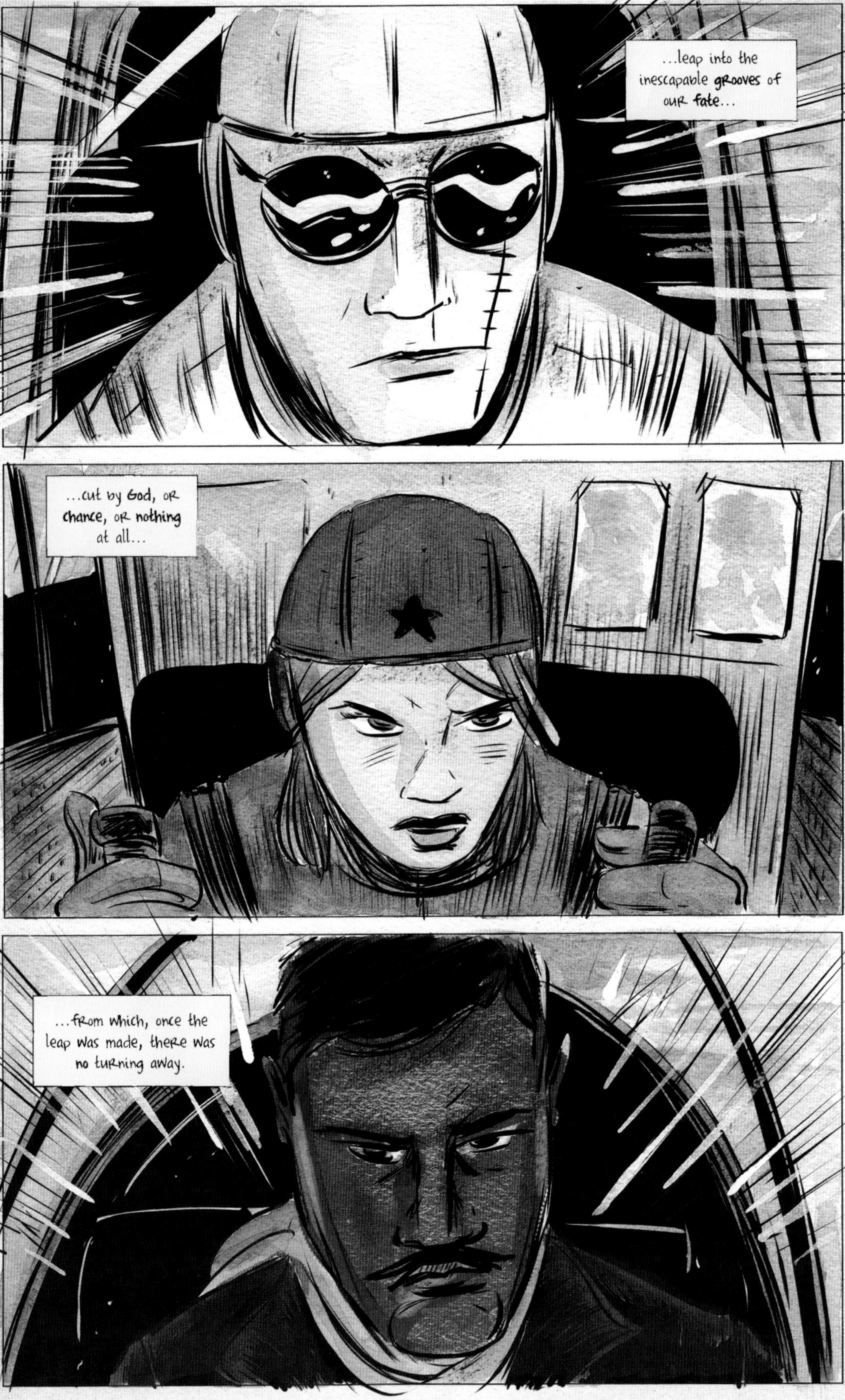
...leap into the inescapable grooves of our fate...
...cut by God, or chance, or nothing at all...
...from which, once the leap was made, there was no turning away.

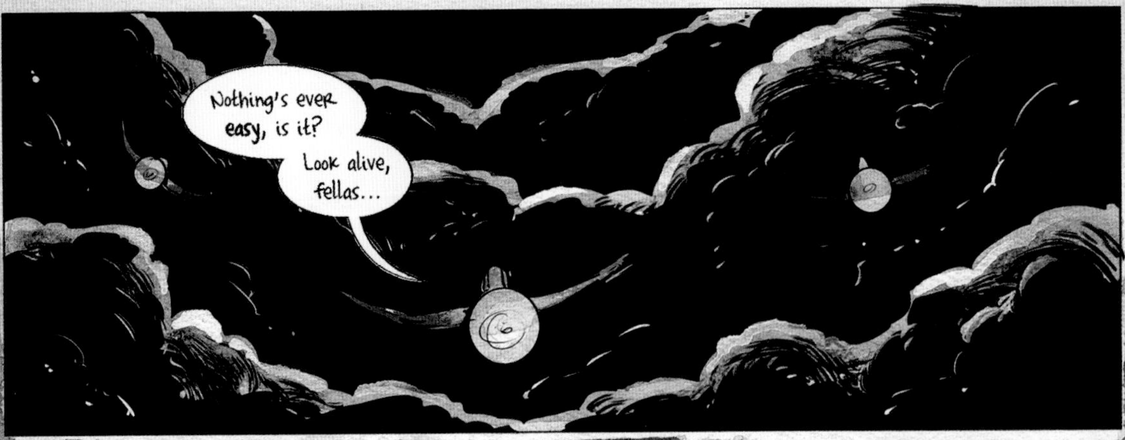
Nothing's ever easy, is it?
Look alive, fellas...

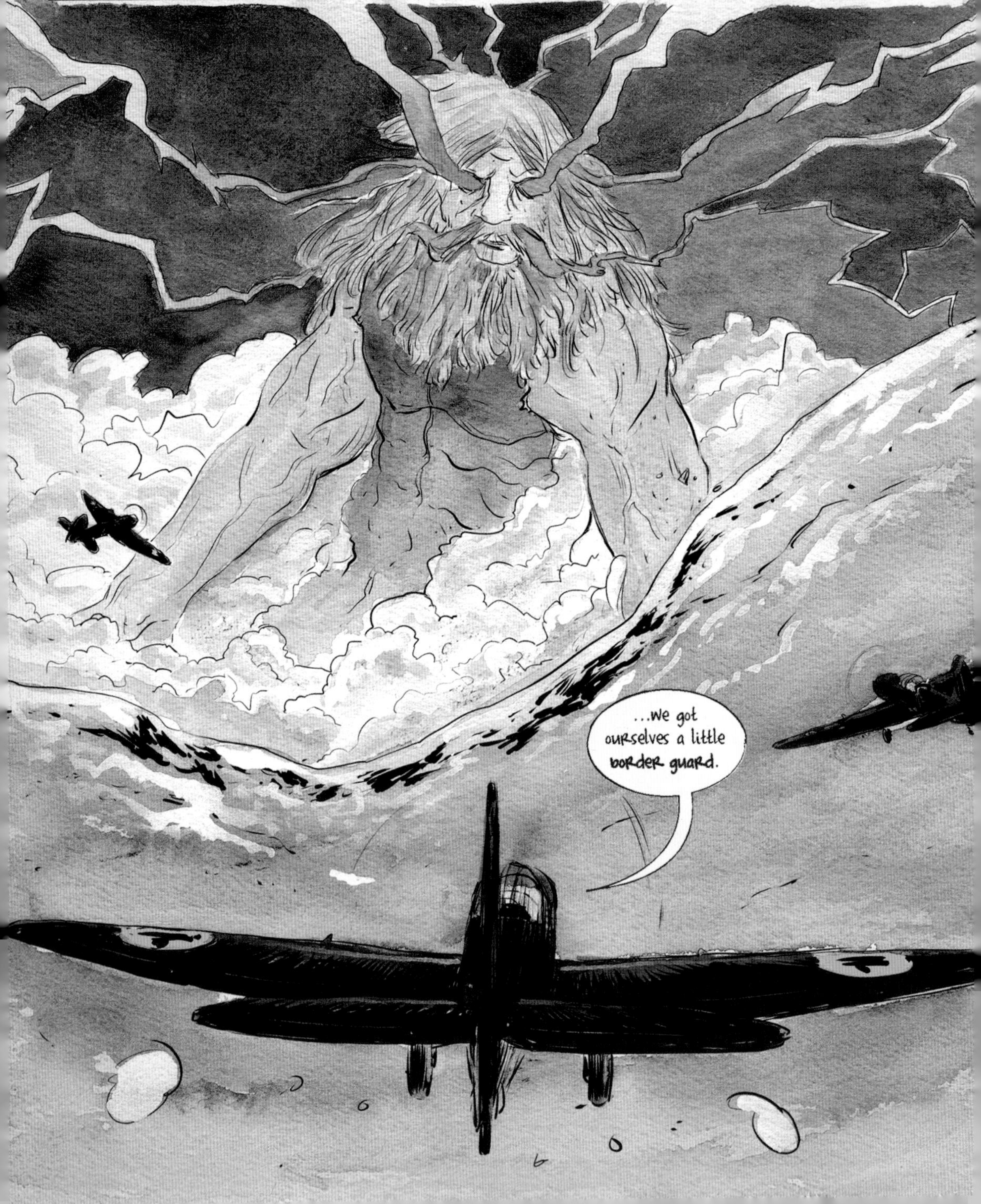
...we got ourselves a little border guard.

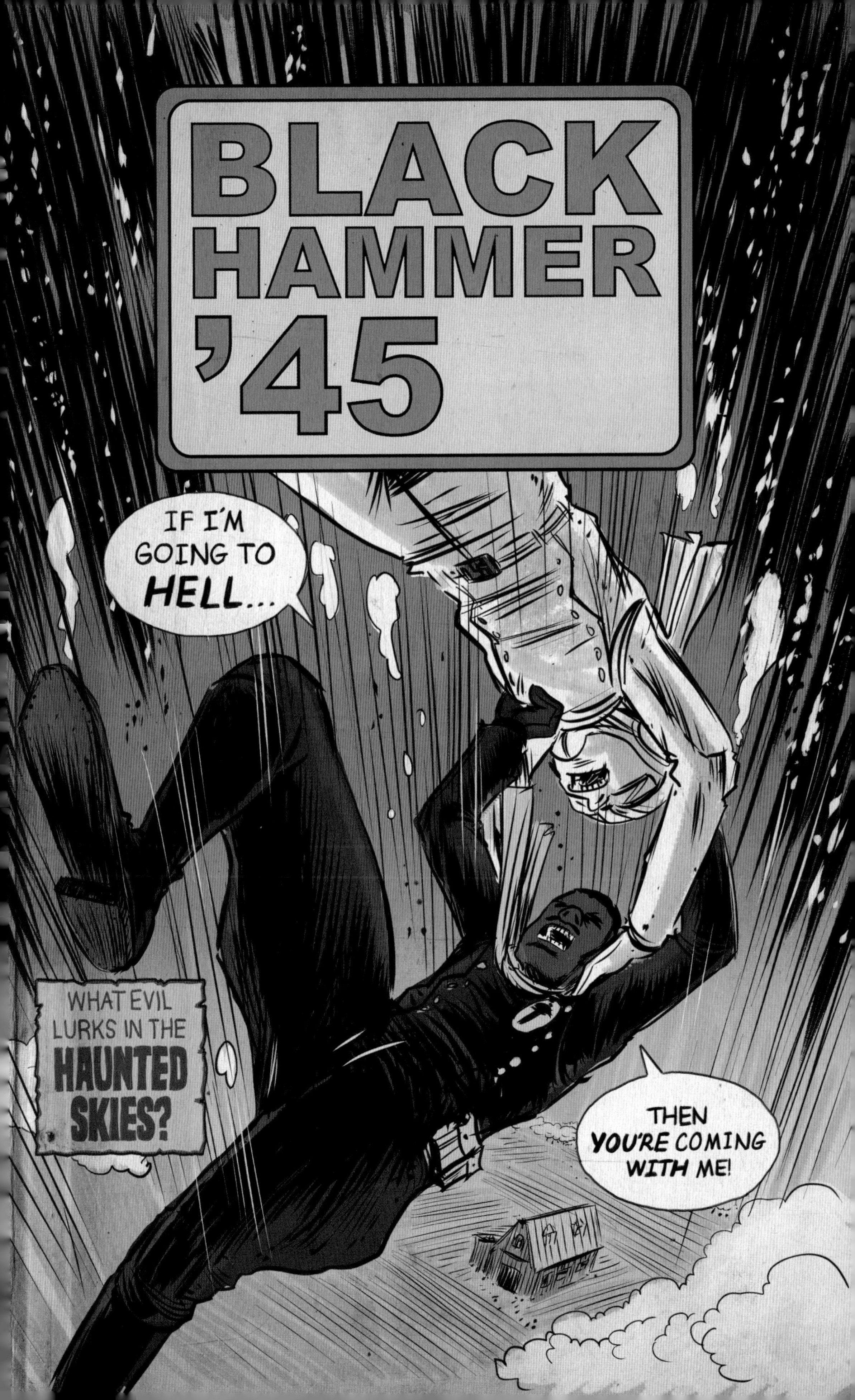
BLACK HAMMER '45
IF I'M GOING TO HELL...
WHAT EVIL LURKS IN THE HAUNTED SKIES?
THEN YOU'RE COMING WITH ME!

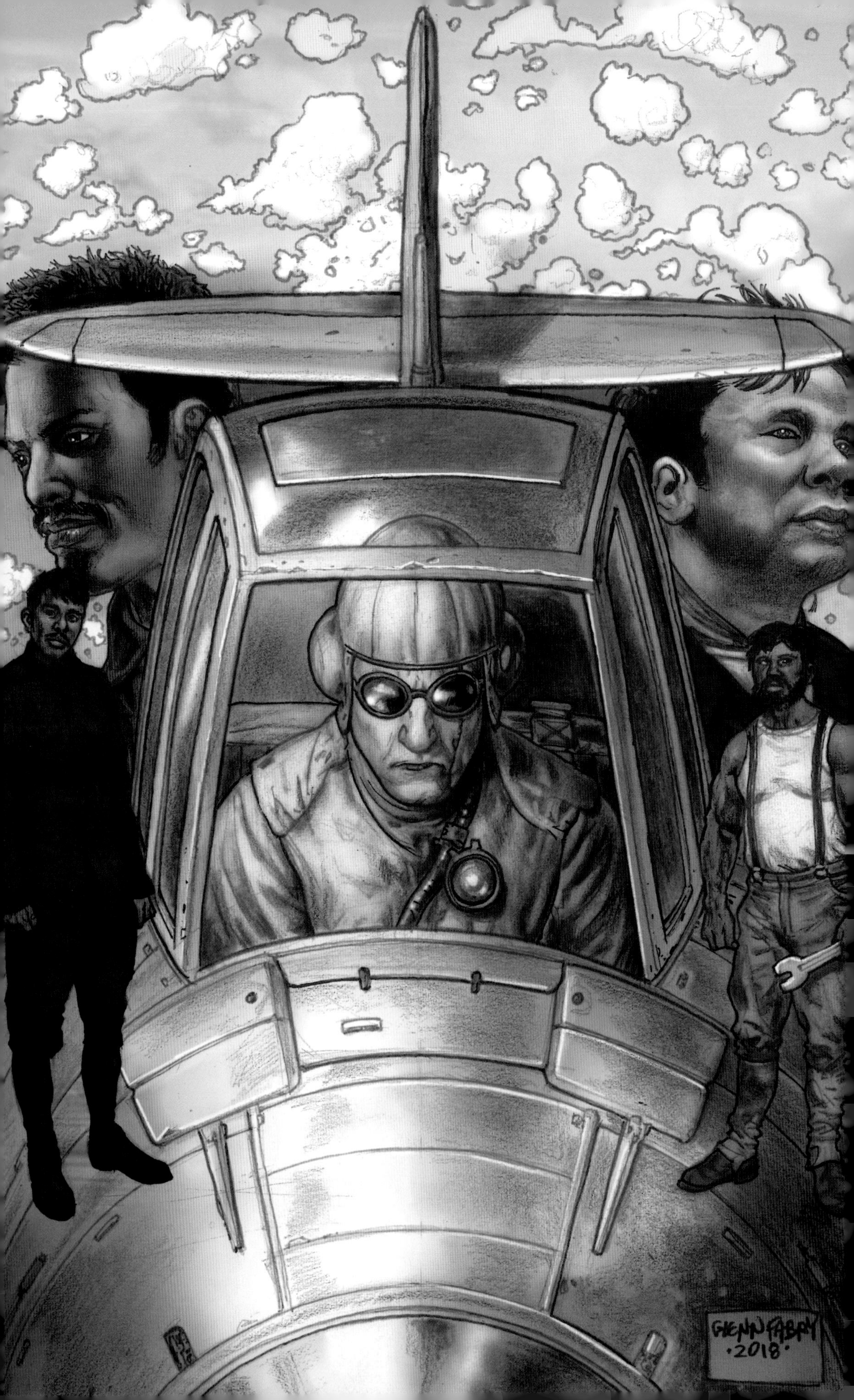
GLENN FABRY
·2018·

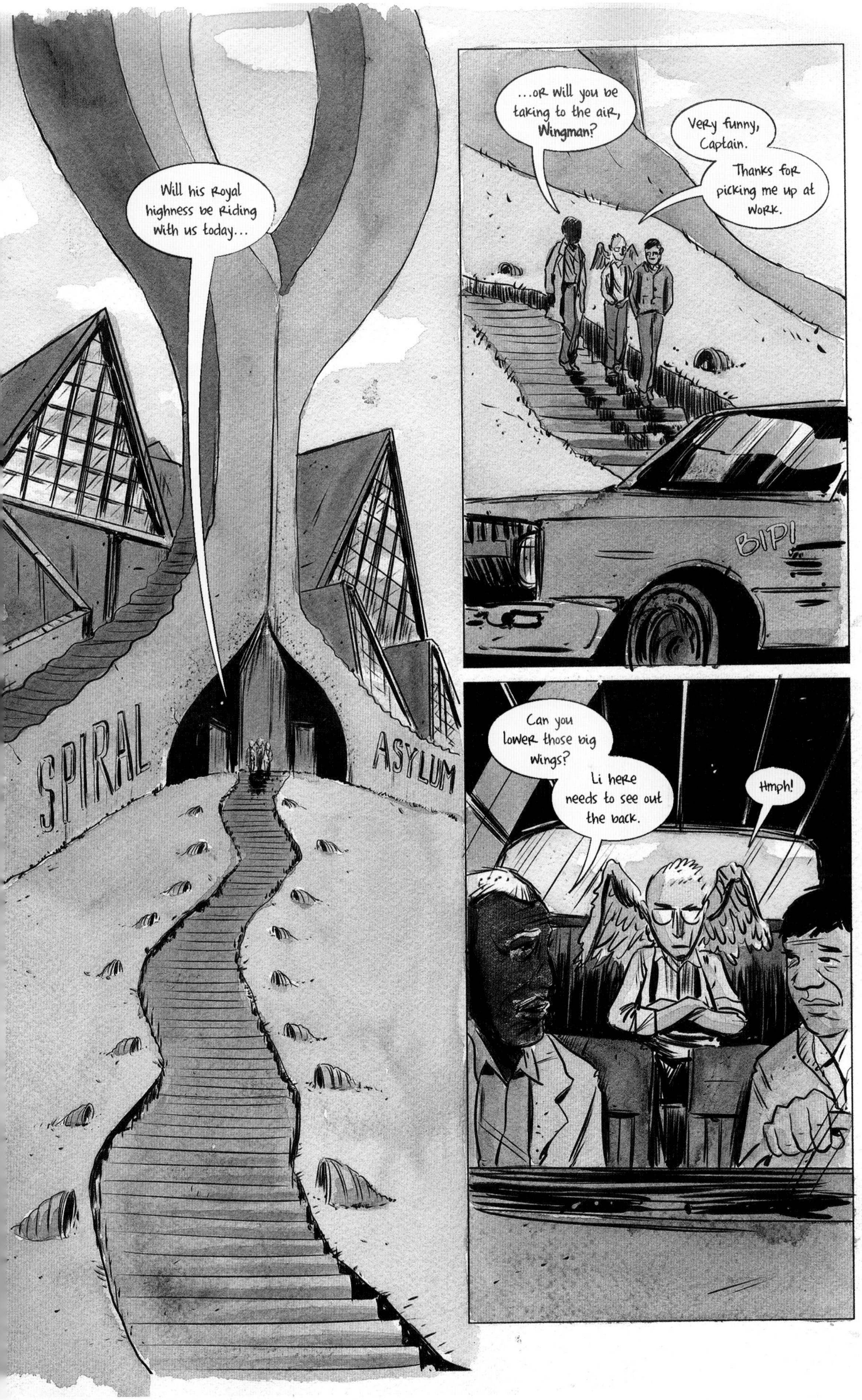

Will his Royal highness be Riding with us today...
SPIRAL
ASYLUM
...oR will you be taking to the aiR, Wingman?
Very funny, Captain.
Thanks for picking me up at work.
BIP!
Can you lower those big wings?
Li here needs to see out the back.
Hmph!

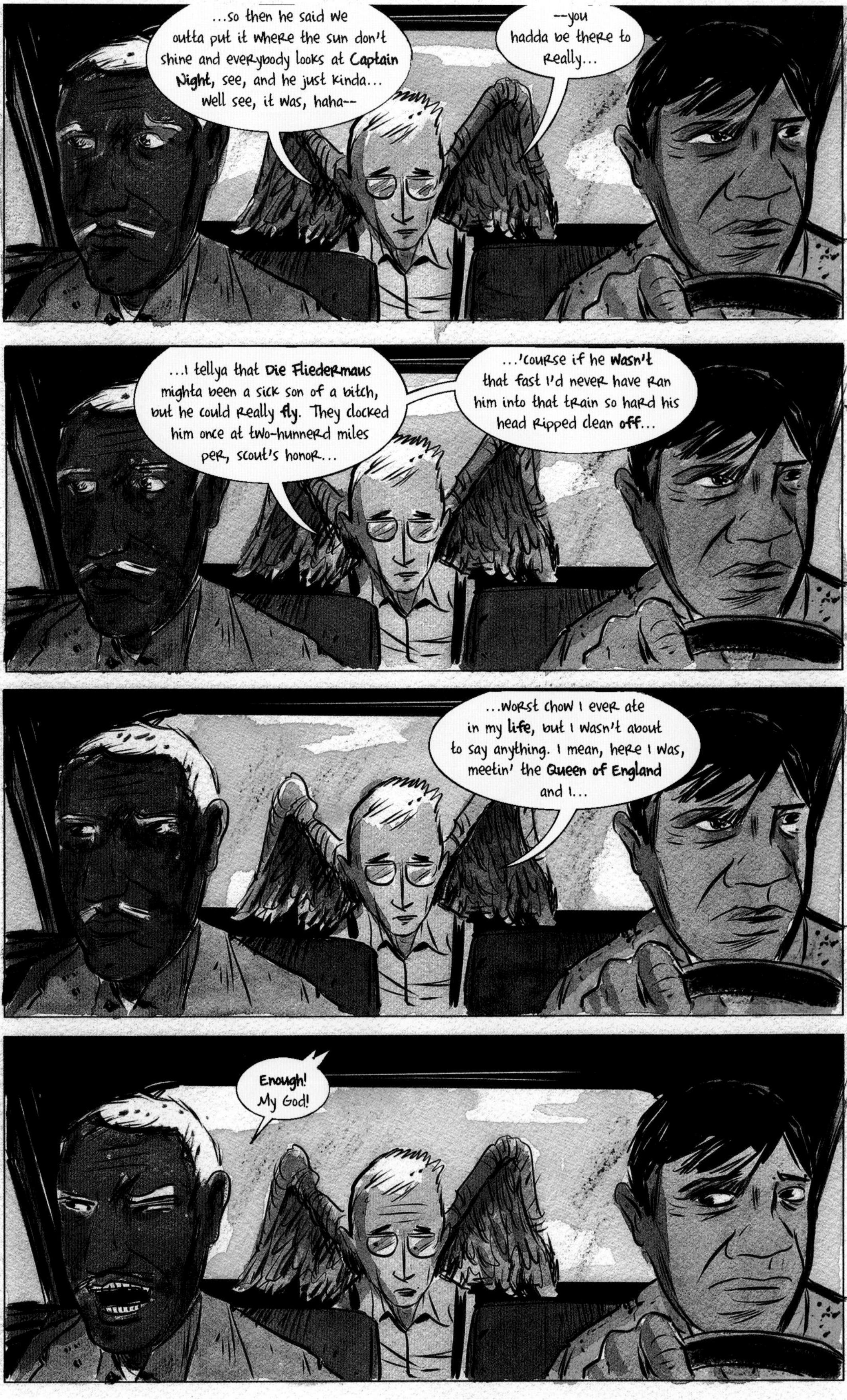
...so then he said we outta put it where the sun don't shine and everybody looks at Captain Night, see, and he just kinda... well see, it was, haha--
--you hadda be there to really...
...I tellya that Die Fliedermaus mighta been a sick son of a bitch, but he could really fly. They clocked him once at two-hunnerd miles per, scout's honor...
...'course if he wasn't that fast I'd never have ran him into that train so hard his head ripped clean off...
...worst chow I ever ate in my life, but I wasn't about to say anything. I mean, here I was, meetin' the Queen of England and I...
Enough! My God!

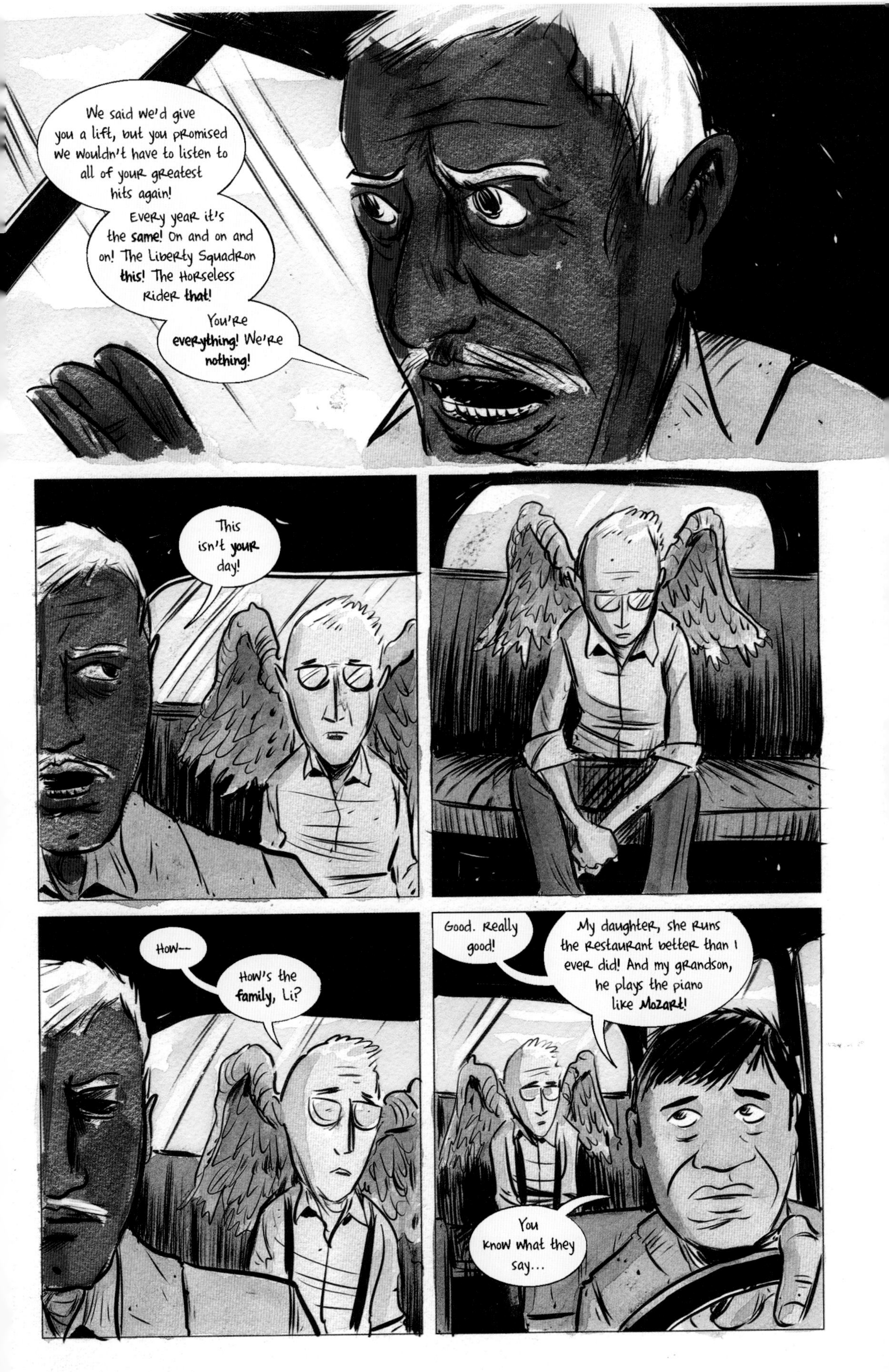
We said we'd give you a lift, but you promised we wouldn't have to listen to all of your greatest hits again!
Every year it's the **same!** On and on and on! The Liberty Squadron **this!** The Horseless Rider **that!**
You're **everything!** We're **nothing!**
This isn't **your** day!
How--
How's the **family**, Li?
Good. Really good!
My daughter, she runs the restaurant better than I ever did! And my grandson, he plays the piano like **Mozart!**
You know what they say...

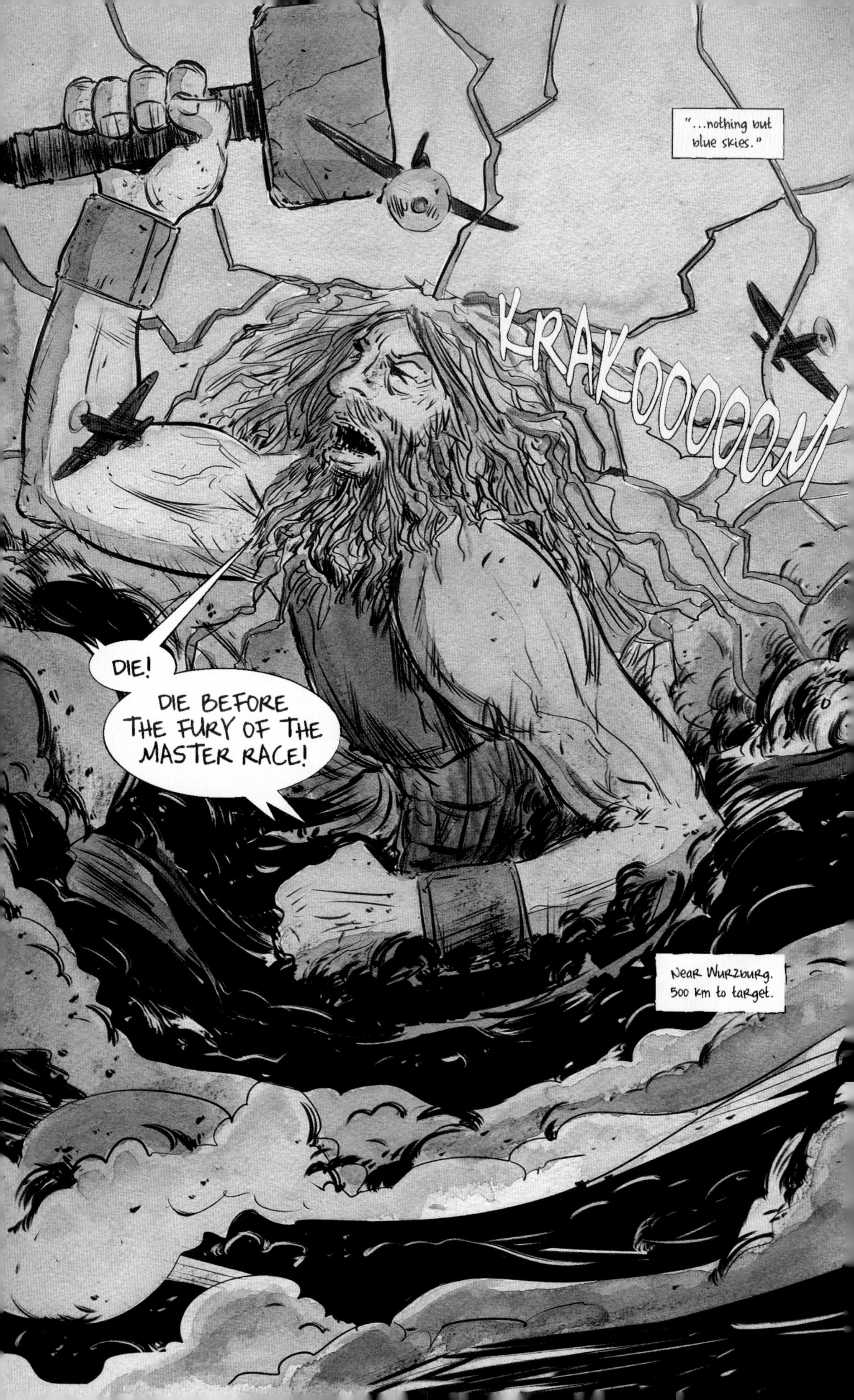
"...nothing but blue skies."
KRAKOOOOOM
DIE!
DIE BEFORE THE FURY OF THE MASTER RACE!
Near Wurzburg. 500 km to target.

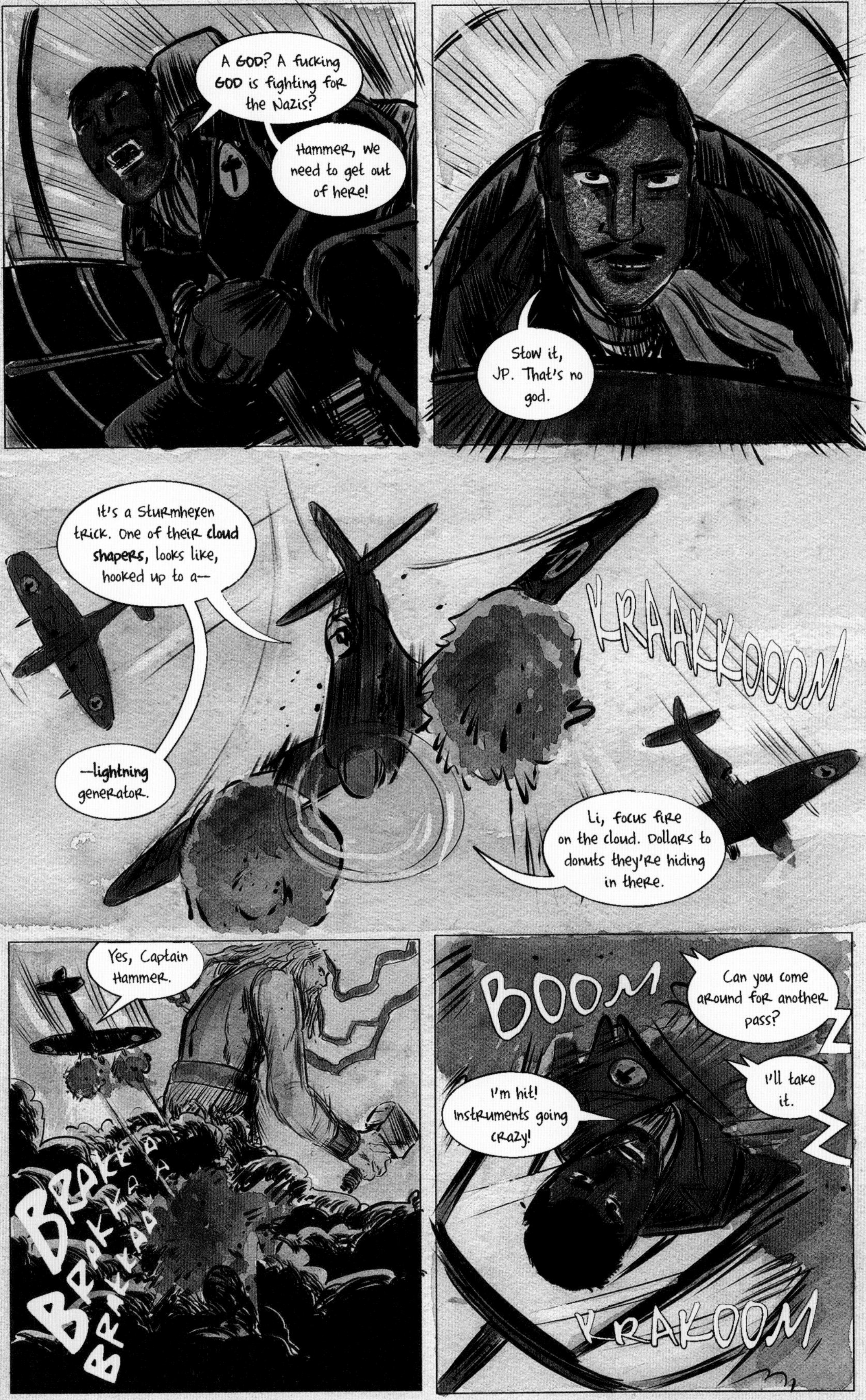

A GOD? A fucking GOD is fighting for the Nazis?
Hammer, we need to get out of here!
Stow it, JP. That's no god.
It's a Sturmhexen trick. One of their cloud shapers, looks like, hooked up to a--
--lightning generator.
KRAAKKOOOM
Li, focus fire on the cloud. Dollars to donuts they're hiding in there.
Yes, Captain Hammer.
BRRAKKA BRRAKKA BRRAKKA
BOOM
Can you come around for another pass?
I'm hit! Instruments going crazy!
I'll take it.
KRAKOOM

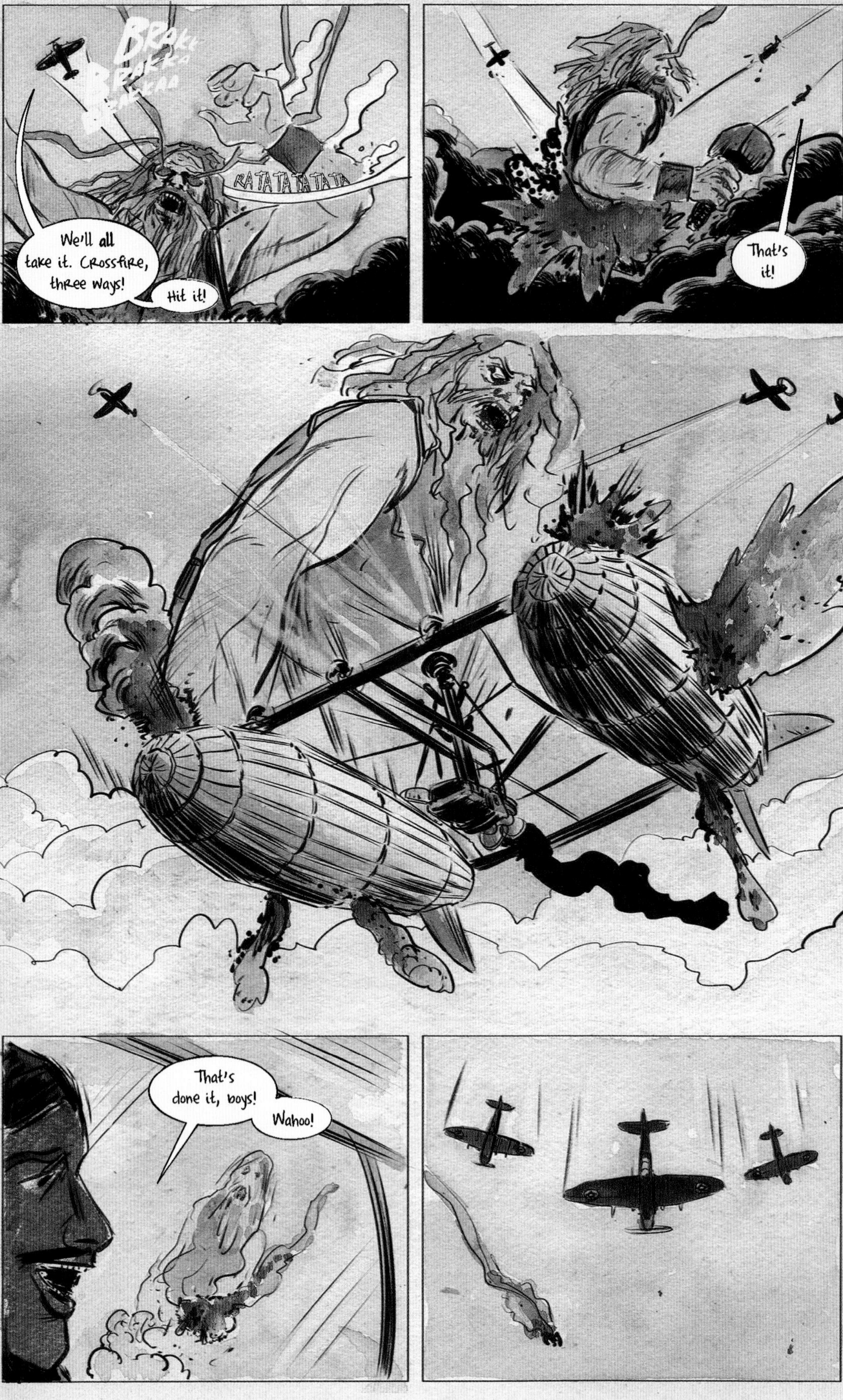
BRAKK
RATATATATATA
We'll all take it. Crossfire, three ways!
Hit it!
That's it!
That's done it, boys!
Wahoo!

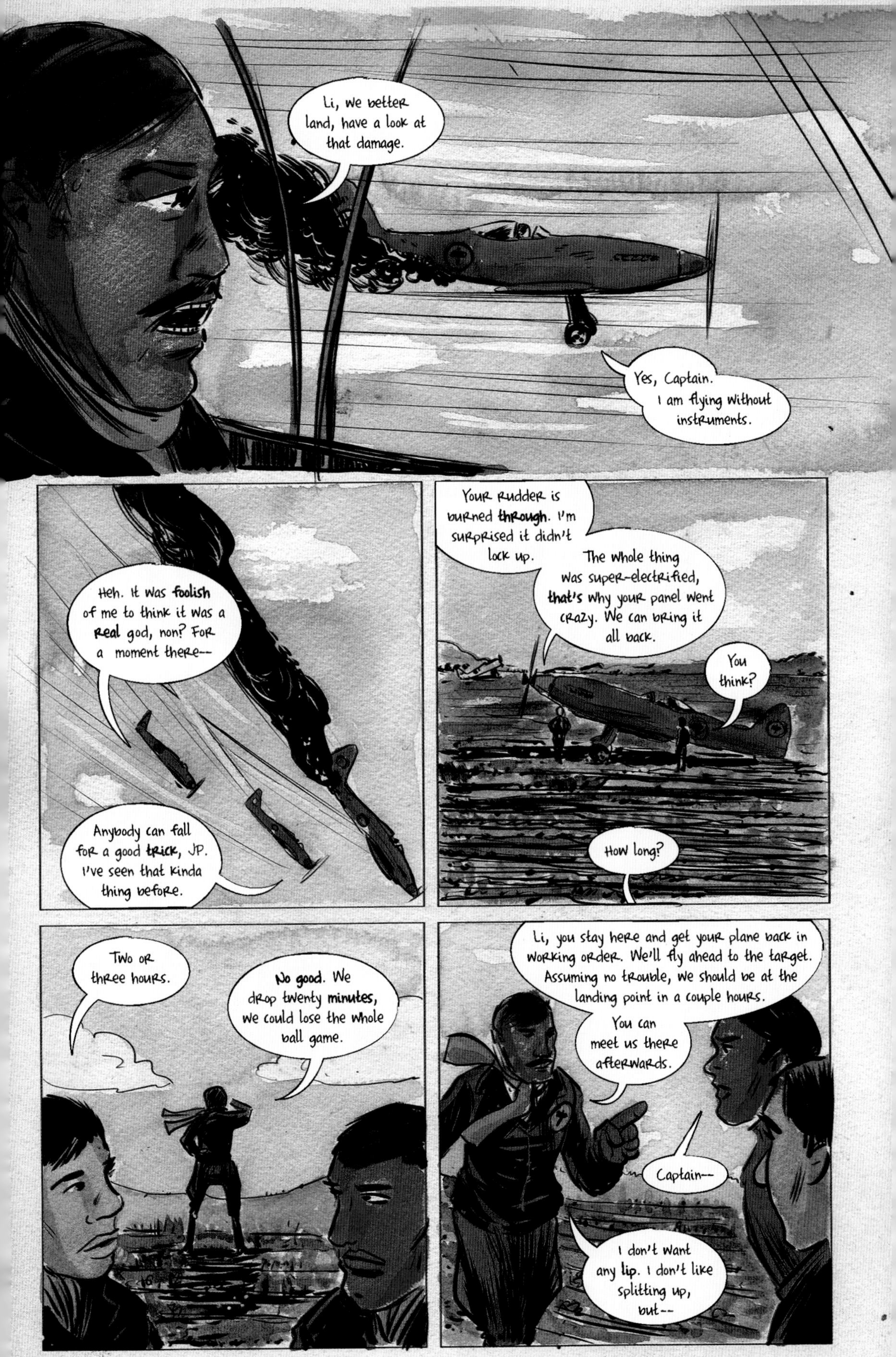
Li, we better land, have a look at that damage.
Yes, Captain. I am flying without instruments.
Heh. It was foolish of me to think it was a real god, non? For a moment there--
Anybody can fall for a good trick, JP. I've seen that kinda thing before.
Your rudder is burned through. I'm surprised it didn't lock up.
The whole thing was super-electrified, that's why your panel went crazy. We can bring it all back.
You think?
How long?
Two or three hours.
No good. We drop twenty minutes, we could lose the whole ball game.
Li, you stay here and get your plane back in working order. We'll fly ahead to the target. Assuming no trouble, we should be at the landing point in a couple hours.
You can meet us there afterwards.
Captain--
I don't want any lip. I don't like splitting up, but--

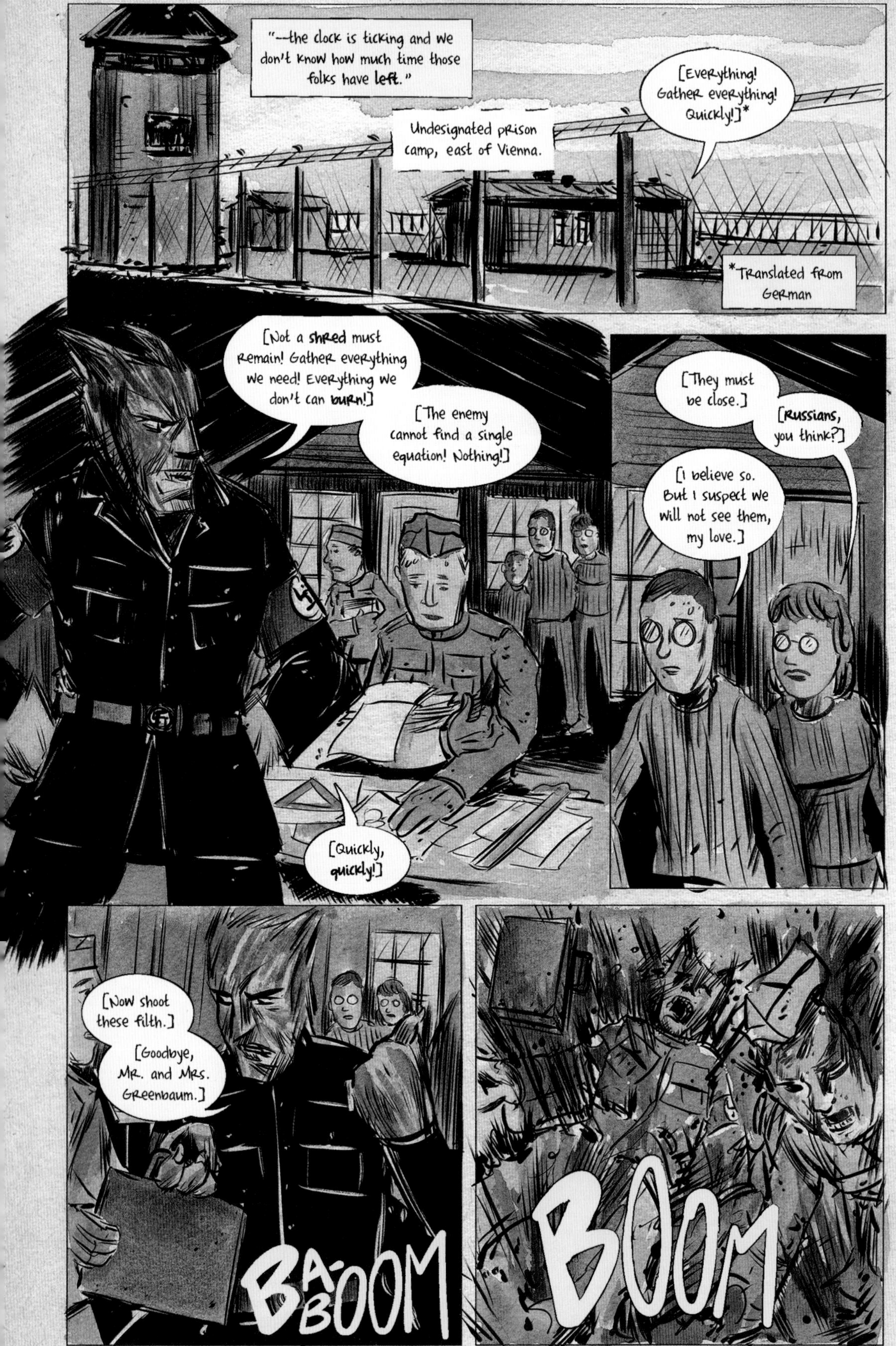
"--the clock is ticking and we don't know how much time those folks have left."
Undesignated prison camp, east of Vienna.
[Everything! Gather everything! Quickly!]*
*Translated from German
[Not a shred must remain! Gather everything we need! Everything we don't can burn!]
[The enemy cannot find a single equation! Nothing!]
[Quickly, quickly!]
[They must be close.]
[Russians, you think?]
[I believe so. But I suspect we will not see them, my love.]
[Now shoot these filth.]
[Goodbye, Mr. and Mrs. Greenbaum.]
BA-BOOM
BOOM

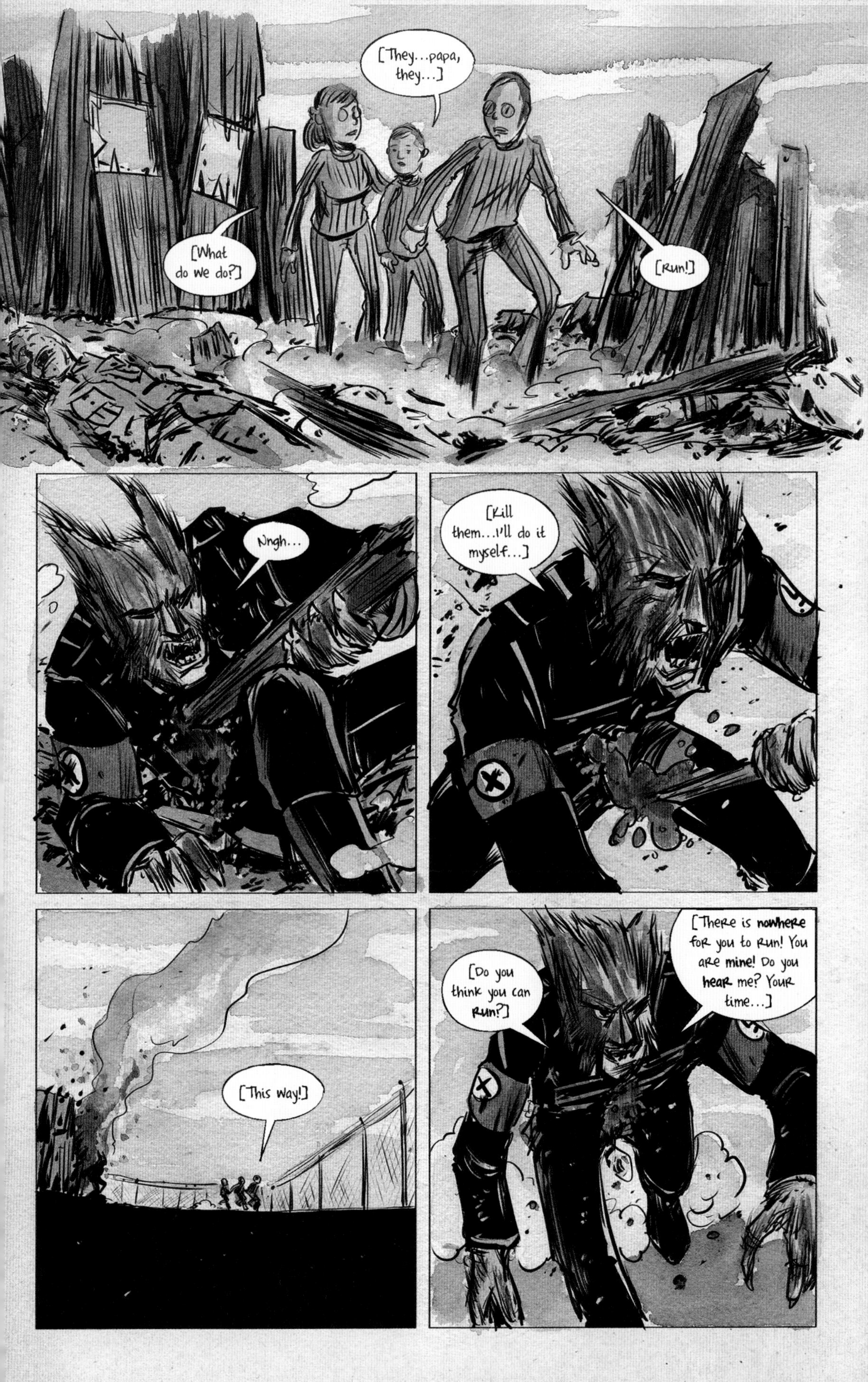
[They...papa, they...]
[What do we do?]
[Run!]
Nngh...
[Kill them...I'll do it myself...]
[This way!]
[Do you think you can run?]
[There is nowhere for you to run! You are mine! Do you hear me? Your time...]

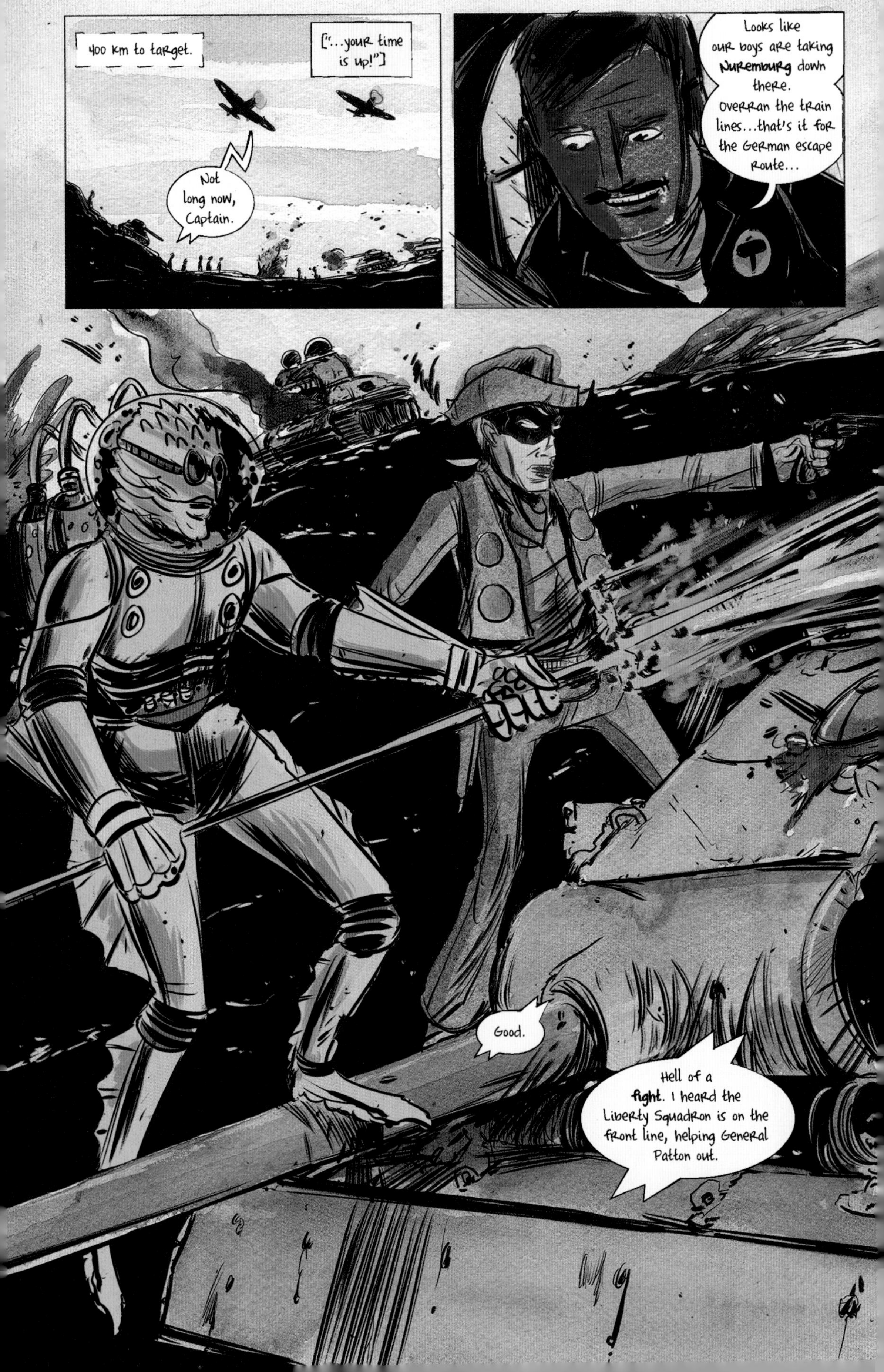
400 km to target.
["...your time is up!"]
Not long now, Captain.
Looks like our boys are taking Nuremburg down there. Overran the train lines...that's it for the German escape route...
Good.
Hell of a fight. I heard the Liberty Squadron is on the front line, helping General Patton out.

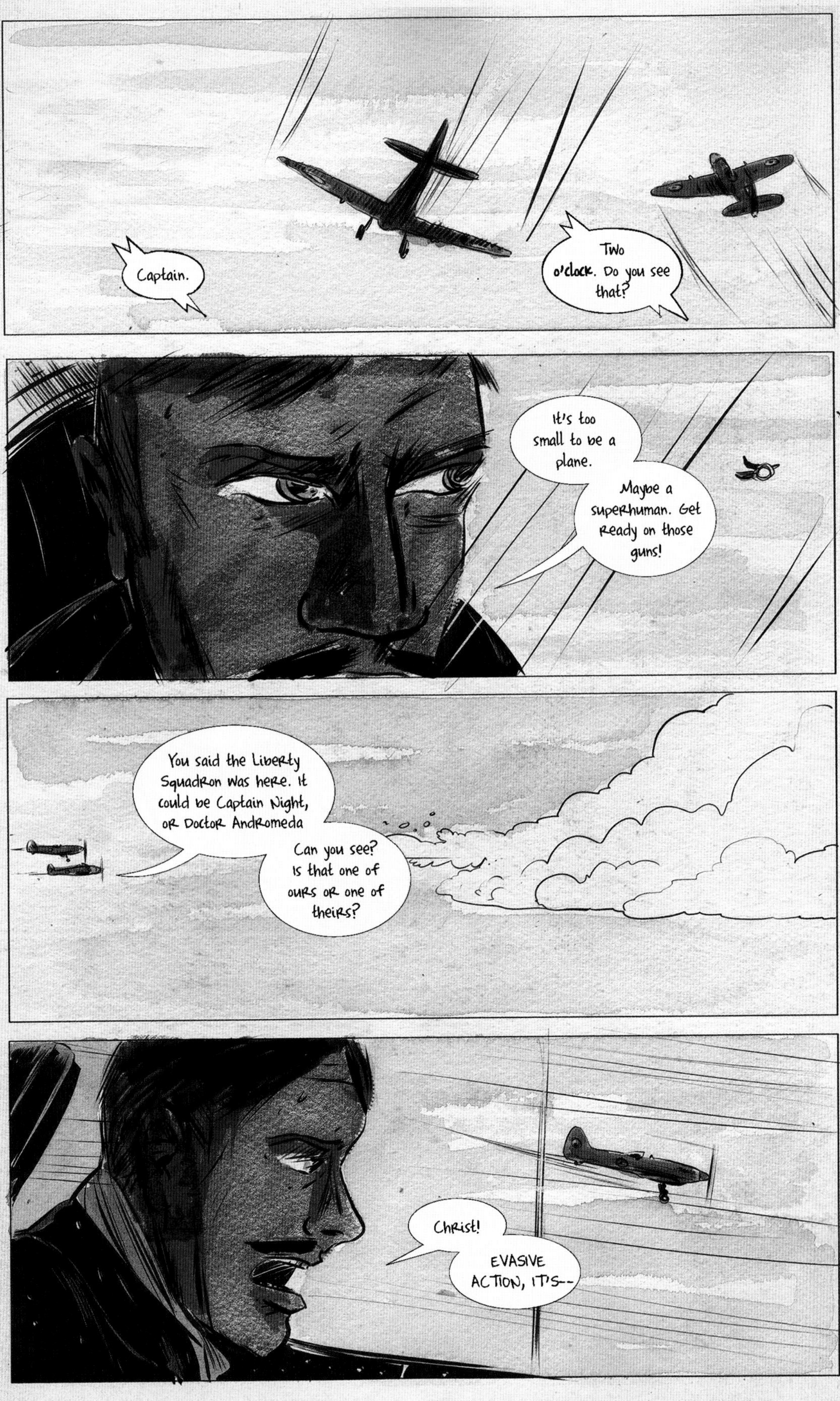
Captain.
Two o'clock. Do you see that?
It's too small to be a plane.
Maybe a superhuman. Get ready on those guns!
You said the Liberty Squadron was here. It could be Captain Night, or Doctor Andromeda
Can you see? Is that one of ours or one of theirs?
Christ!
EVASIVE ACTION, IT'S--

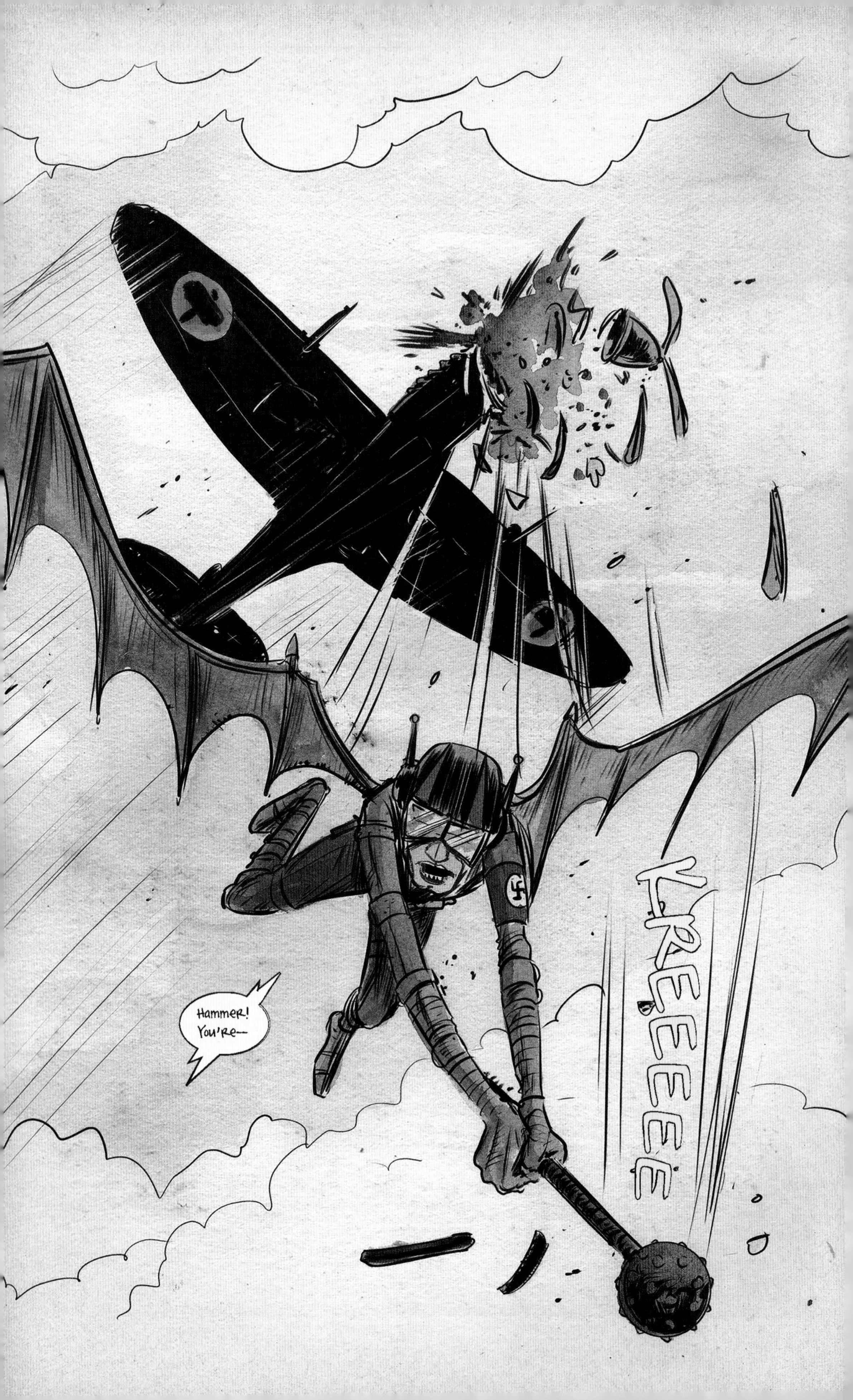
Hammer! You're--
VREEEEEE

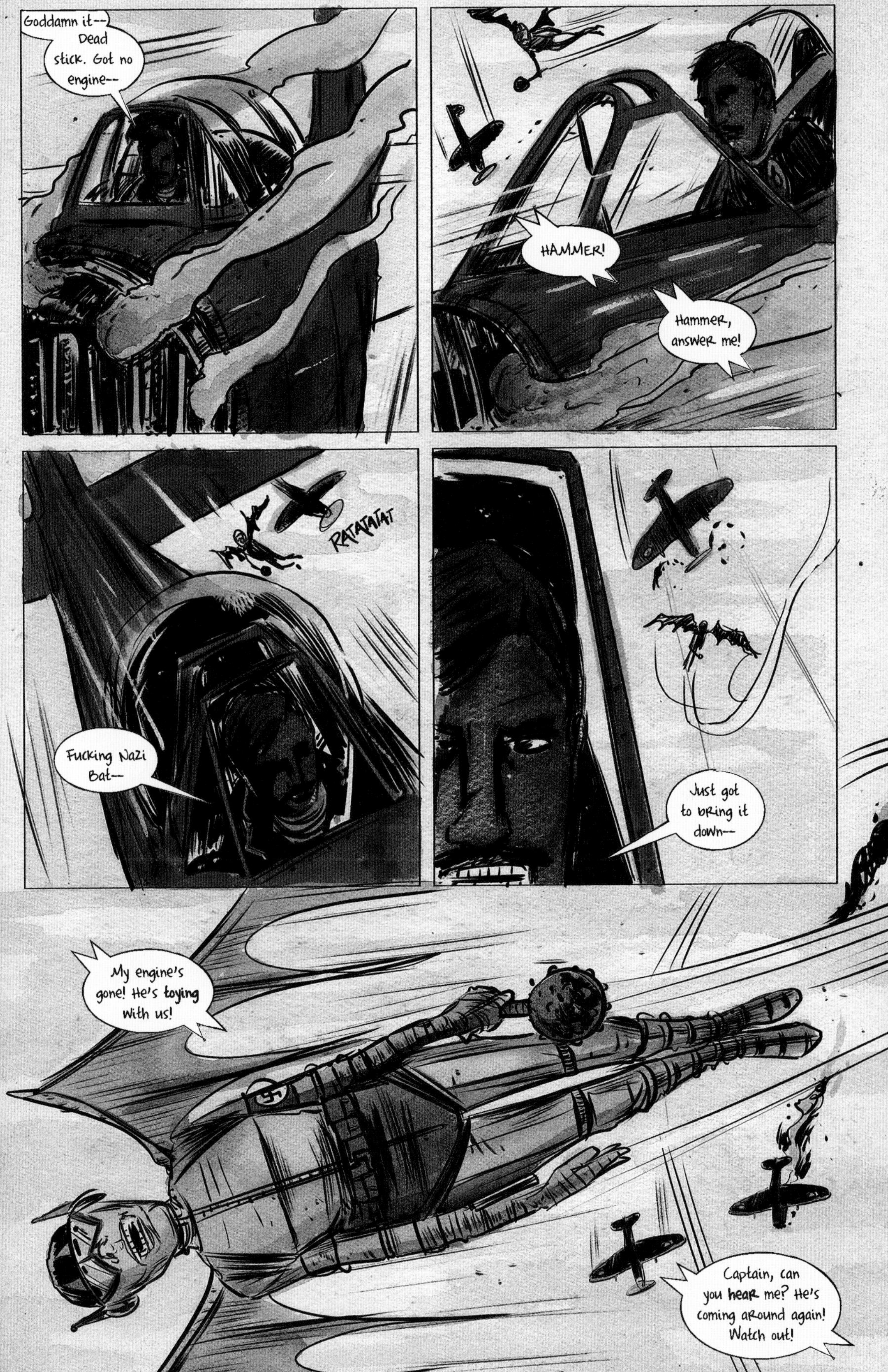
Goddamn it-- Dead stick. Got no engine--
HAMMER!
Hammer, answer me!
RATATATAT
Fucking Nazi Bat--
Just got to bring it down--
My engine's gone! He's toying with us!
Captain, can you hear me? He's coming around again! Watch out!

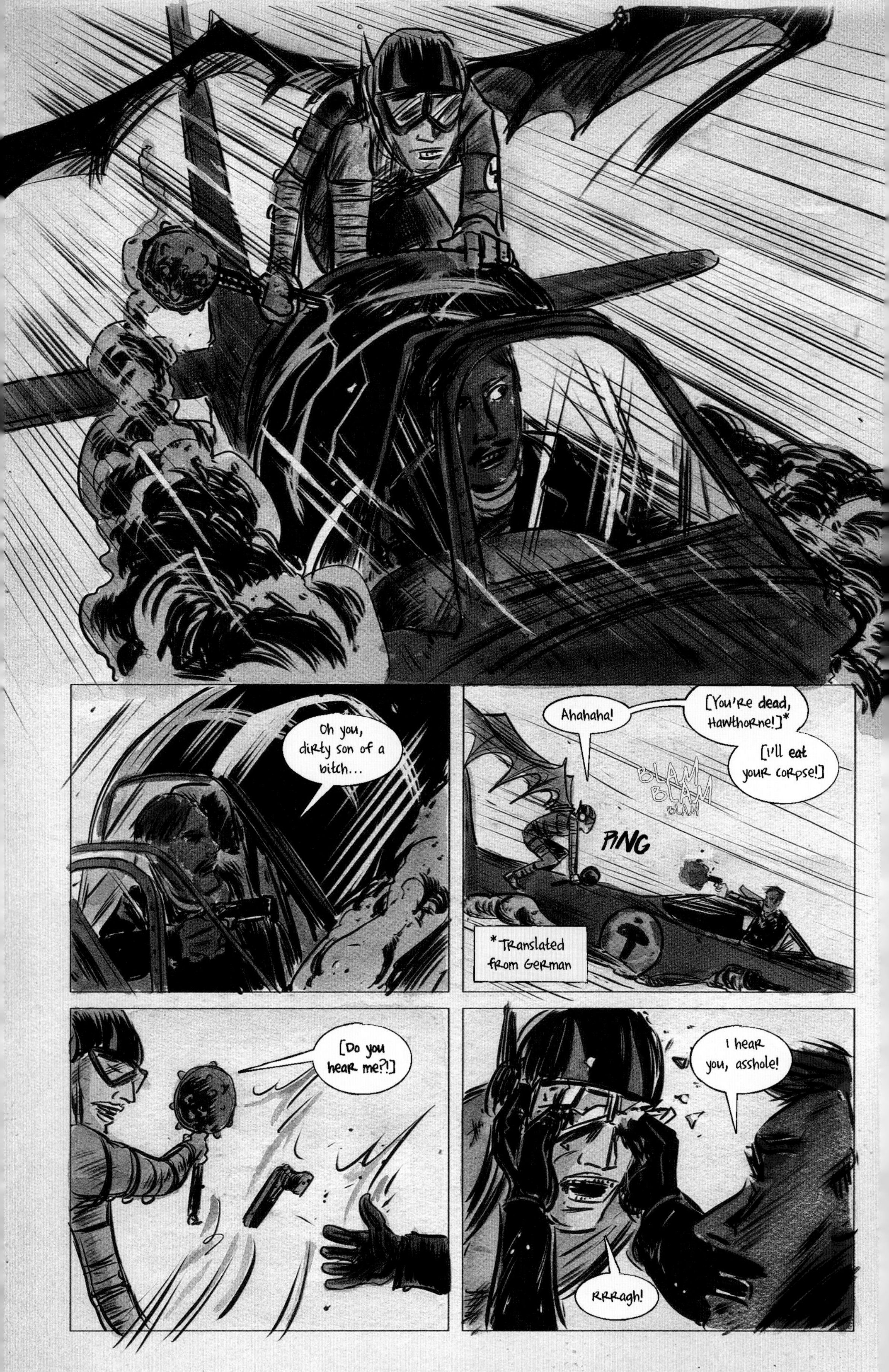
Oh you, dirty son of a bitch...
Ahahaha!
[You're dead, Hawthorne!]*
[I'll eat your corpse!]
BLAM BLAM BLAM
PING
*Translated from German
[Do you hear me?!]
I hear you, asshole!
RRRagh!

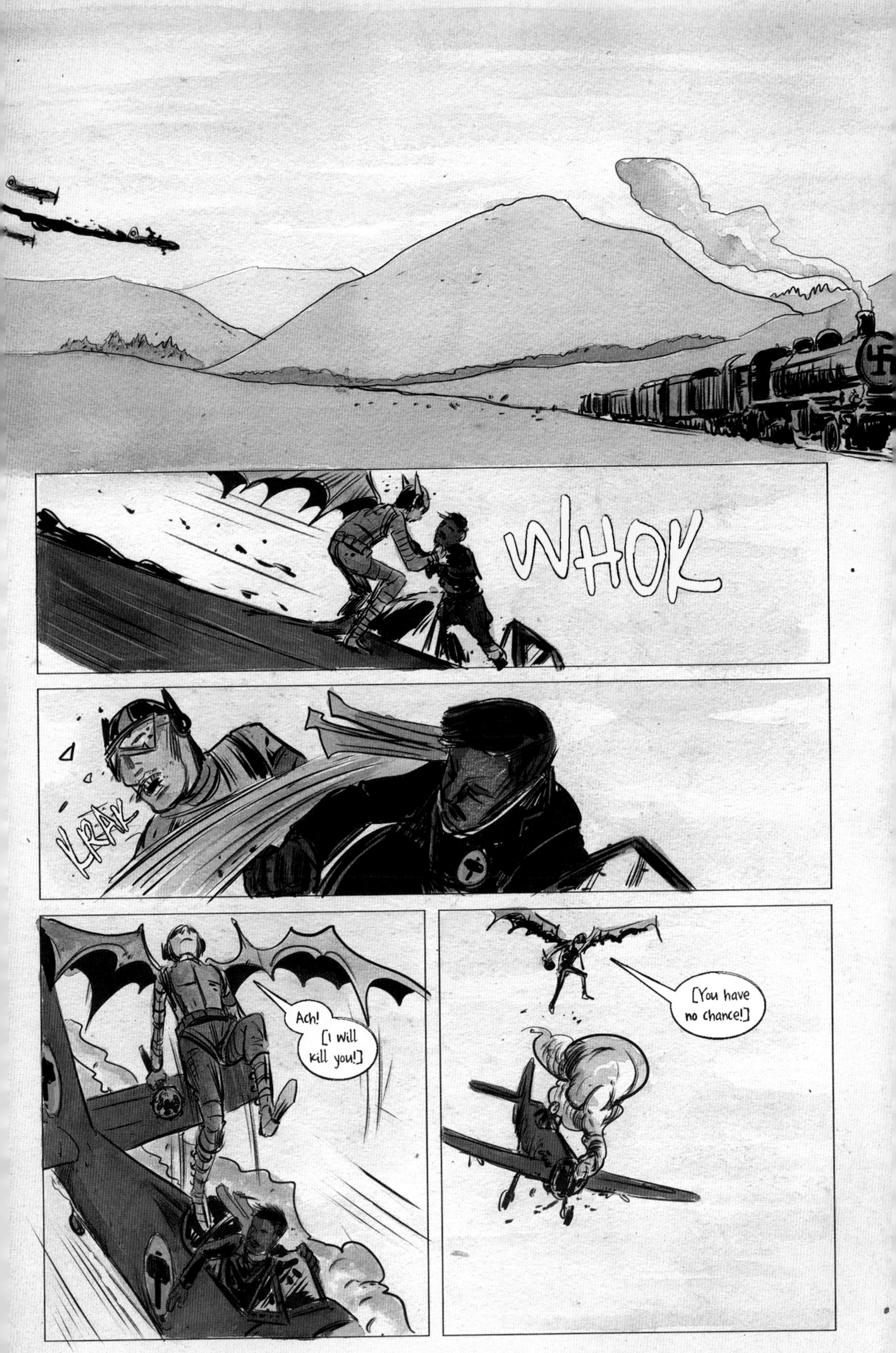
WHOK
KRAK
Ach! [I will kill you!]
[You have no chance!]

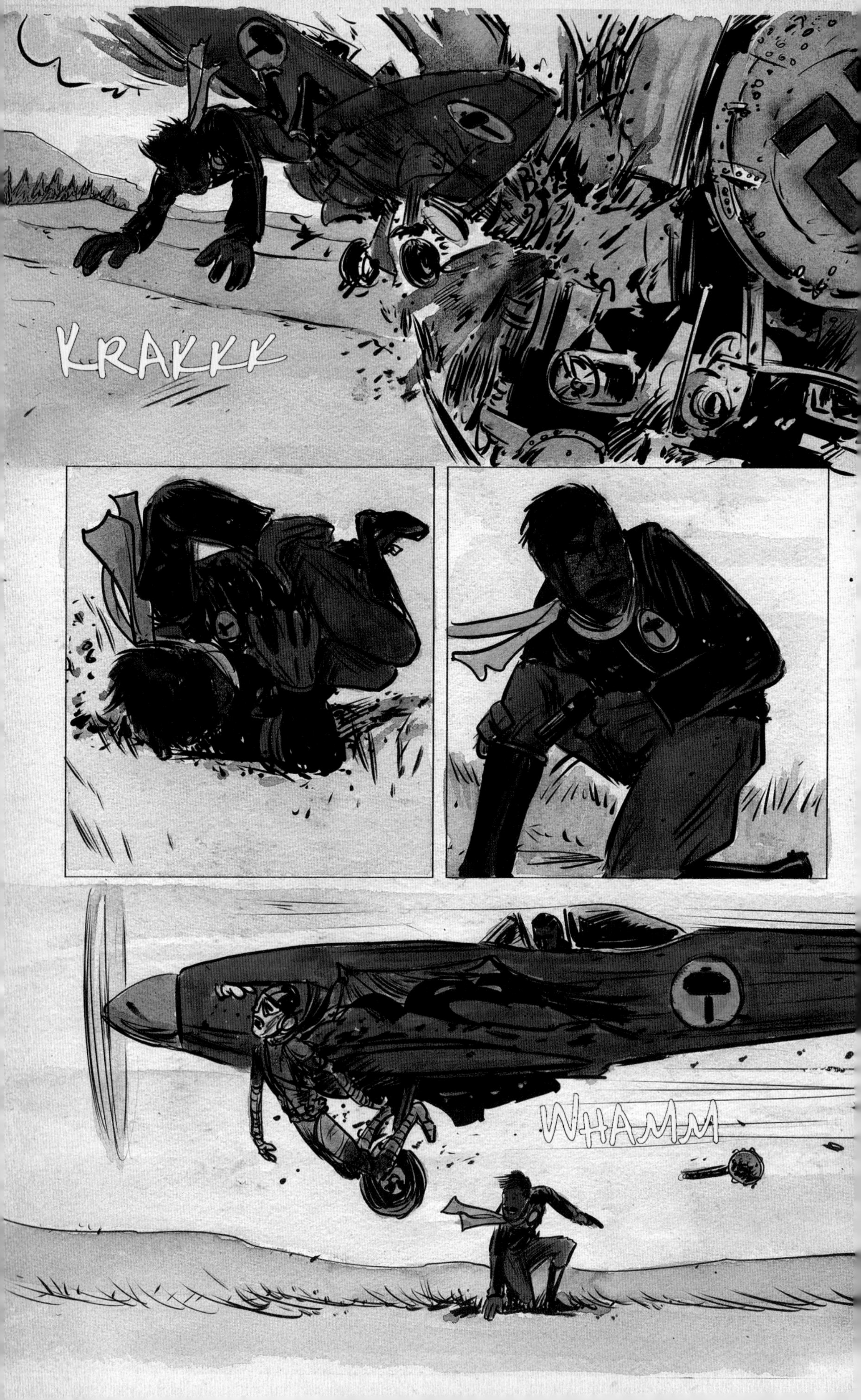
KRAKKK
WHAMM

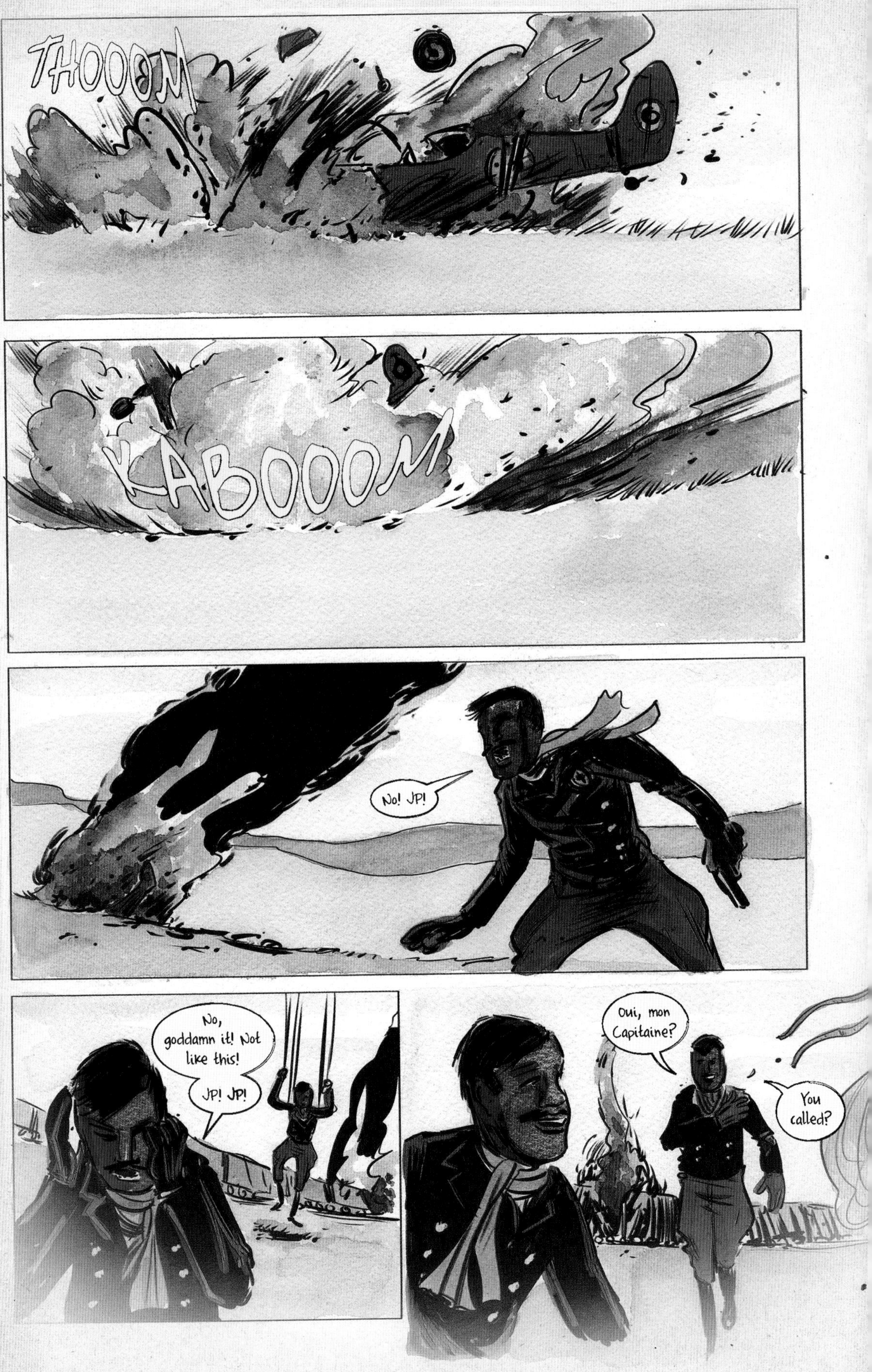

THOOOM
KABOOOM
No! JP!
No, goddamn it! Not like this!
JP! JP!
Oui, mon Capitaine?
You called?

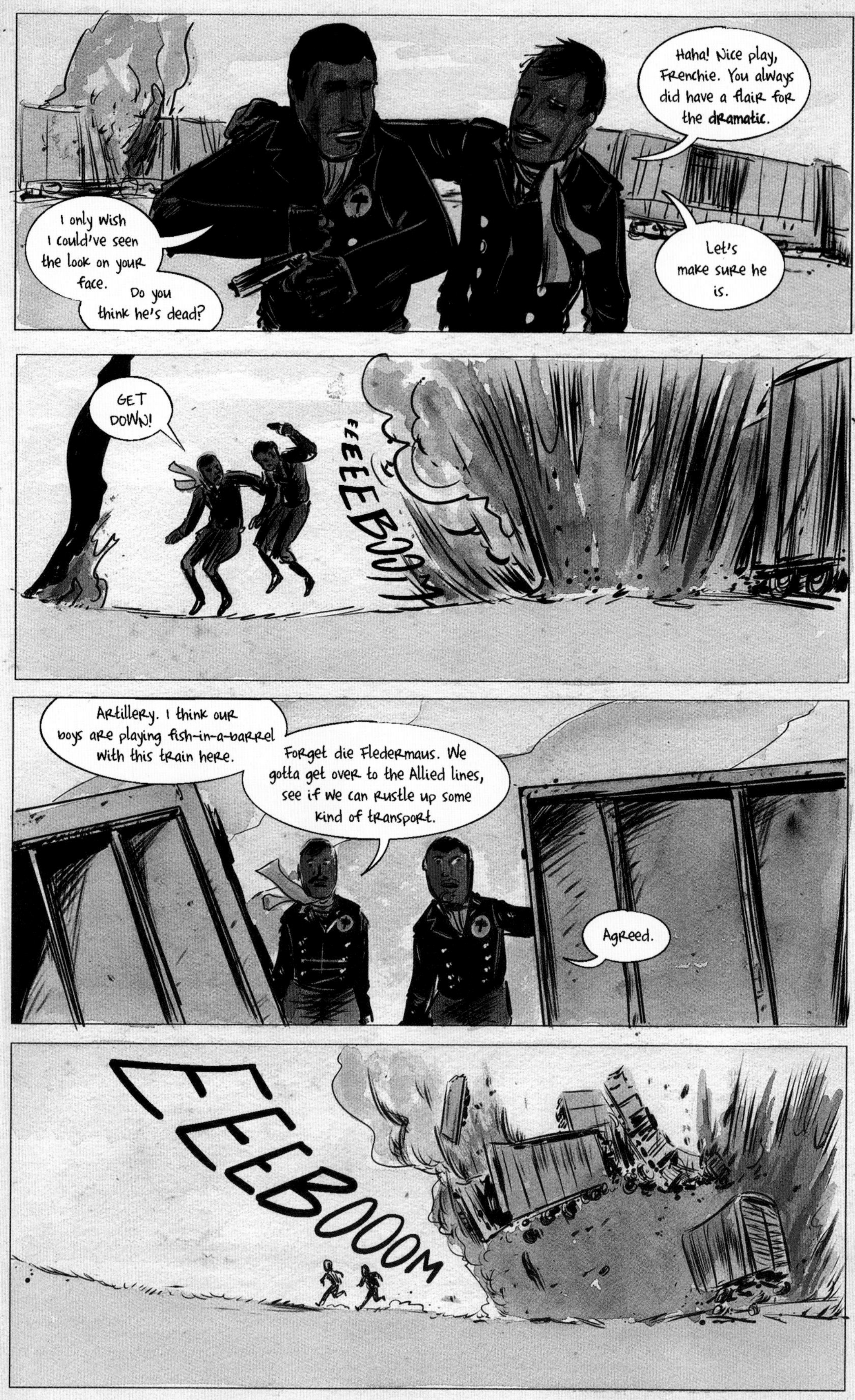
Haha! Nice play, Frenchie. You always did have a flair for the **dramatic**.
I only wish I could've seen the look on your face.
Do you think he's dead?
Let's make sure he is.
GET DOWN!
EEEEEEBOOM
Artillery. I think our boys are playing fish-in-a-barrel with this train here.
Forget die Fledermaus. We gotta get over to the Allied lines, see if we can rustle up some kind of transport.
Agreed.
EEEBOOOM

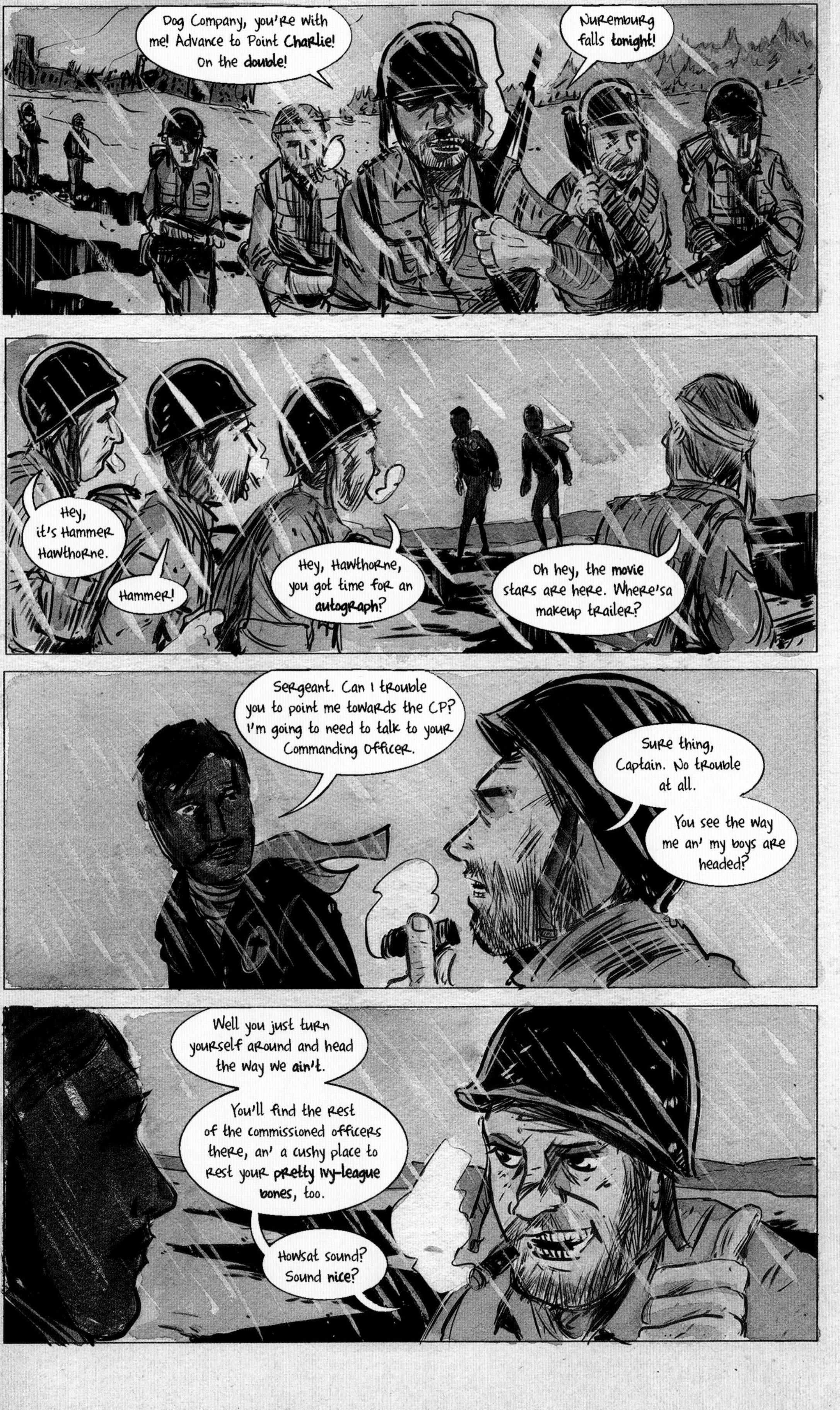
Dog Company, you're with me! Advance to Point Charlie! On the double!
Nuremburg falls tonight!
Hey, it's Hammer Hawthorne.
Hammer!
Hey, Hawthorne, you got time for an autograph?
Oh hey, the movie stars are here. Where'sa makeup trailer?
Sergeant. Can I trouble you to point me towards the CP? I'm going to need to talk to your Commanding Officer.
Sure thing, Captain. No trouble at all.
You see the way me an' my boys are headed?
Well you just turn yourself around and head the way we ain't.
You'll find the rest of the commissioned officers there, an' a cushy place to rest your pretty Ivy-league bones, too.
Howsat sound? Sound nice?

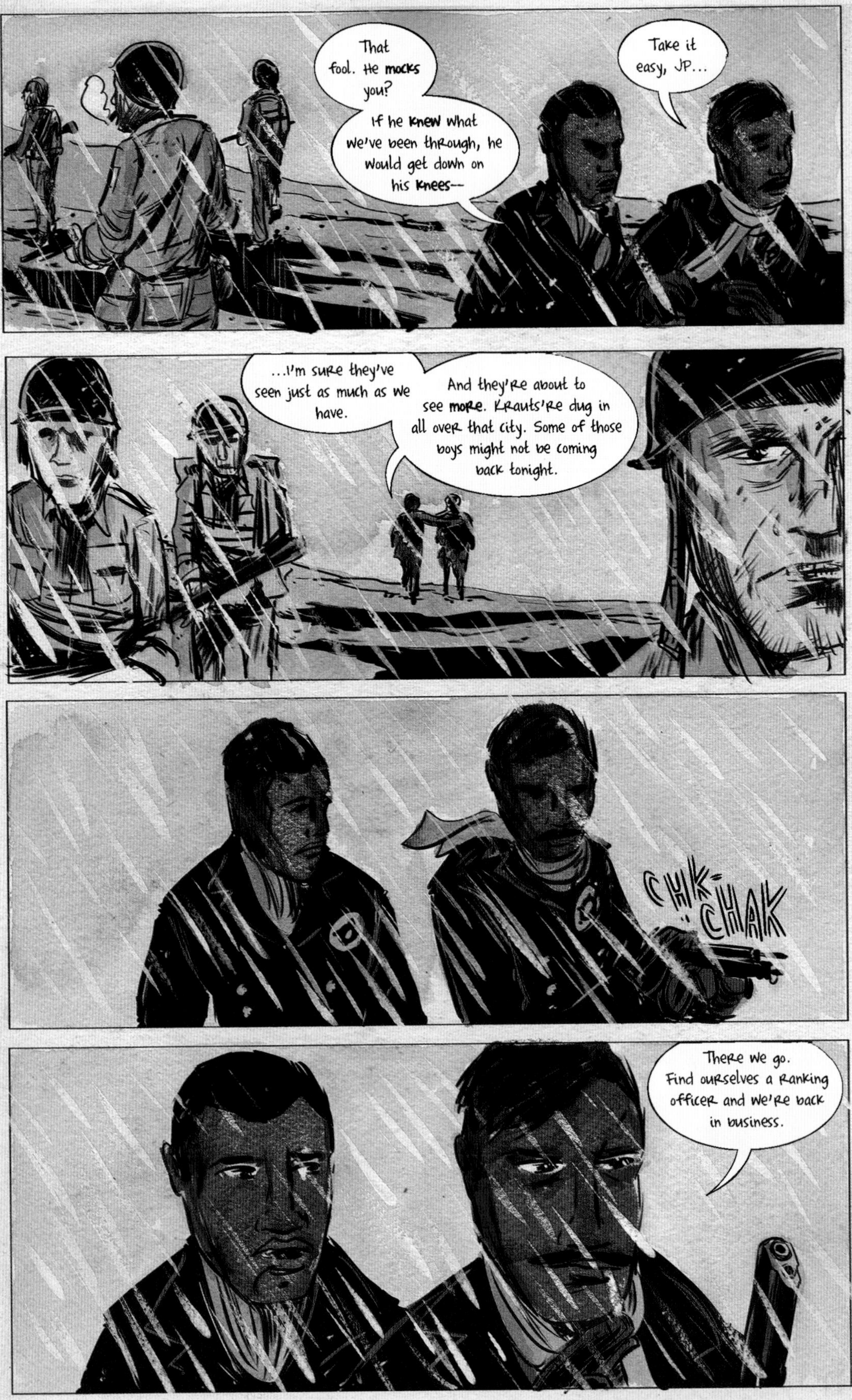
That fool. He mocks you?
If he knew what we've been through, he would get down on his knees--
Take it easy, JP...
...I'm sure they've seen just as much as we have.
And they're about to see more. Krauts're dug in all over that city. Some of those boys might not be coming back tonight.
CHK-CHAK
There we go. Find ourselves a ranking officer and we're back in business.

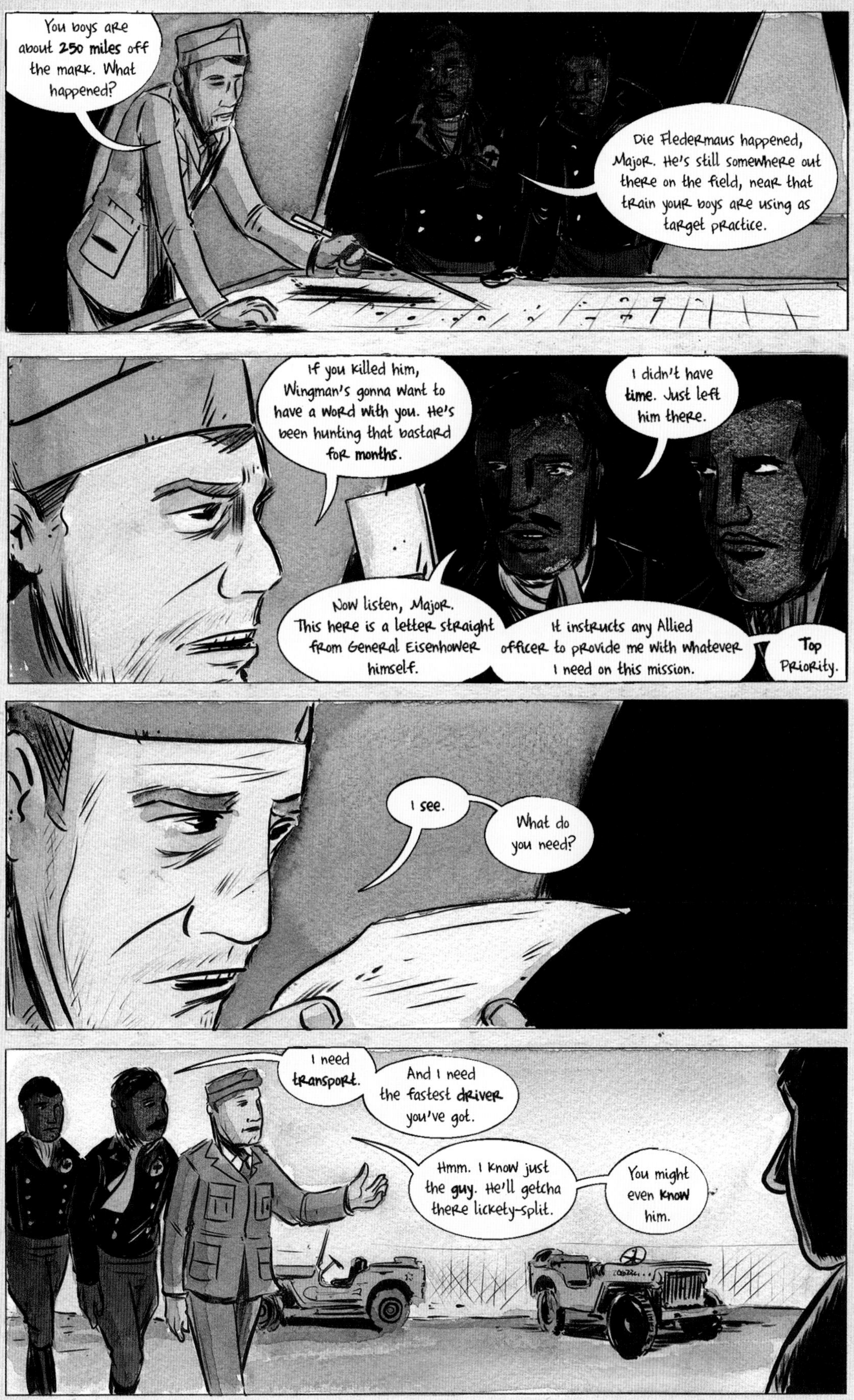
You boys are about 250 miles off the mark. What happened?
Die Fledermaus happened, Major. He's still somewhere out there on the field, near that train your boys are using as target practice.
If you killed him, Wingman's gonna want to have a word with you. He's been hunting that bastard for months.
I didn't have time. Just left him there.
Now listen, Major. This here is a letter straight from General Eisenhower himself.
It instructs any Allied officer to provide me with whatever I need on this mission.
Top Priority.
I see.
What do you need?
I need transport.
And I need the fastest driver you've got.
Hmm. I know just the guy. He'll getcha there lickety-split.
You might even know him.

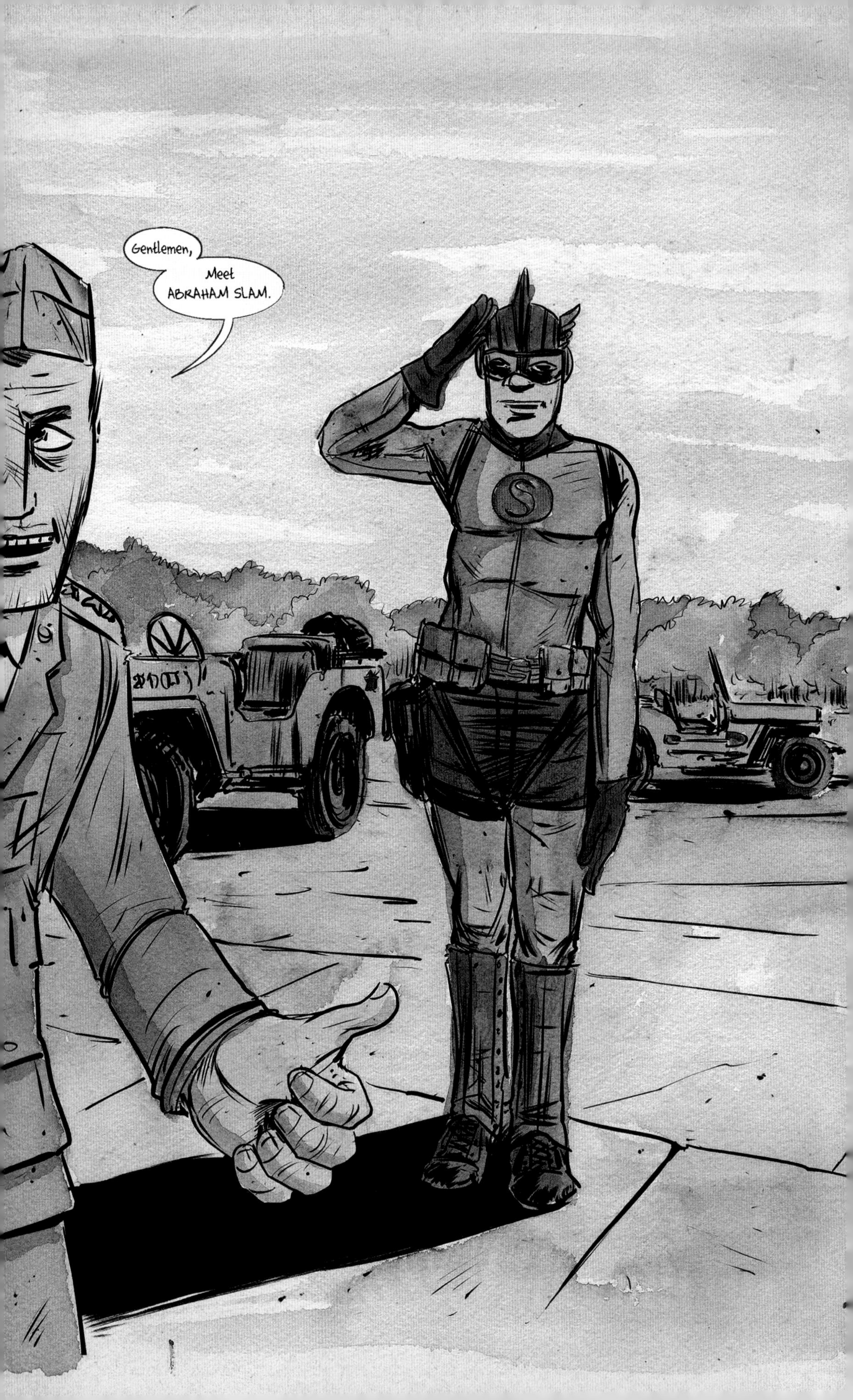
Gentlemen,
Meet ABRAHAM SLAM.

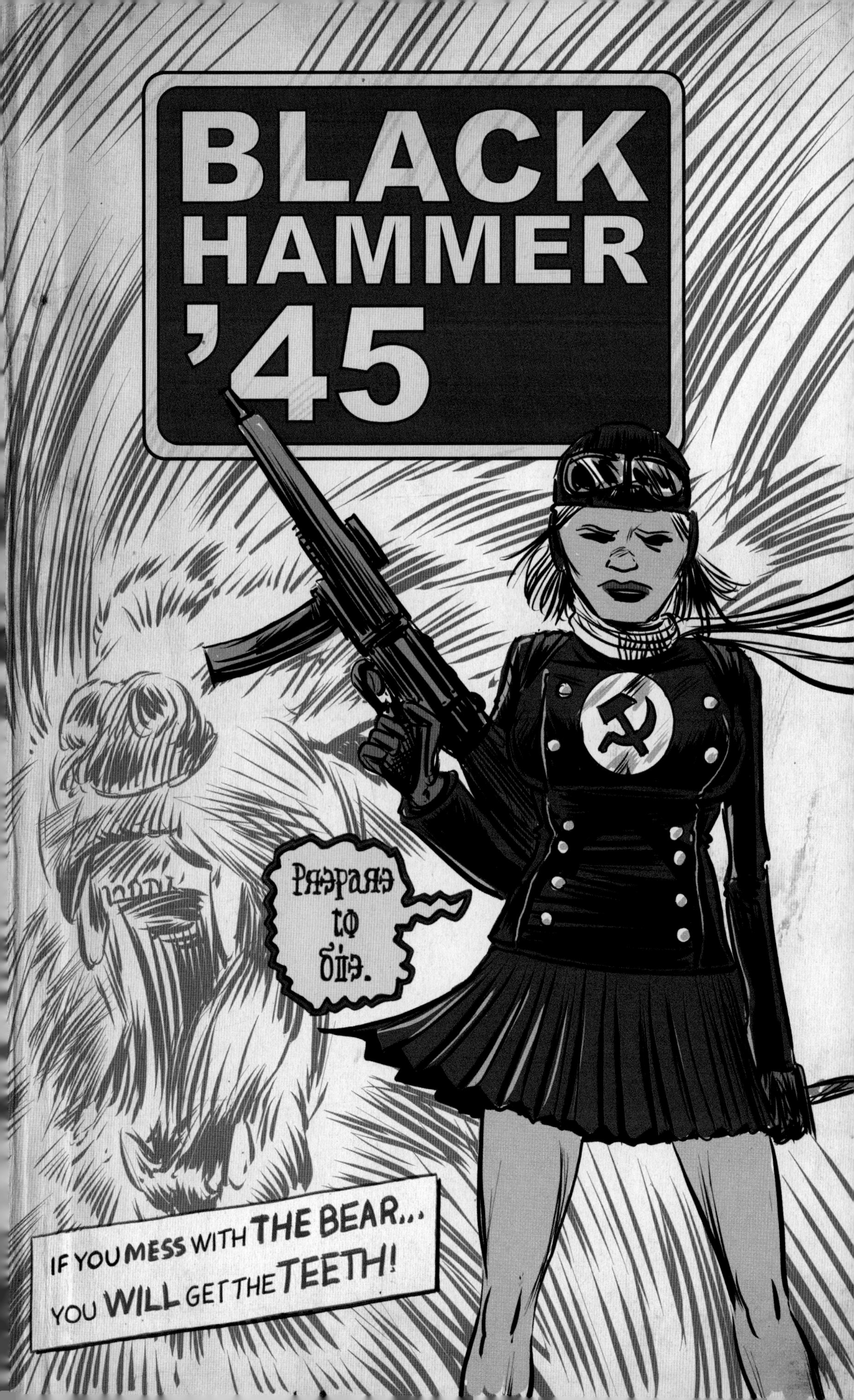
BLACK HAMMER '45
Pяэpaяэ tφ бїпэ.
IF YOU MESS WITH THE BEAR...
YOU WILL GET THE TEETH!

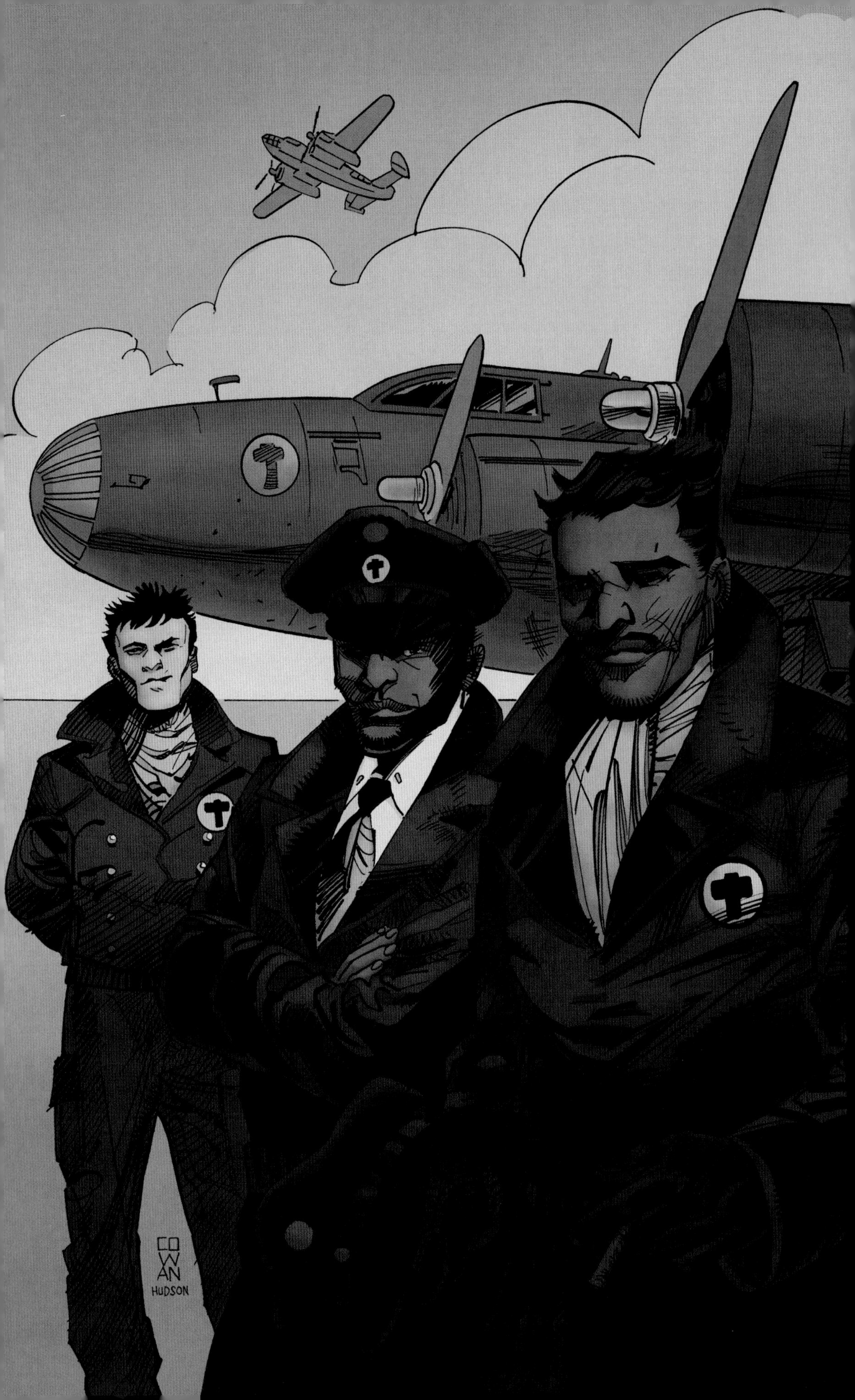
COWAN
HUDSON

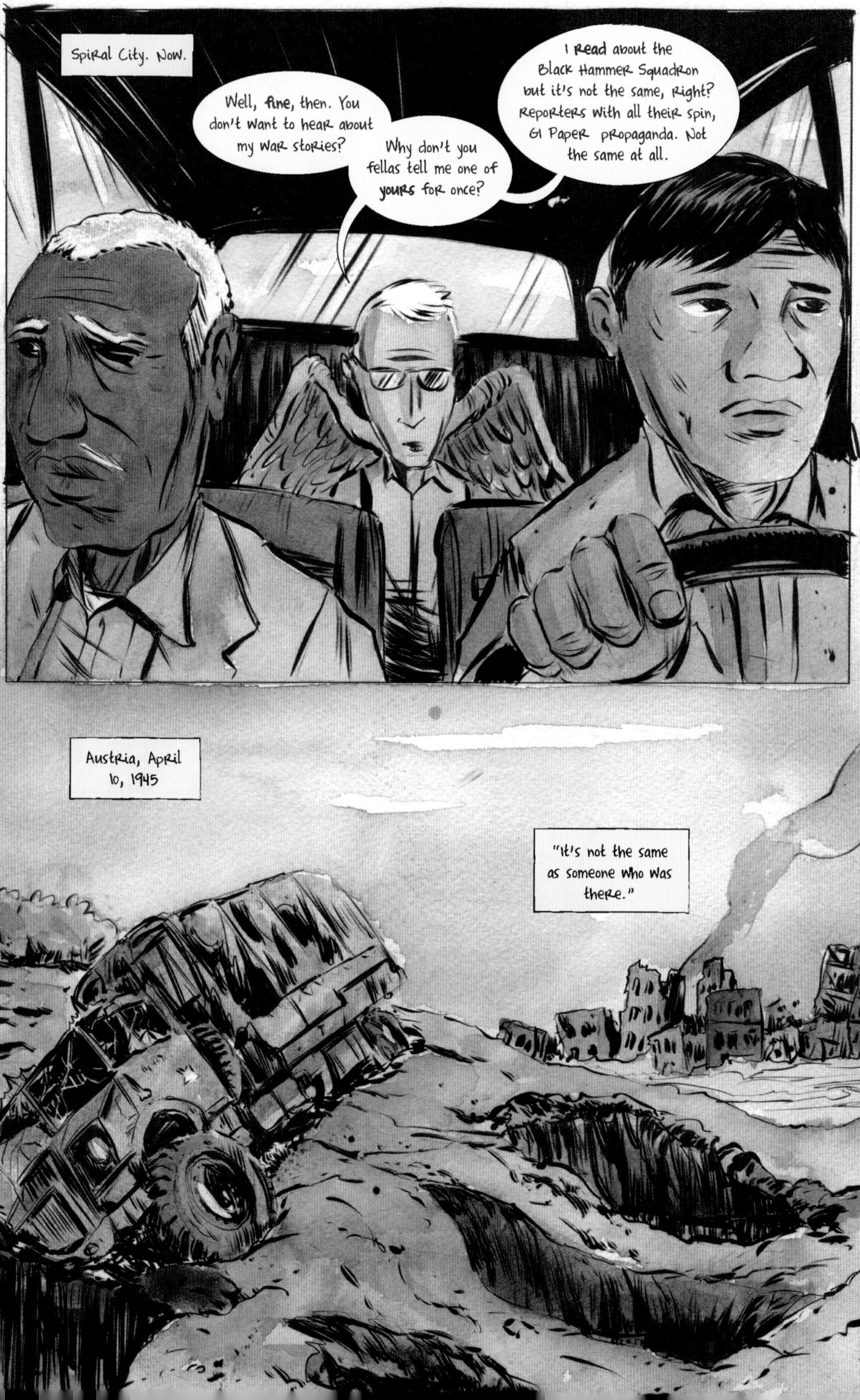
Spiral City. Now.
Well, fine, then. You don't want to hear about my war stories?
Why don't you fellas tell me one of yours for once?
I read about the Black Hammer Squadron but it's not the same, right? Reporters with all their spin, GI Paper propaganda. Not the same at all.
Austria, April 10, 1945
"It's not the same as someone who was there."

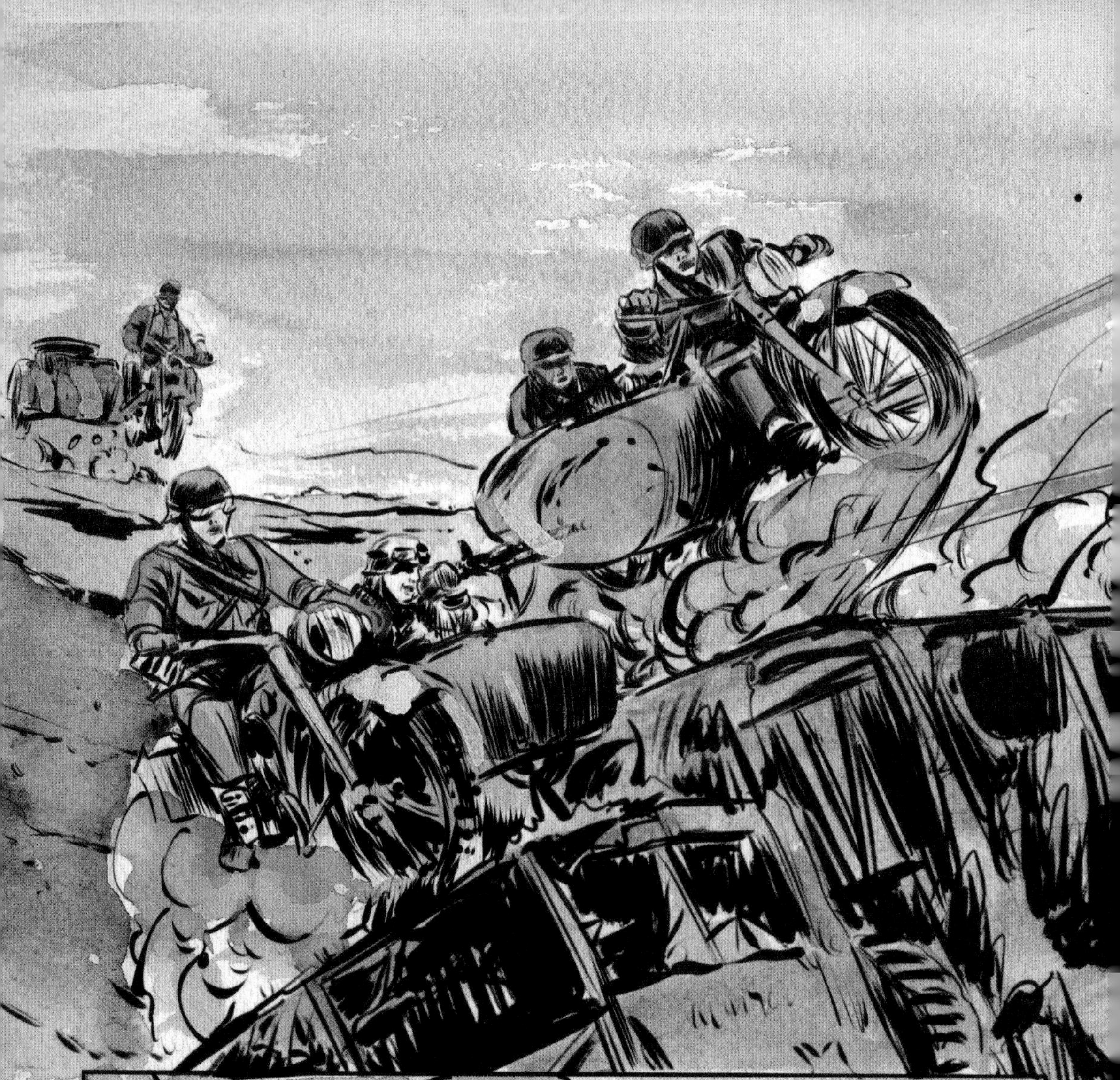

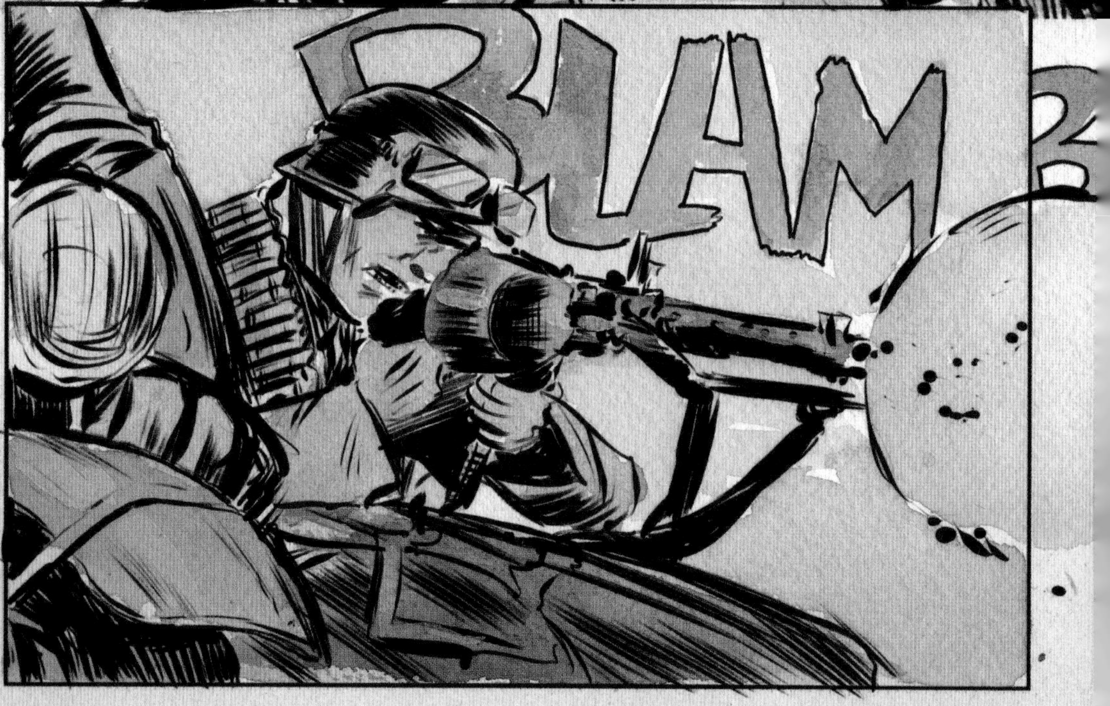
BLAM

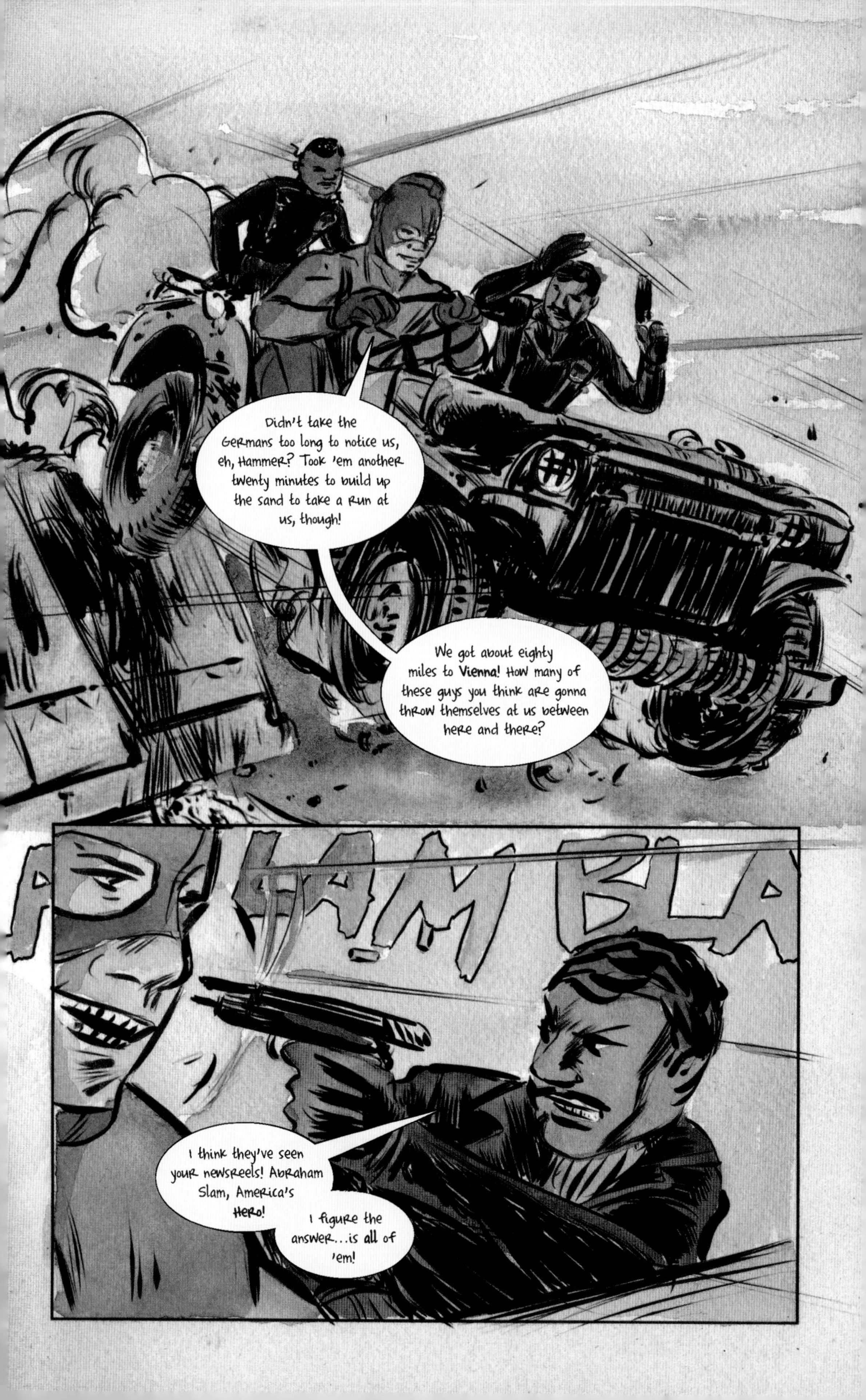
Didn't take the Germans too long to notice us, eh, Hammer? Took 'em another twenty minutes to build up the sand to take a run at us, though!
We got about eighty miles to **Vienna!** How many of these guys you think are gonna throw themselves at us between here and there?
I think they've seen your newsreels! Abraham Slam, America's **Hero**!
I figure the answer...is **all** of 'em!

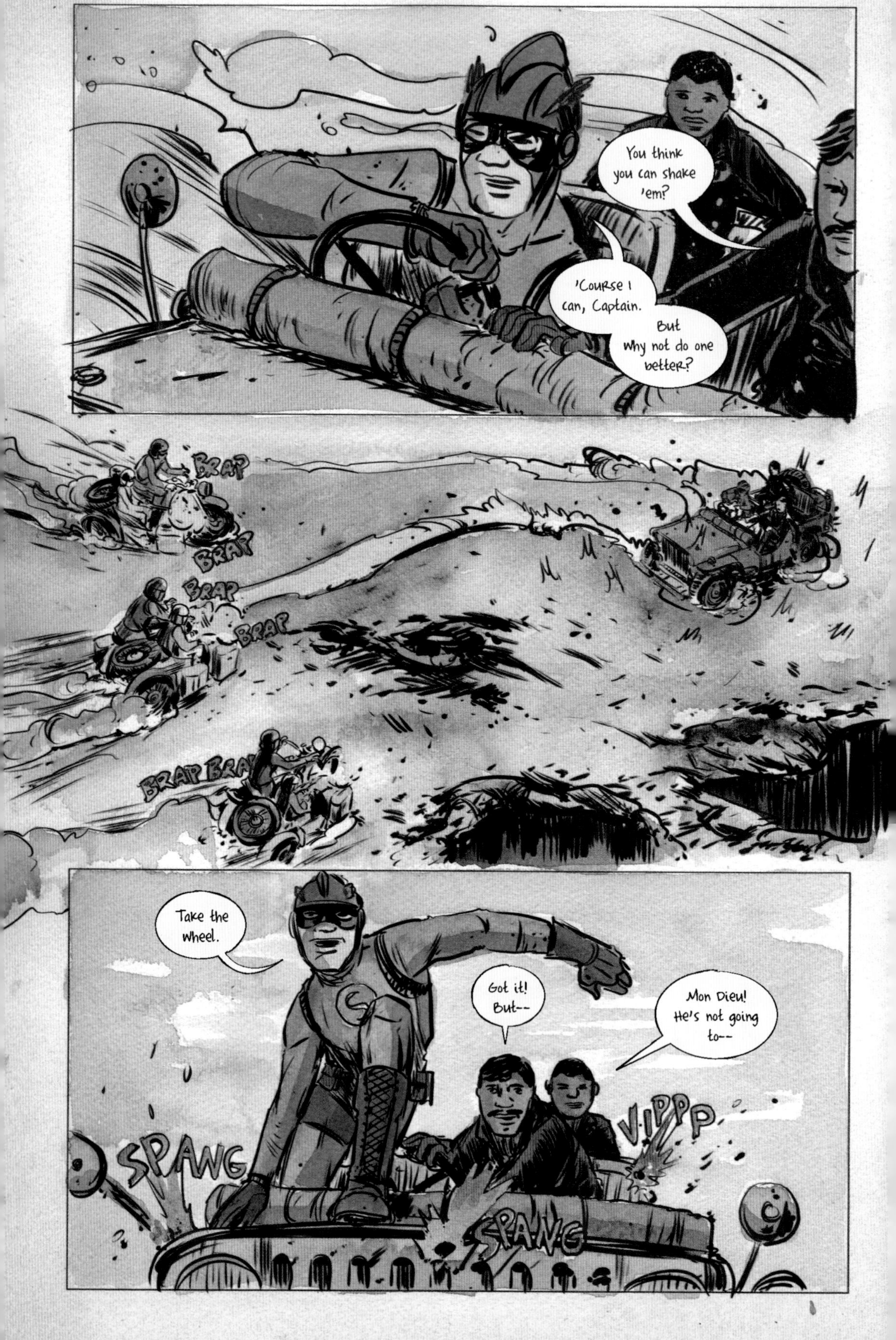
You think you can shake 'em?
'Course I can, Captain.
But why not do one better?
BRAP
BRAP
BRAP
BRAP
BRAP BRAP
Take the wheel.
Got it! But--
Mon Dieu! He's not going to--
SPANG
VIPPP
SPANG

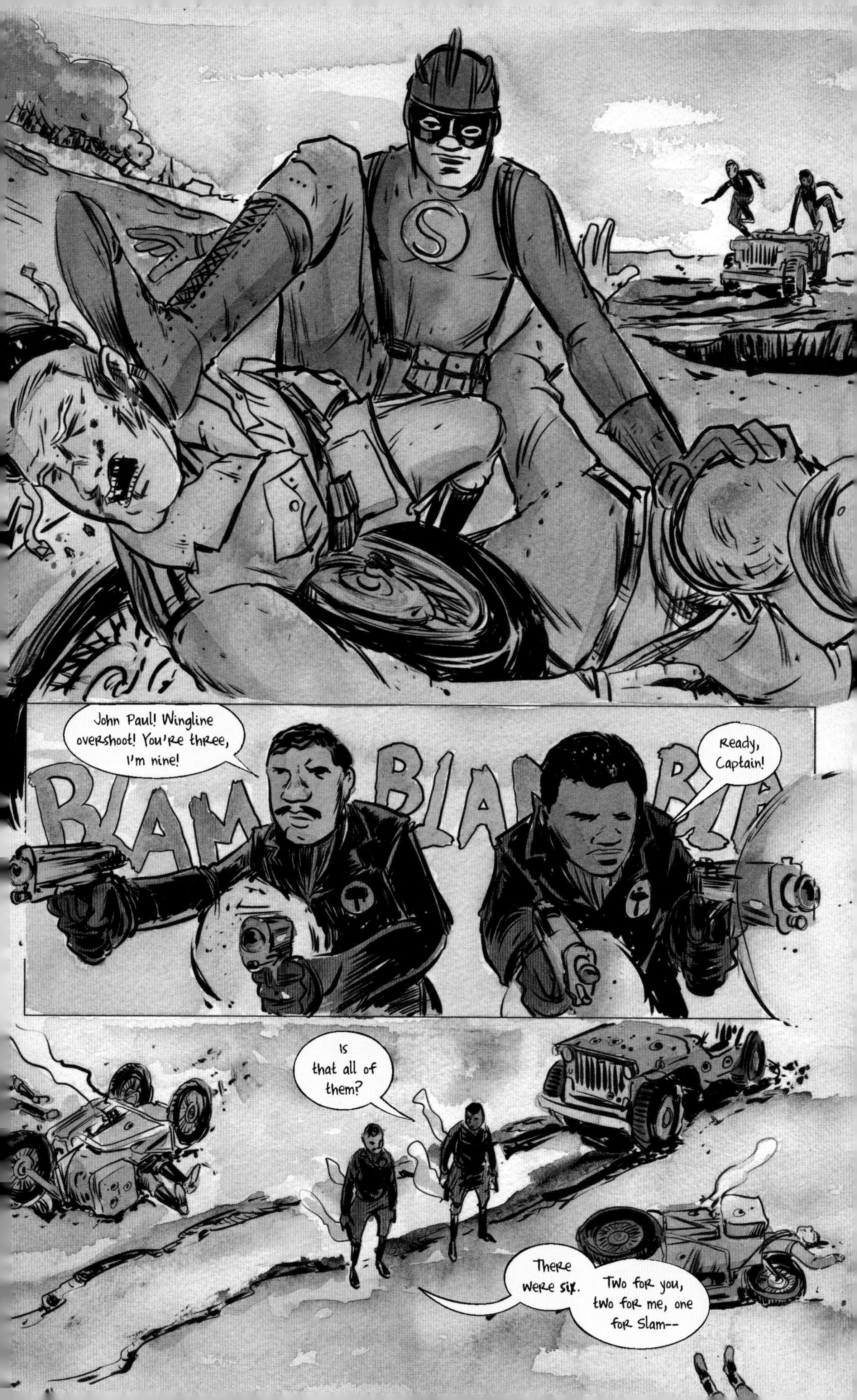
John Paul! Wingline overshoot! You're three, I'm nine!
Ready, Captain!
BLAM
BLAM
Is that all of them?
There were six.
Two for you, two for me, one for Slam--

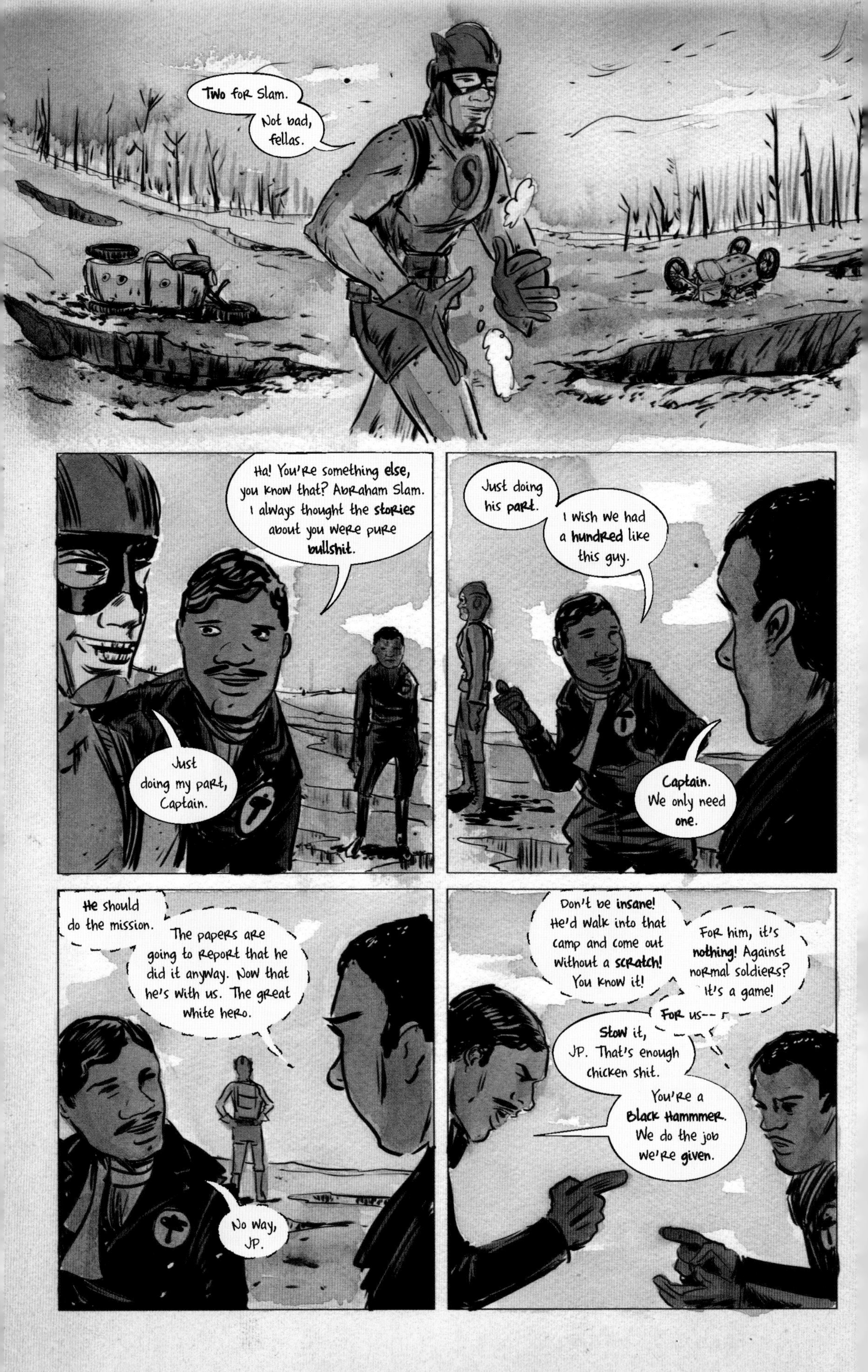

Two for Slam.
Not bad, fellas.
Ha! You're something else, you know that? Abraham Slam. I always thought the stories about you were pure bullshit.
Just doing my part, Captain.
Just doing his part.
I wish we had a hundred like this guy.
Captain. We only need one.
He should do the mission.
The papers are going to report that he did it anyway. Now that he's with us. The great white hero.
No way, JP.
Don't be insane! He'd walk into that camp and come out without a scratch! You know it!
For him, it's nothing! Against normal soldiers? It's a game!
For us--
Stow it, JP. That's enough chicken shit.
You're a Black Hammmer. We do the job we're given.

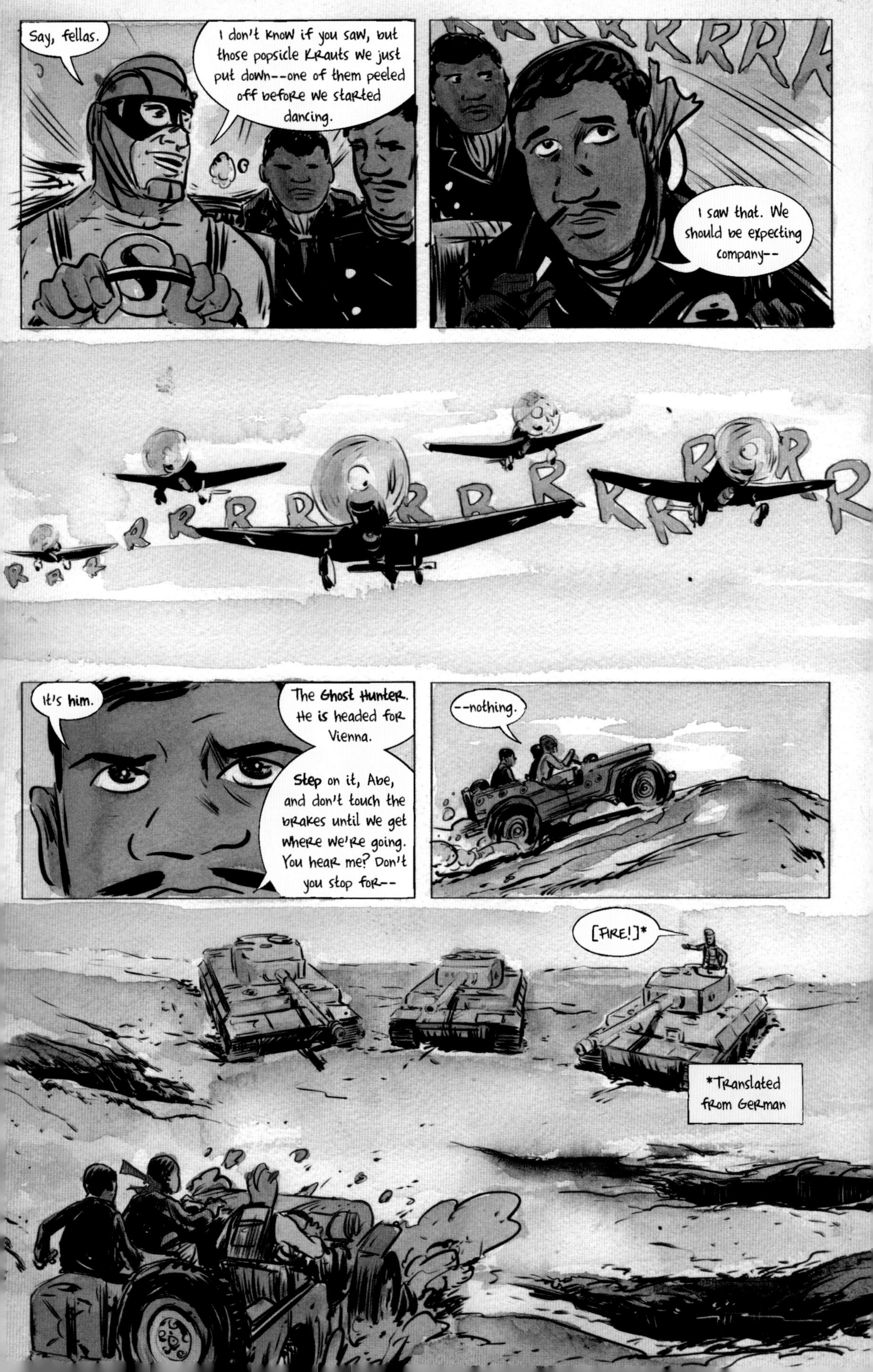
Say, fellas.
I don't know if you saw, but those popsicle Krauts we just put down--one of them peeled off before we started dancing.
RRRRRRRRR
I saw that. We should be expecting company--
RRRRRRRRRRRRRR
It's him.
The Ghost Hunter. He is headed for Vienna.
Step on it, Abe, and don't touch the brakes until we get where we're going. You hear me? Don't you stop for--
--nothing.
[FIRE!]*
*Translated from German

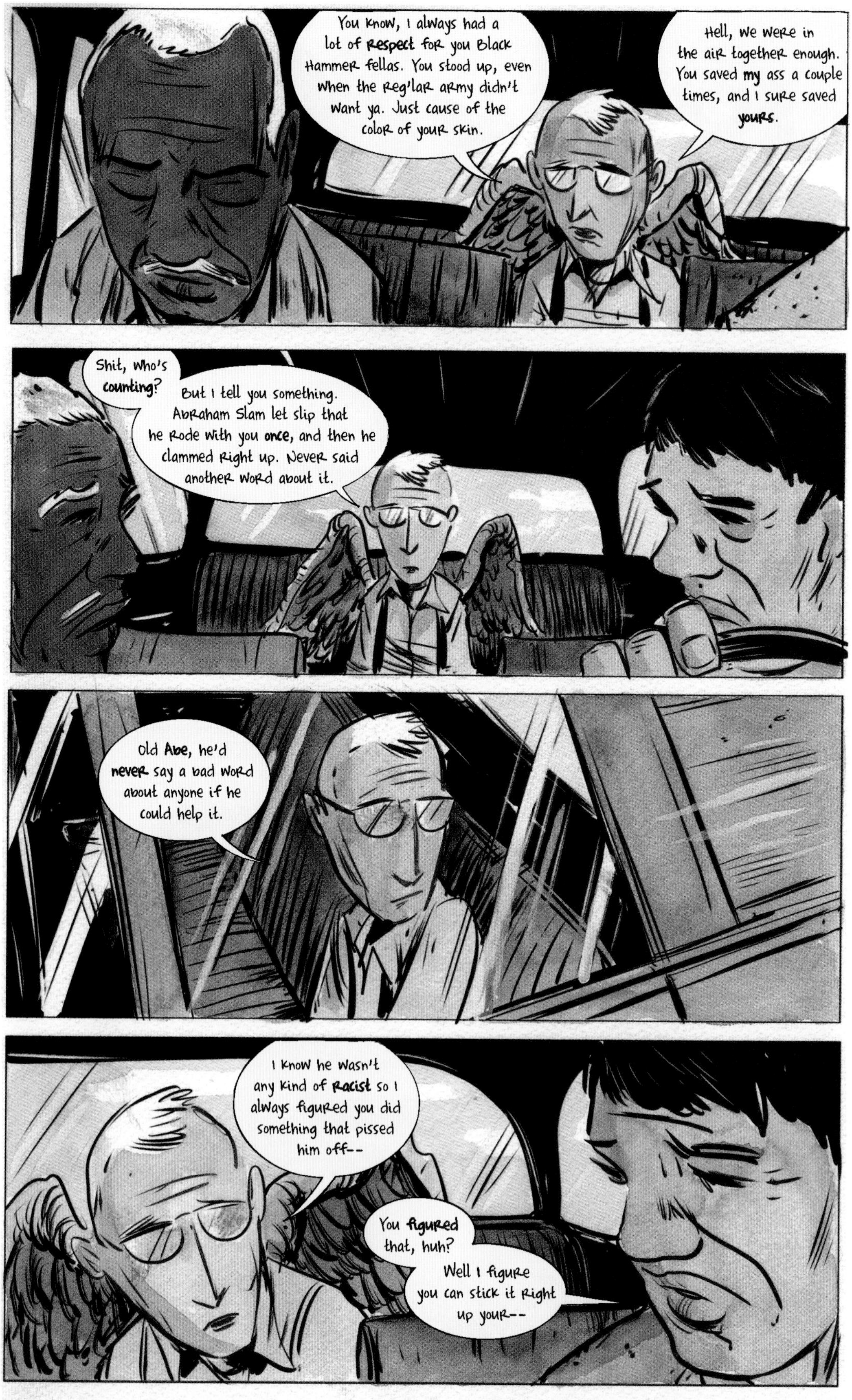
You know, I always had a lot of respect for you Black Hammer fellas. You stood up, even when the reg'lar army didn't want ya. Just cause of the color of your skin.
Hell, we were in the air together enough. You saved my ass a couple times, and I sure saved yours.
Shit, who's counting?
But I tell you something. Abraham Slam let slip that he rode with you once, and then he clammed right up. Never said another word about it.
Old Abe, he'd never say a bad word about anyone if he could help it.
I know he wasn't any kind of racist so I always figured you did something that pissed him off--
You figured that, huh?
Well I figure you can stick it right up your--

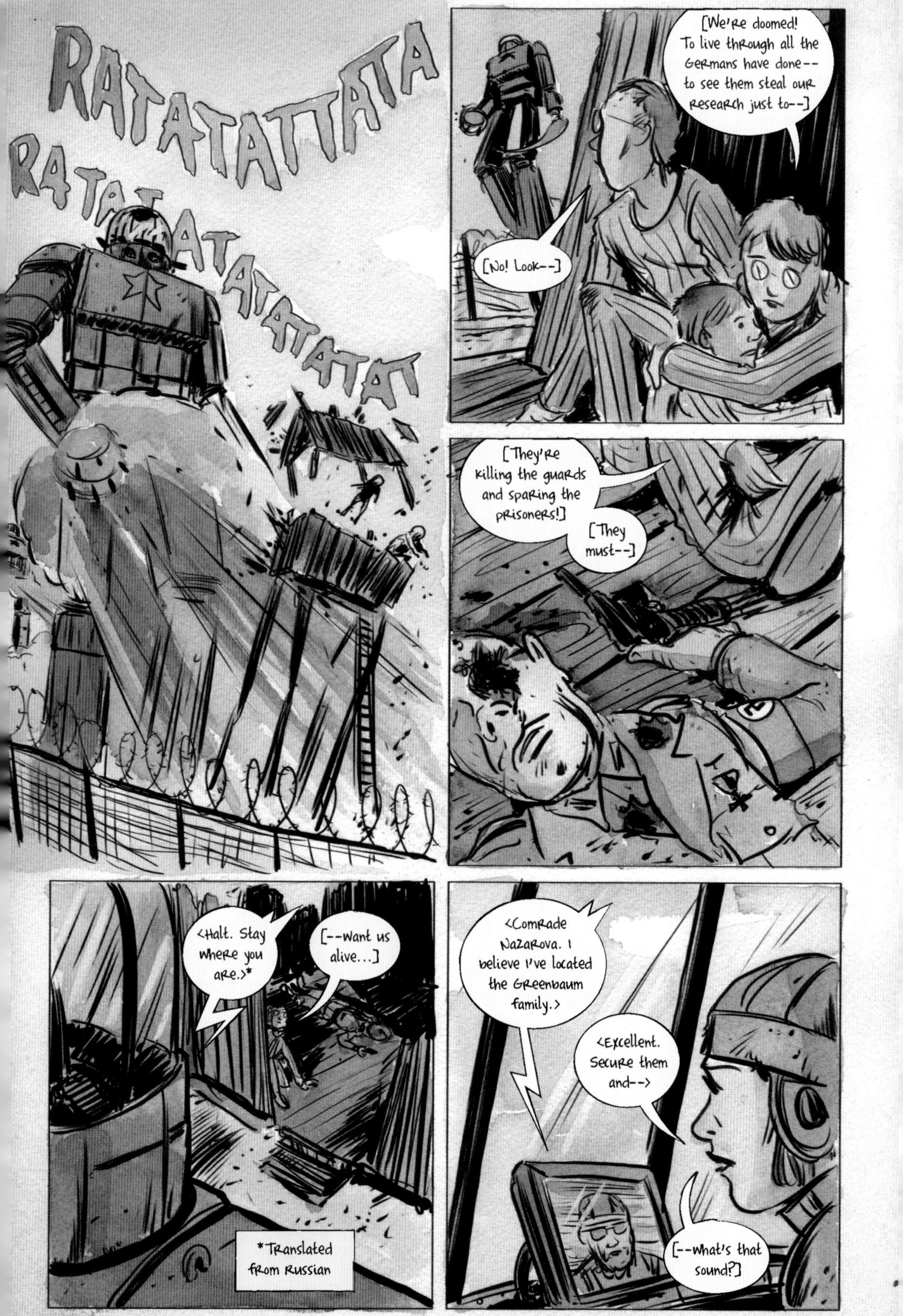
RATATATTATA
RATATATATATATATAT
[We're doomed! To live through all the Germans have done-- to see them steal our research just to--]
[No! Look--]
[They're killing the guards and sparing the prisoners!]
[They must--]
<Halt. Stay where you are.>*
[--want us alive...]
*Translated from Russian
<Comrade Nazarova. I believe I've located the Greenbaum family.>
<Excellent. Secure them and-->
[--what's that sound?]

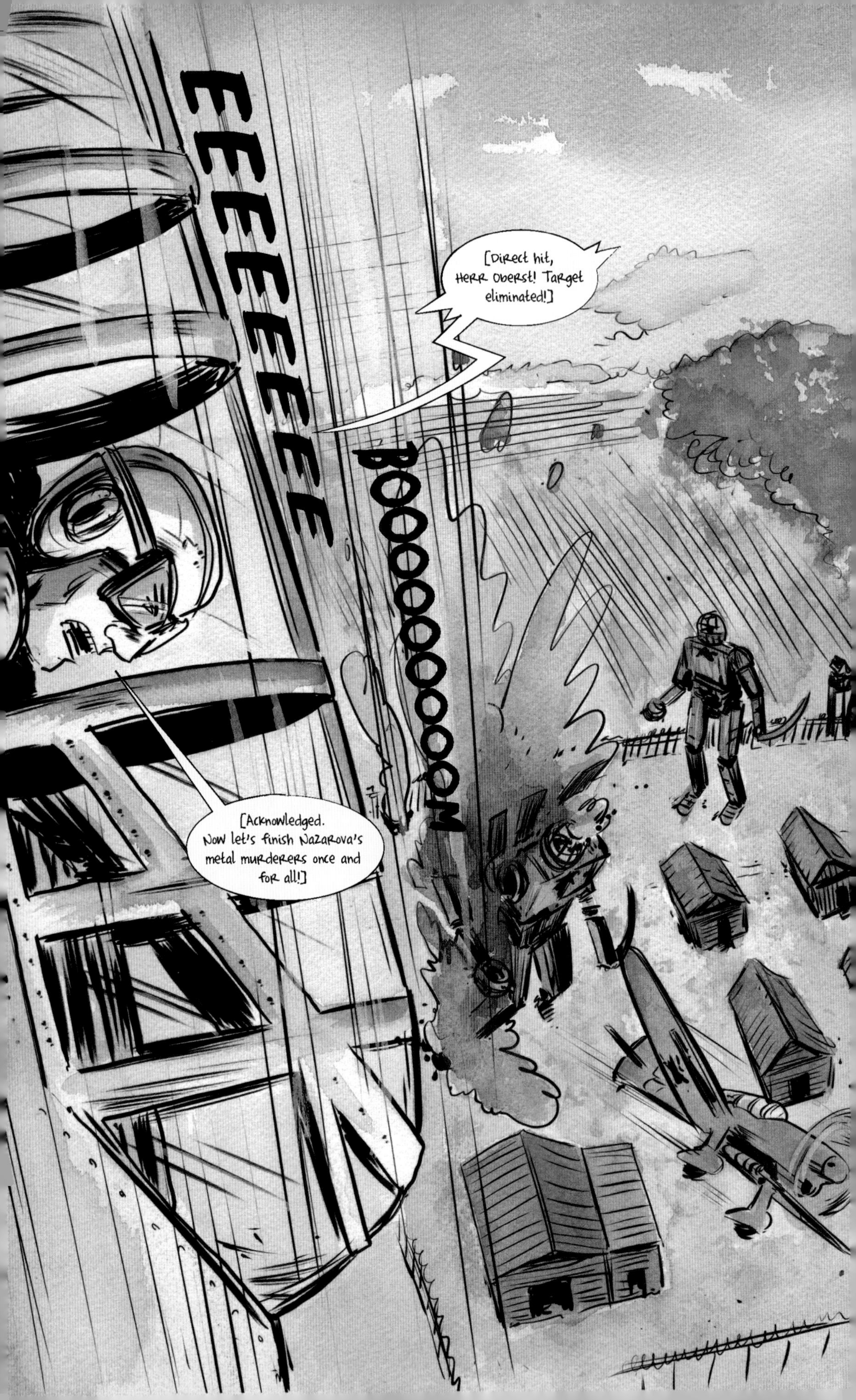
EEEEEEEEEEE
[Direct hit, Herr Oberst! Target eliminated!]
BOOOOOOOOOOM
[Acknowledged. Now let's finish Nazarova's metal murderers once and for all!]

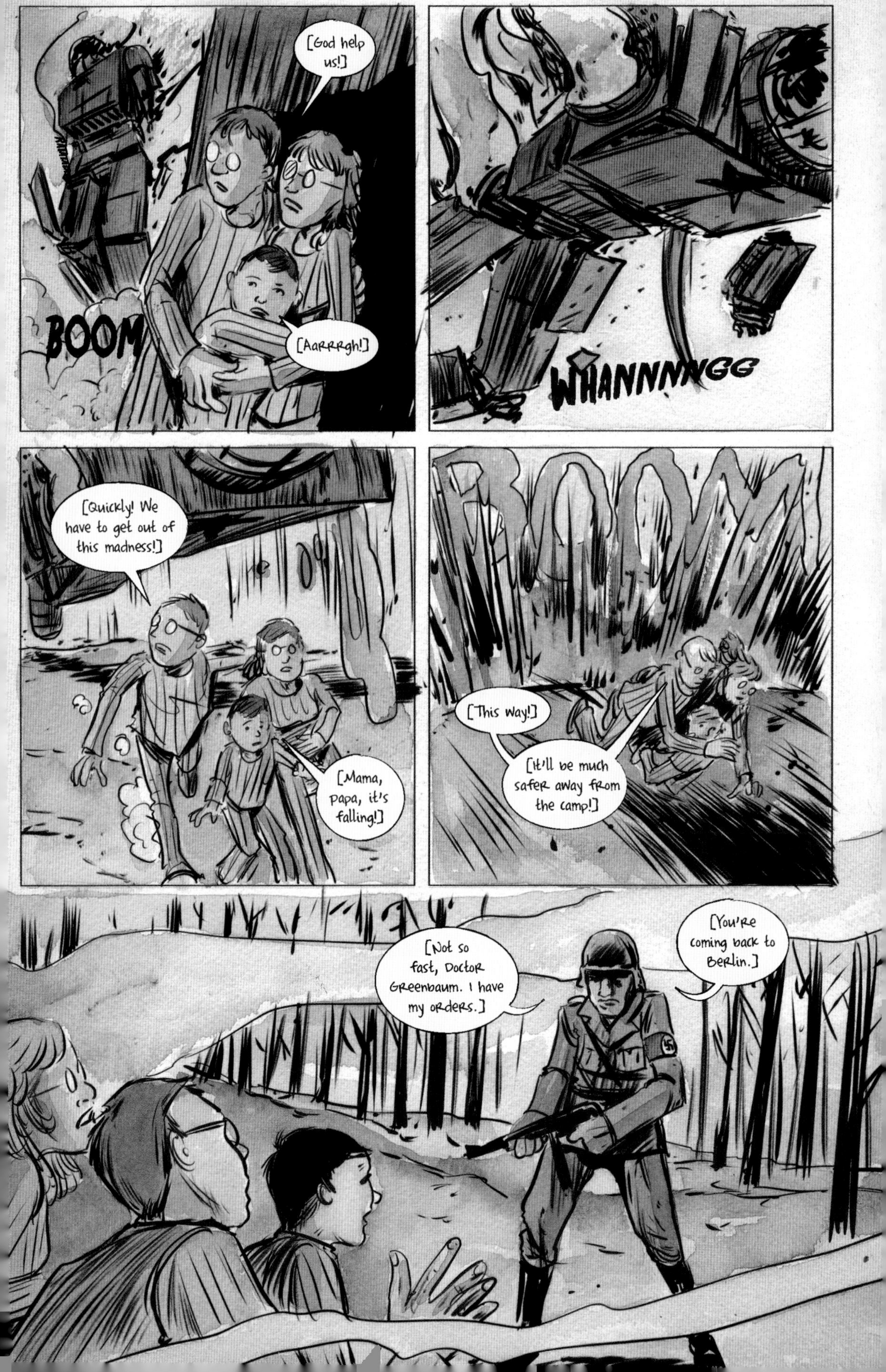
[God help us!]
BOOM
[Aarrrgh!]
WHANNNNGG
[Quickly! We have to get out of this madness!]
[Mama, papa, it's falling!]
BOOM
[This way!]
[It'll be much safer away from the camp!]
[Not so fast, Doctor Greenbaum. I have my orders.]
[You're coming back to Berlin.]

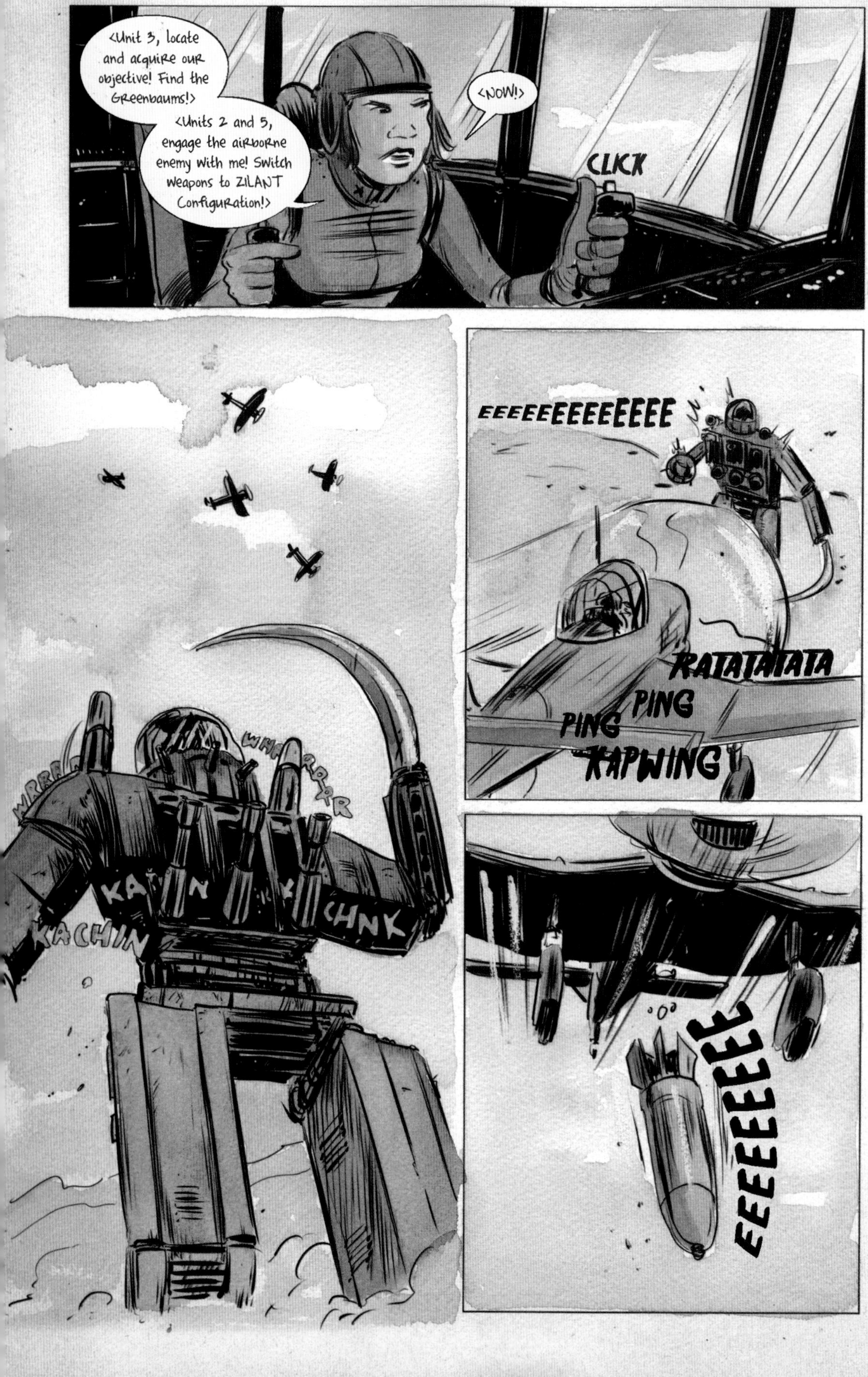
<Unit 3, locate and acquire our objective! Find the Greenbaums!>
<Units 2 and 5, engage the airborne enemy with me! Switch weapons to ZILANT Configuration!>
<NOW!>
CLICK
WRRR
WHRRRRR
KACHIN
CHNK
EEEEEEEEEEEEE
RATATATATA
PING
PING
KAPWING
EEEEEEEEEEE

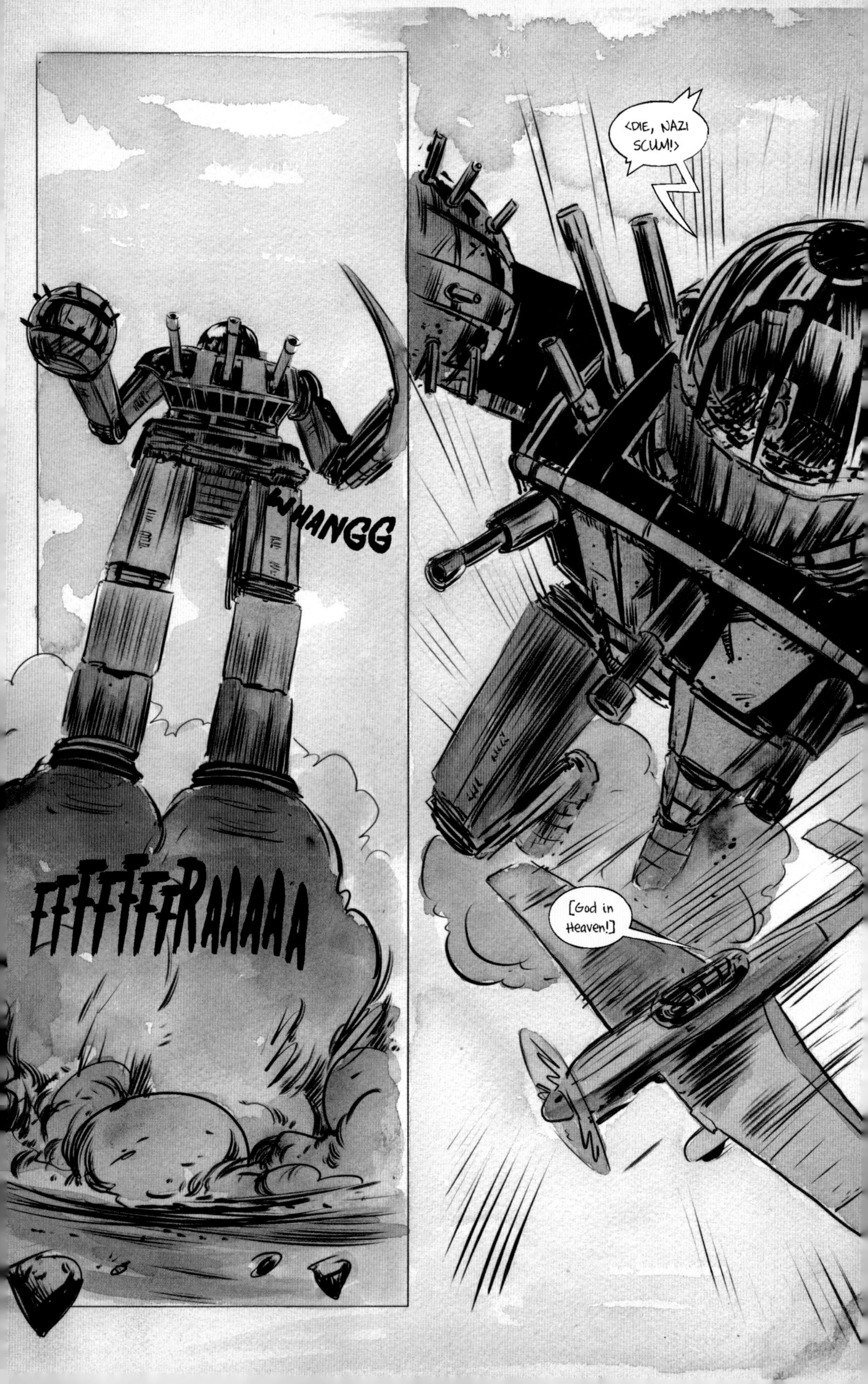
WHANGG
EFFFFFFRAAAAA
<DIE, NAZI SCUM!>
[God in Heaven!]

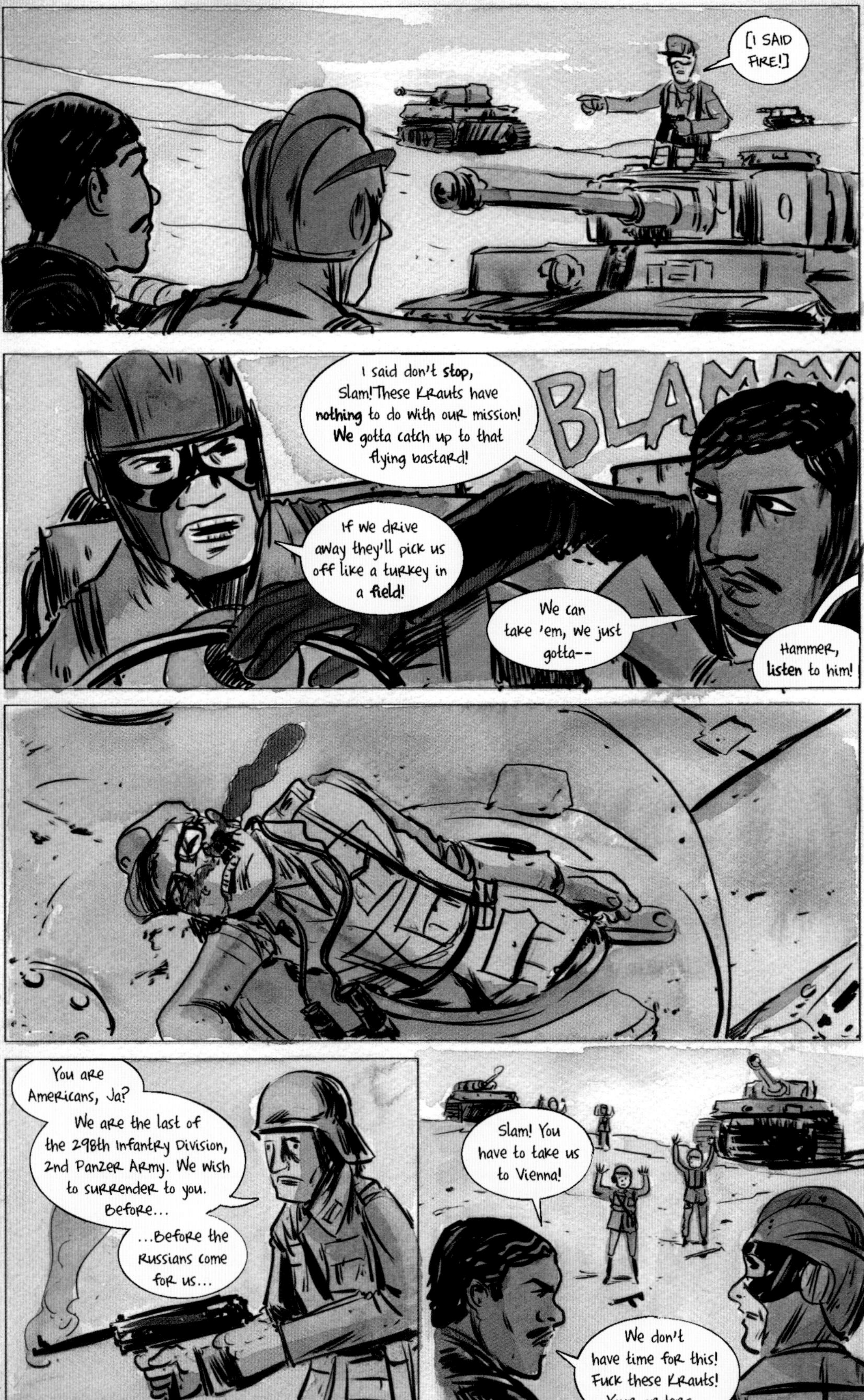
[I SAID FIRE!]
I said don't **stop**, Slam! These Krauts have **nothing** to do with our mission! **We** gotta catch up to that flying bastard!
BLAM
If we drive away they'll pick us off like a turkey in a **field**!
We can take 'em, we just gotta--
Hammer, **listen** to him!
You are Americans, Ja?
We are the last of the 298th Infantry Division, 2nd Panzer Army. We wish to surrender to you. Before...
...Before the Russians come for us...
Slam! You have to take us to Vienna!
We don't have time for this! Fuck these Krauts! Your orders--

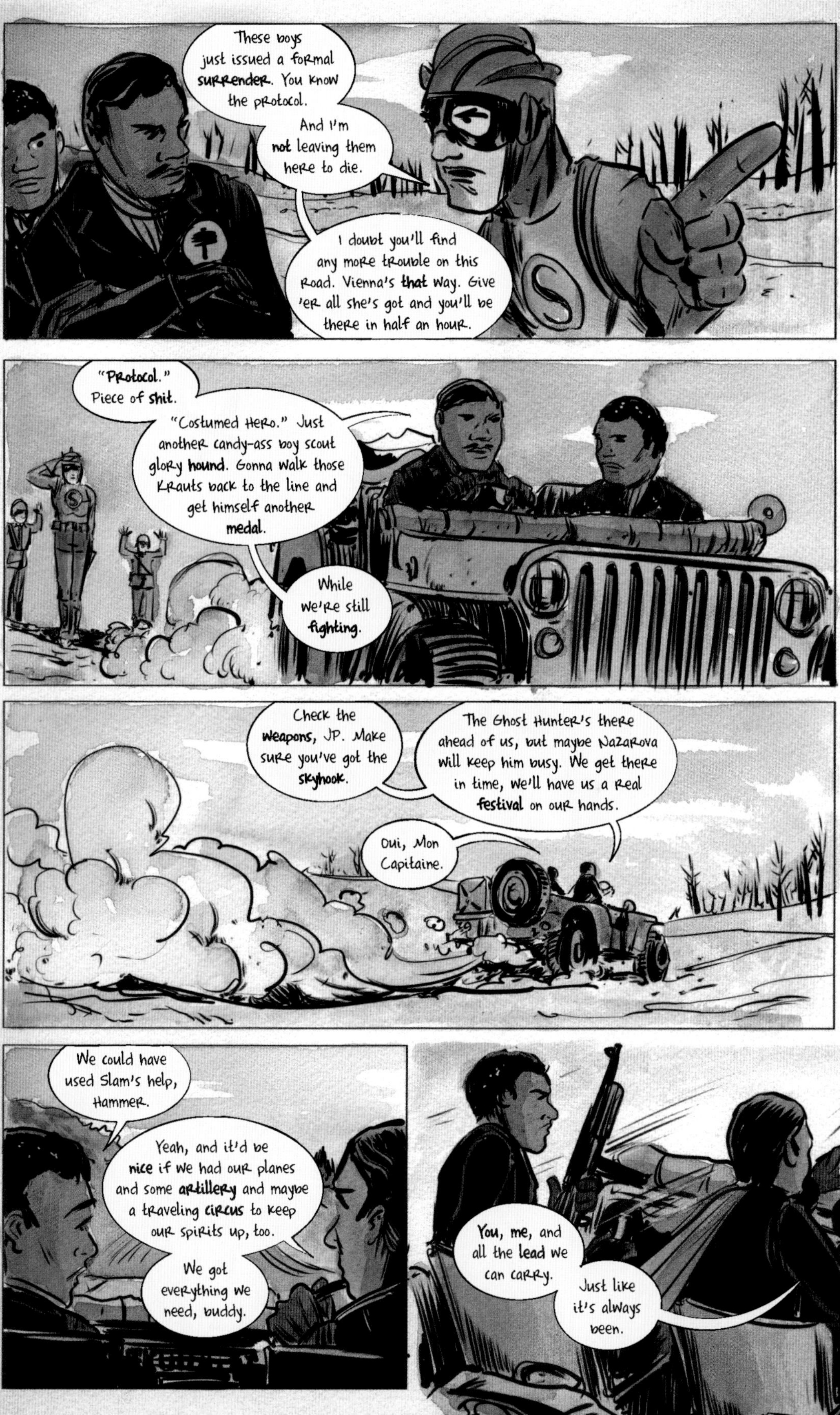
These boys just issued a formal surrender. You know the protocol.
And I'm not leaving them here to die.
I doubt you'll find any more trouble on this road. Vienna's that way. Give 'er all she's got and you'll be there in half an hour.
"Protocol." Piece of shit.
"Costumed Hero." Just another candy-ass boy scout glory hound. Gonna walk those Krauts back to the line and get himself another medal.
While we're still fighting.
Check the weapons, JP. Make sure you've got the skyhook.
The Ghost Hunter's there ahead of us, but maybe Nazarova will keep him busy. We get there in time, we'll have us a real festival on our hands.
Oui, Mon Capitaine.
We could have used Slam's help, Hammer.
Yeah, and it'd be nice if we had our planes and some artillery and maybe a traveling circus to keep our spirits up, too.
We got everything we need, buddy.
You, me, and all the lead we can carry.
Just like it's always been.

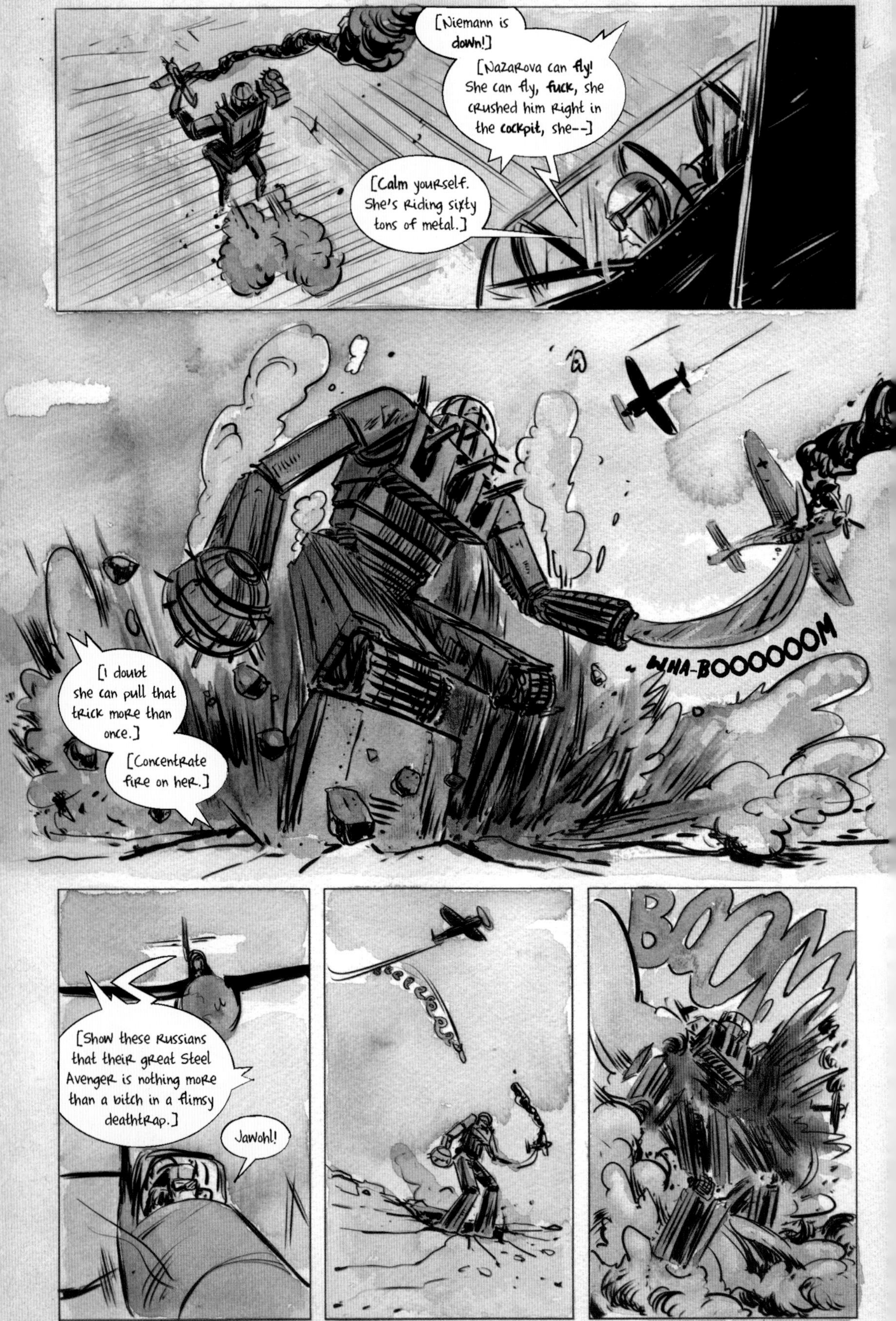
[Niemann is down!]
[Nazarova can fly! She can fly, fuck, she crushed him right in the cockpit, she--]
[Calm yourself. She's riding sixty tons of metal.]
WHA-BOOOOOOM
[I doubt she can pull that trick more than once.]
[Concentrate fire on her.]
[Show these Russians that their great Steel Avenger is nothing more than a bitch in a flimsy deathtrap.]
Jawohl!
BOOM

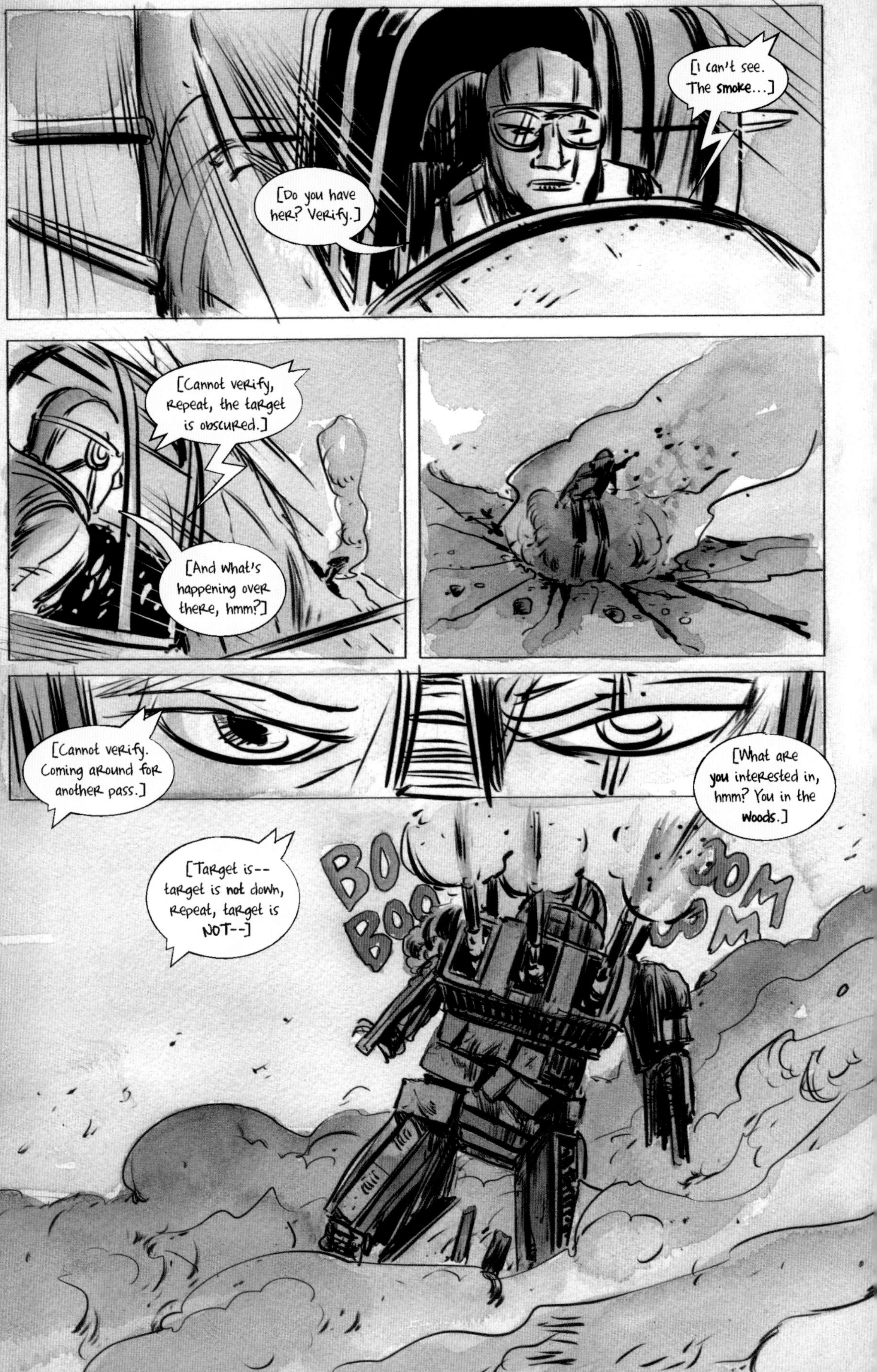
[I can't see. The smoke...]
[Do you have her? Verify.]
[Cannot verify, repeat, the target is obscured.]
[And what's happening over there, hmm?]
[Cannot verify. Coming around for another pass.]
[What are you interested in, hmm? You in the woods.]
[Target is-- target is not down, repeat, target is NOT--]
BOOM BOOM
BOOM BOOM

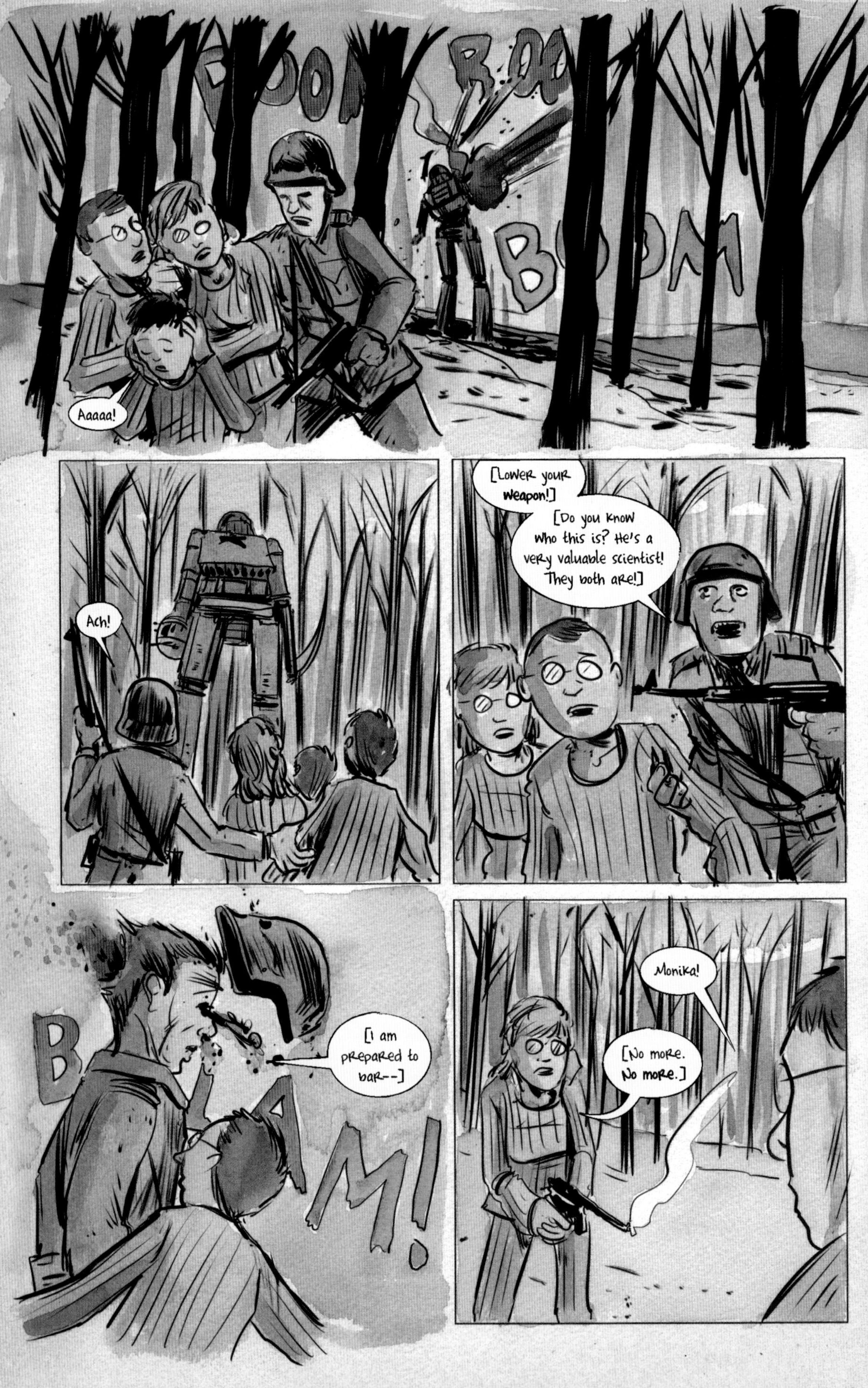
BOOM
BOOM
BOOM
Aaaaa!
Ach!
[Lower your weapon!]
[Do you know who this is? He's a very valuable scientist! They both are!]
B
[I am prepared to bar--]
AM!
Monika!
[No more. No more.]

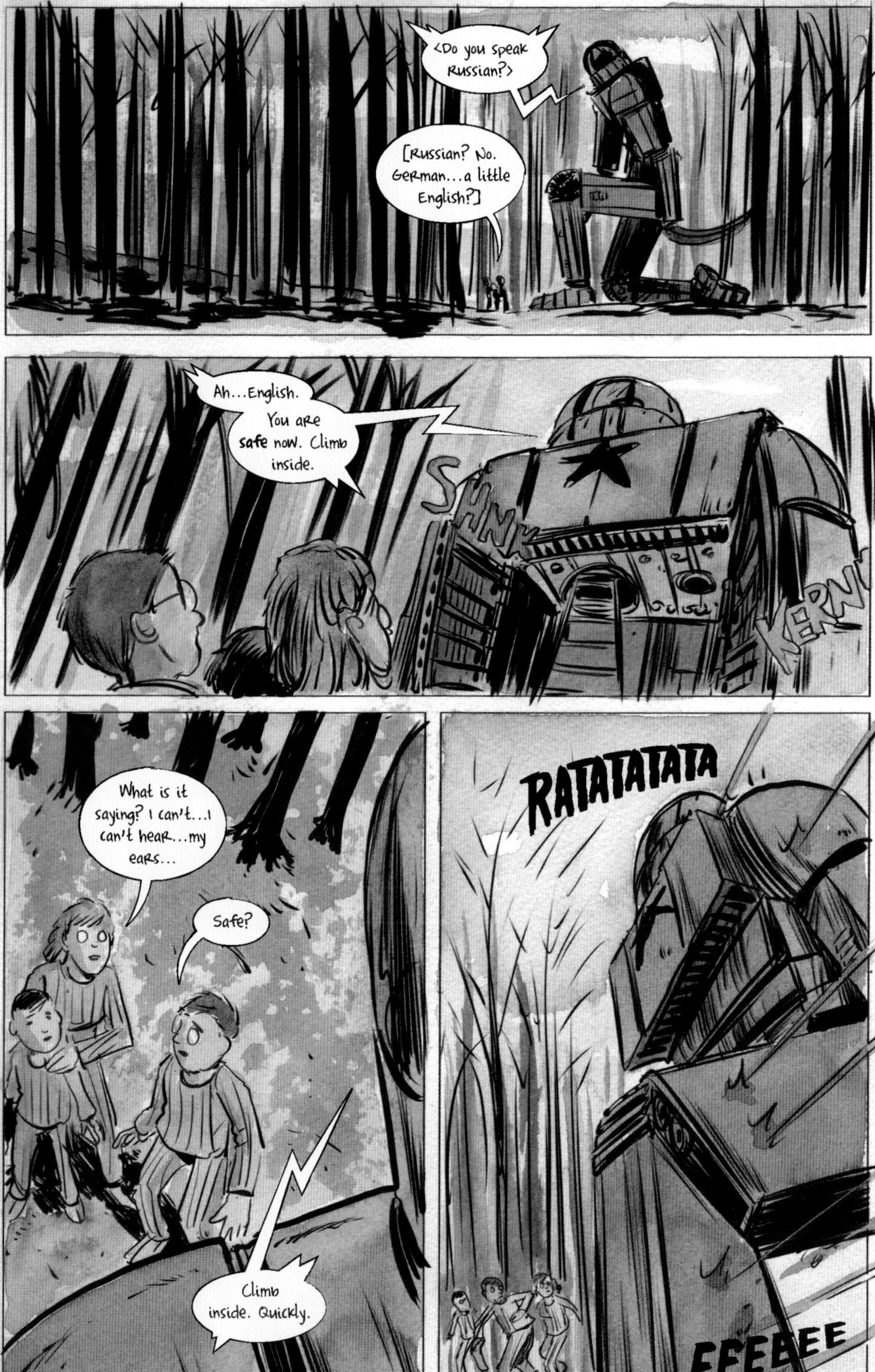
<Do you speak Russian?>
[Russian? No. German...a little English?]
Ah...English. You are **safe** now. Climb inside.
What is it saying? I can't...I can't hear...my ears...
Safe?
Climb inside. Quickly.
RATATATATA
EEEEEE

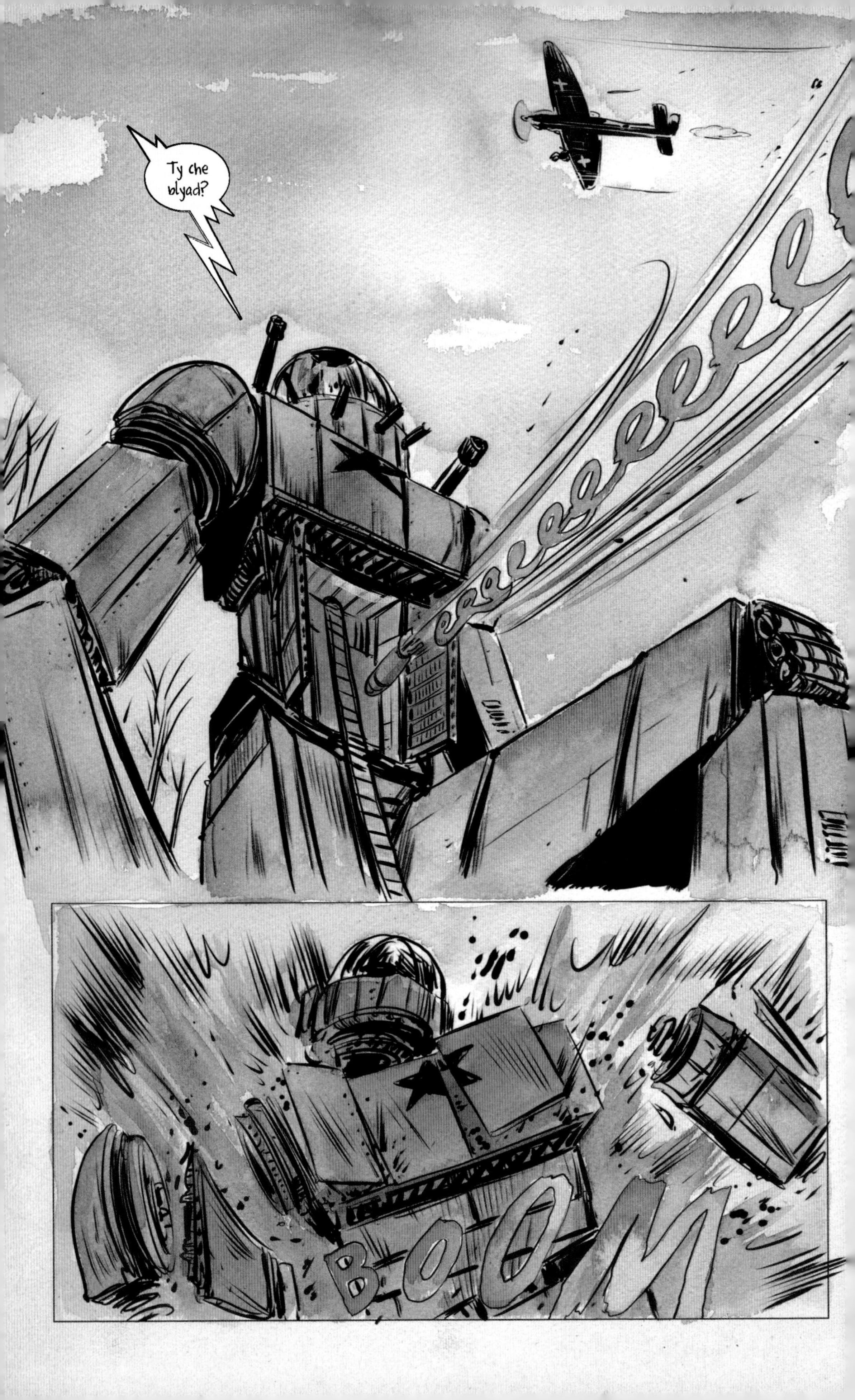
Ty che blyad?
BOOM

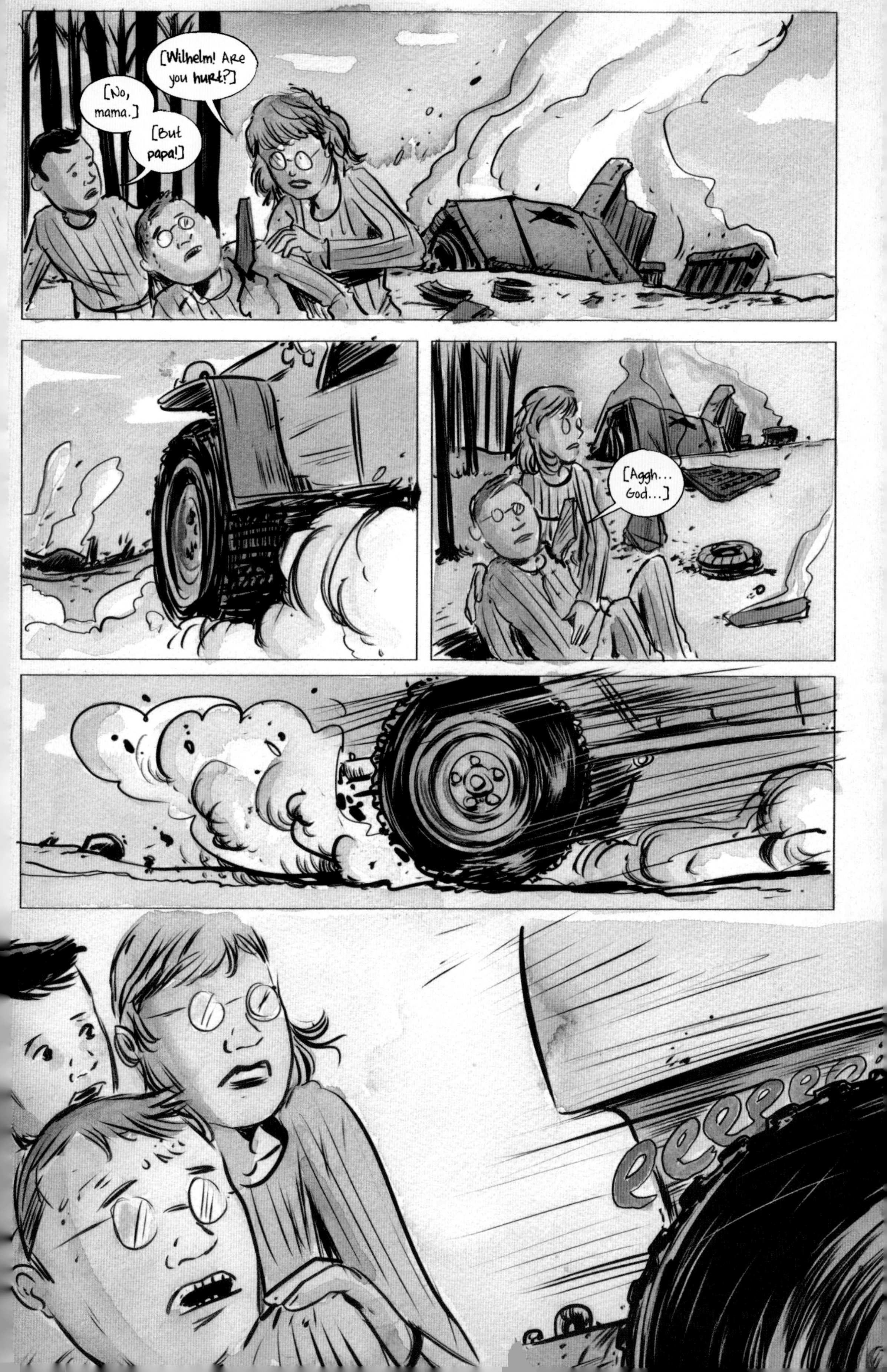
[Wilhelm! Are you hurt?]
[No, mama.]
[But papa!]
[Aggh... God...]

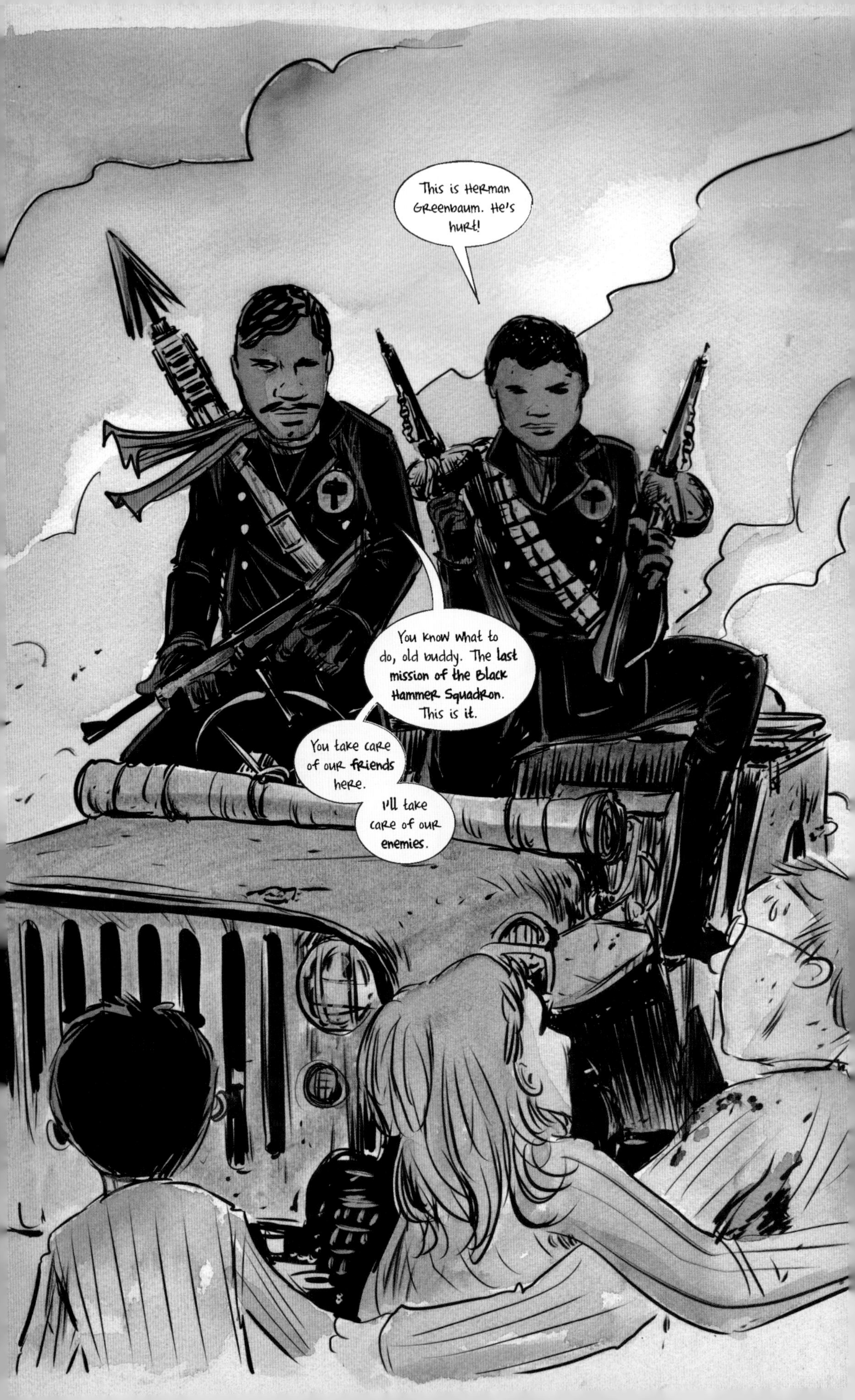
This is Herman Greenbaum. He's hurt!
You know what to do, old buddy. The **last mission of the Black Hammer Squadron.** This is **it.**
You take care of our **friends** here.
I'll take care of our **enemies.**

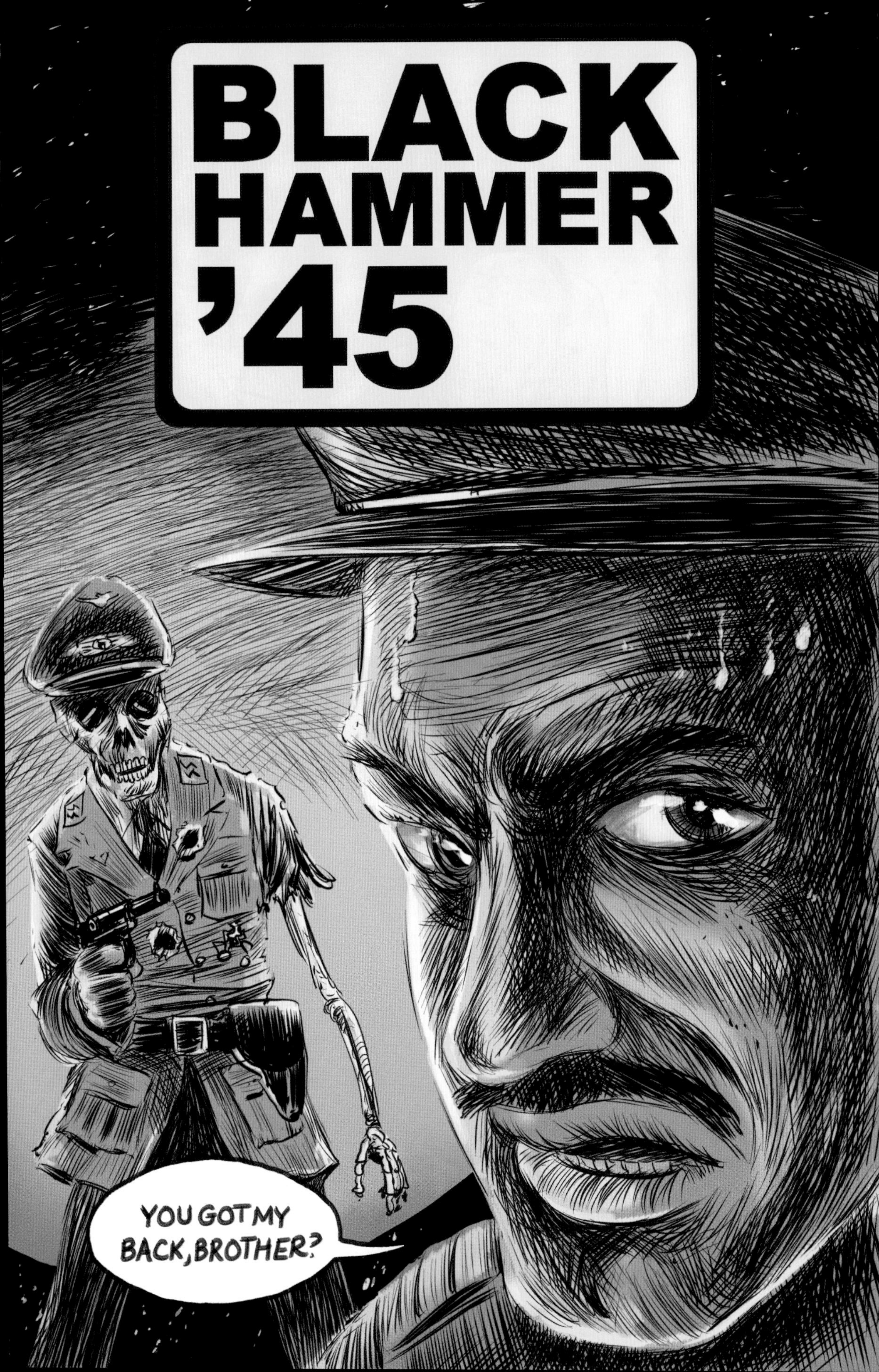
BLACK HAMMER '45
YOU GOT MY BACK, BROTHER?

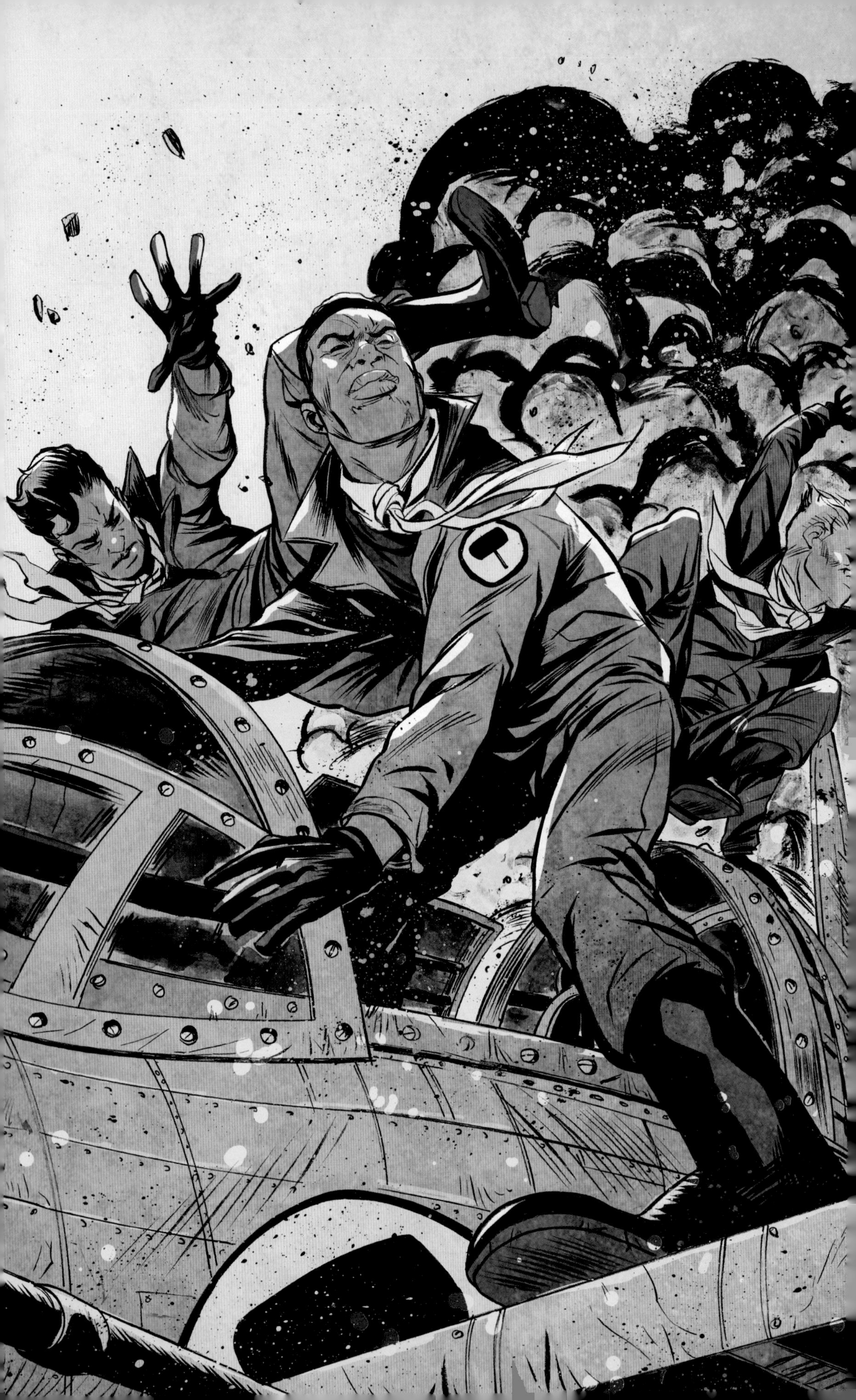

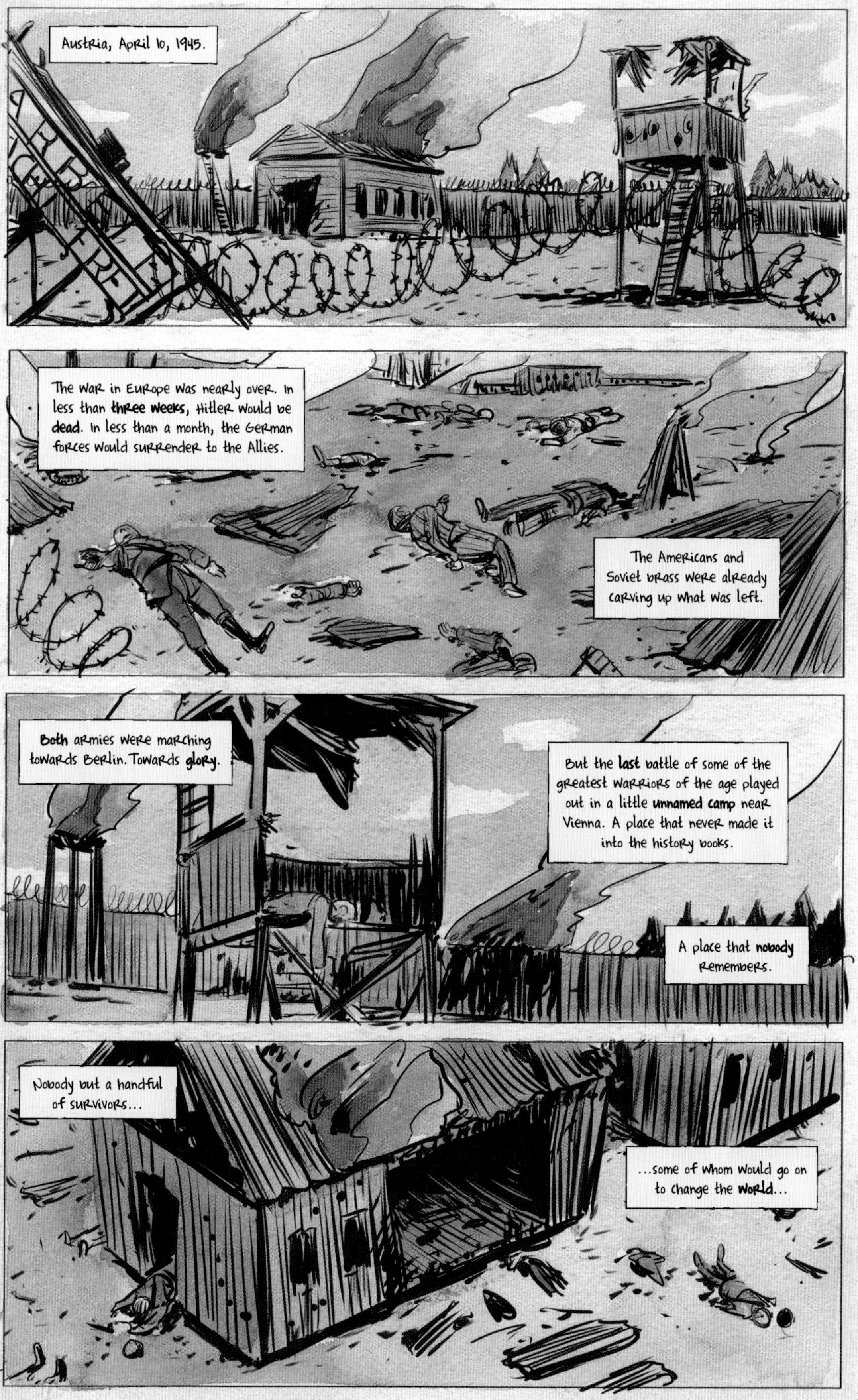
Austria, April 10, 1945.
The war in Europe was nearly over. In less than three weeks, Hitler would be dead. In less than a month, the German forces would surrender to the Allies.
The Americans and Soviet brass were already carving up what was left.
Both armies were marching towards Berlin. Towards glory.
But the last battle of some of the greatest warriors of the age played out in a little unnamed camp near Vienna. A place that never made it into the history books.
A place that nobody remembers.
Nobody but a handful of survivors...
...some of whom would go on to change the world...

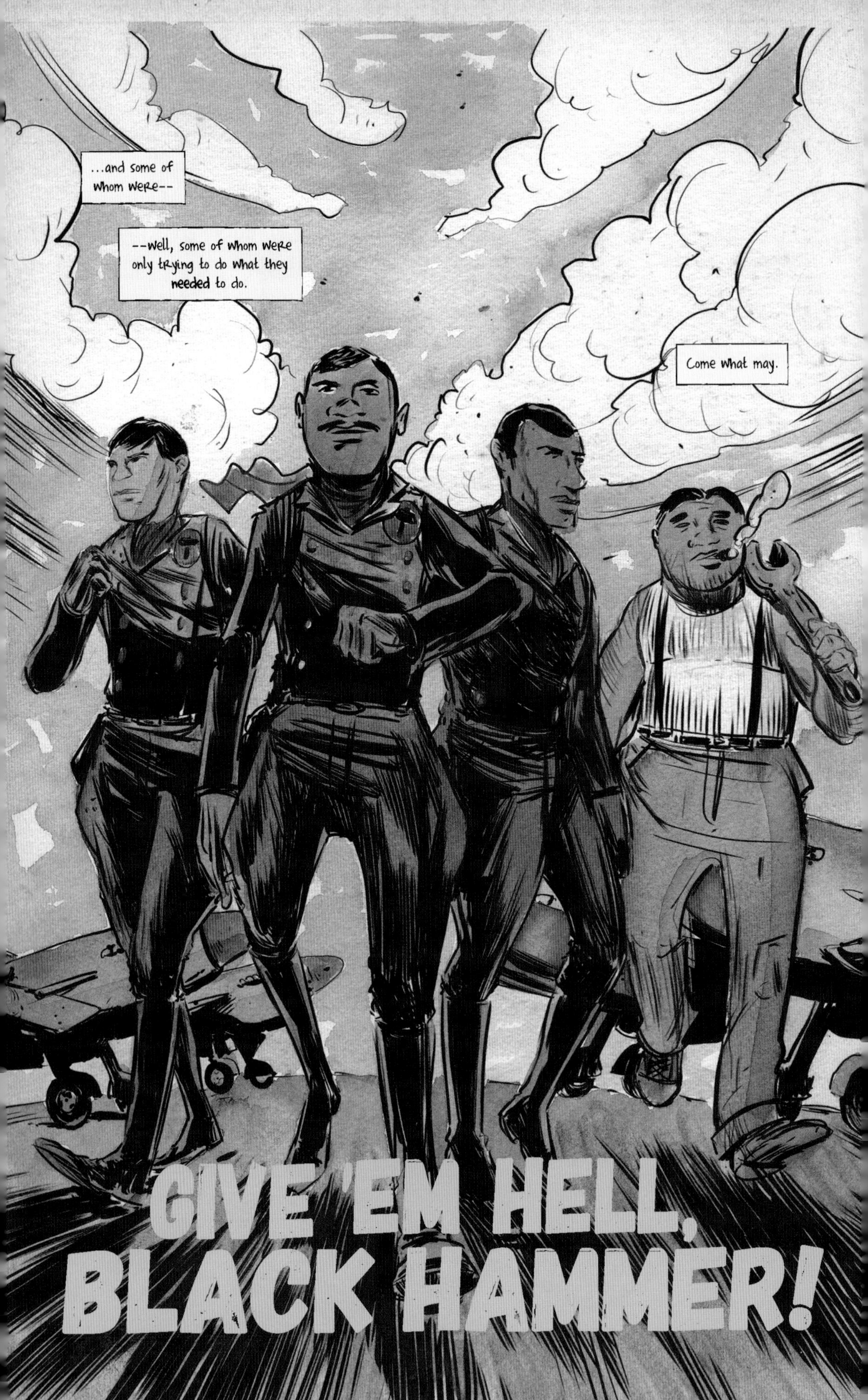
...and some of whom were--
--well, some of whom were only trying to do what they needed to do.
Come what may.
GIVE 'EM HELL, BLACK HAMMER!

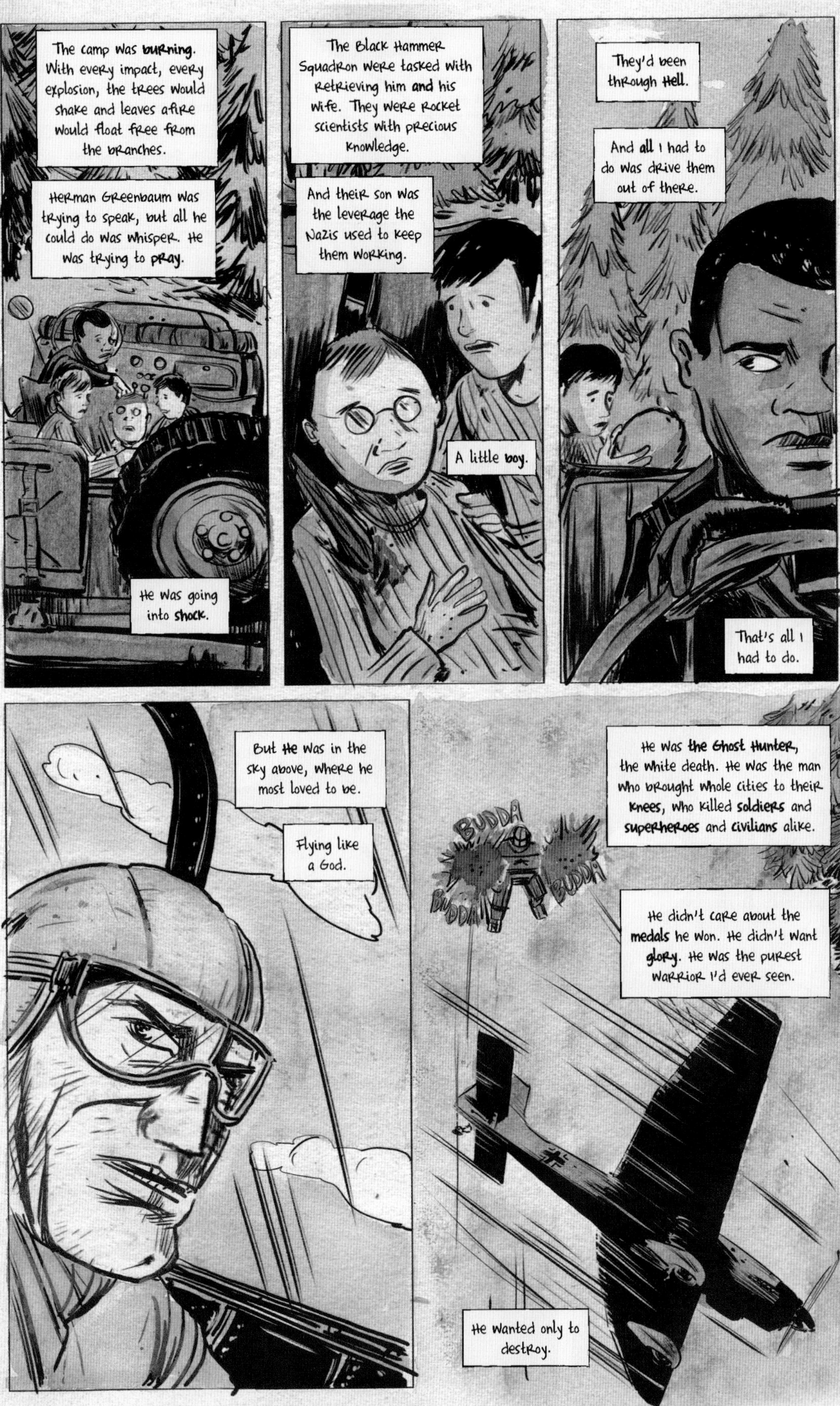

The camp was burning. With every impact, every explosion, the trees would shake and leaves afire would float free from the branches.
Herman Greenbaum was trying to speak, but all he could do was whisper. He was trying to pray.
He was going into shock.
The Black Hammer Squadron were tasked with retrieving him and his wife. They were rocket scientists with precious knowledge.
And their son was the leverage the Nazis used to keep them working.
A little boy.
They'd been through Hell.
And all I had to do was drive them out of there.
That's all I had to do.
But he was in the sky above, where he most loved to be.
Flying like a God.
He was the Ghost Hunter, the white death. He was the man who brought whole cities to their knees, who killed soldiers and superheroes and civilians alike.
BUDDA
BUDDA
BUDDA
He didn't care about the medals he won. He didn't want glory. He was the purest warrior I'd ever seen.
He wanted only to destroy.

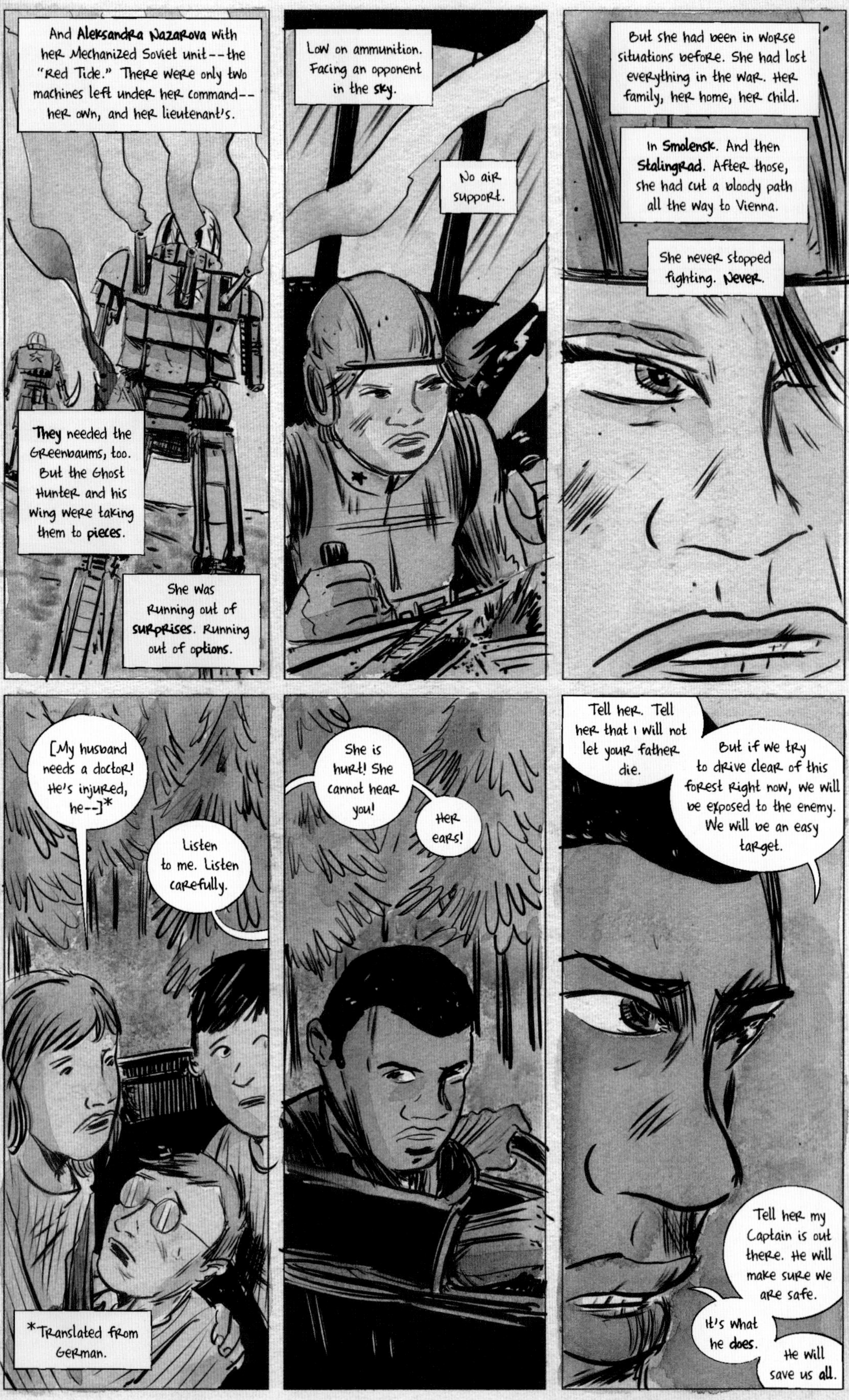
And Aleksandra Nazarova with her Mechanized Soviet unit--the "Red Tide." There were only two machines left under her command--her own, and her lieutenant's.
They needed the Greenbaums, too. But the Ghost Hunter and his wing were taking them to pieces.
She was running out of surprises. Running out of options.
Low on ammunition. Facing an opponent in the sky.
No air support.
But she had been in worse situations before. She had lost everything in the war. Her family, her home, her child.
In Smolensk. And then Stalingrad. After those, she had cut a bloody path all the way to Vienna.
She never stopped fighting. Never.
[My husband needs a doctor! He's injured, he--]*
Listen to me. Listen carefully.
*Translated from German.
She is hurt! She cannot hear you!
Her ears!
Tell her. Tell her that I will not let your father die.
But if we try to drive clear of this forest right now, we will be exposed to the enemy. We will be an easy target.
Tell her my Captain is out there. He will make sure we are safe.
It's what he does.
He will save us all.

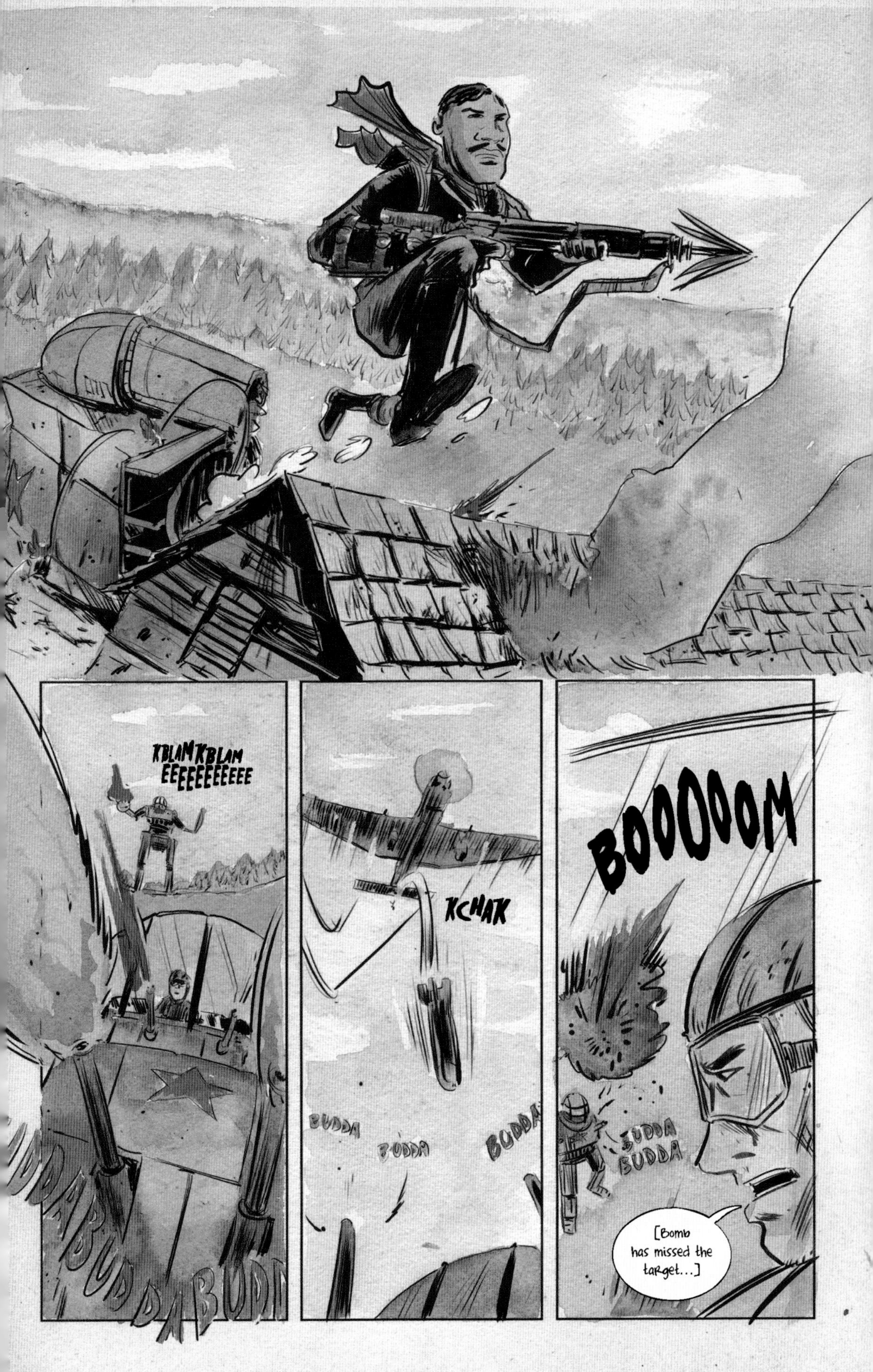
KBLAM KBLAM
EEEEEEEEEE
BUDDA BUDDA BUDD
KCHAK
BUDDA
BUDDA
BUDDA
BOOOOOM
BUDDA
BUDDA
[Bomb has missed the target...]

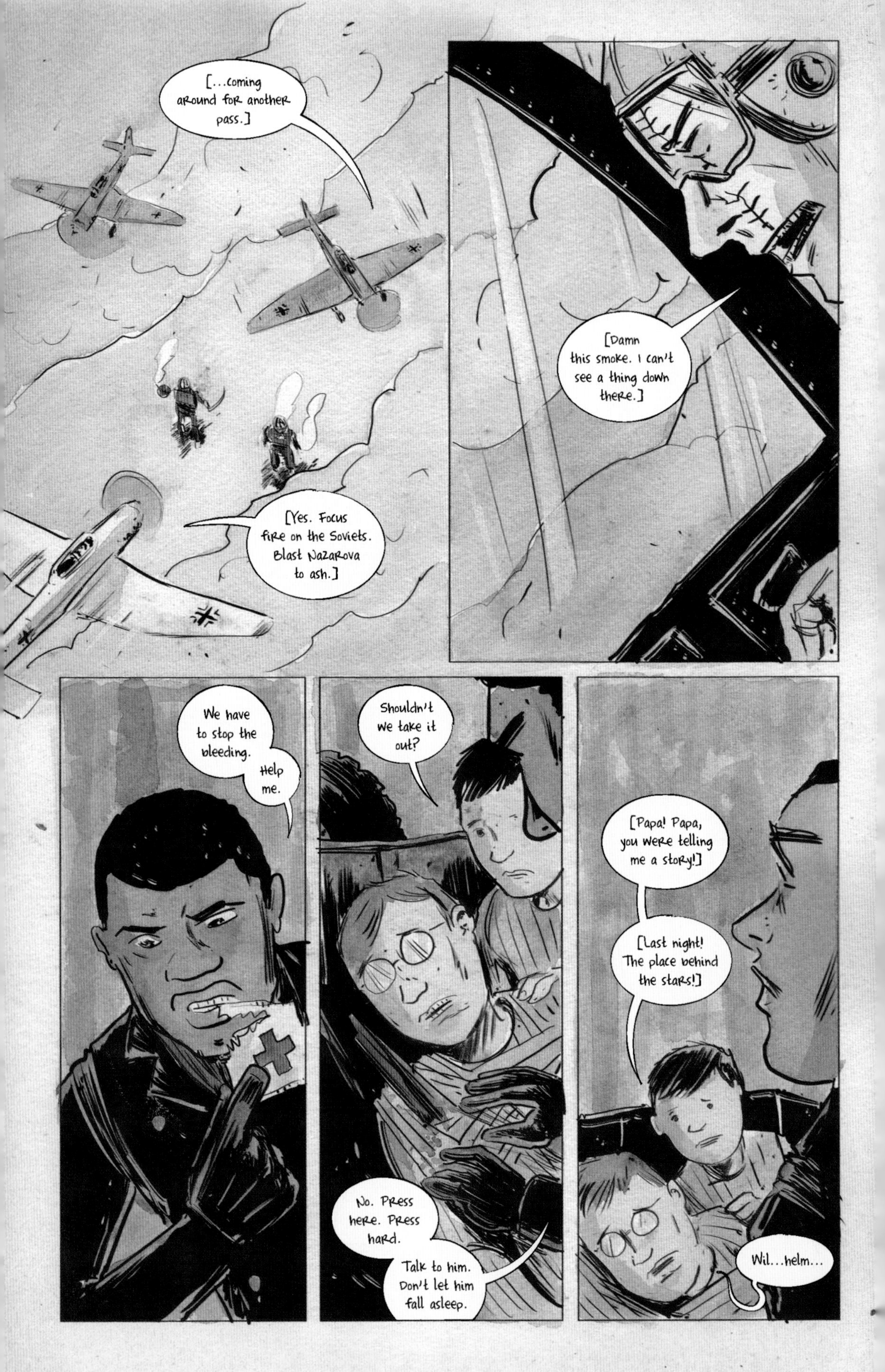
[...coming around for another pass.]
[Yes. Focus fire on the Soviets. Blast Nazarova to ash.]
[Damn this smoke. I can't see a thing down there.]
We have to stop the bleeding.
Help me.
Shouldn't we take it out?
No. Press here. Press hard.
Talk to him. Don't let him fall asleep.
[Papa! Papa, you were telling me a story!]
[Last night! The place behind the stars!]
Wil...helm...

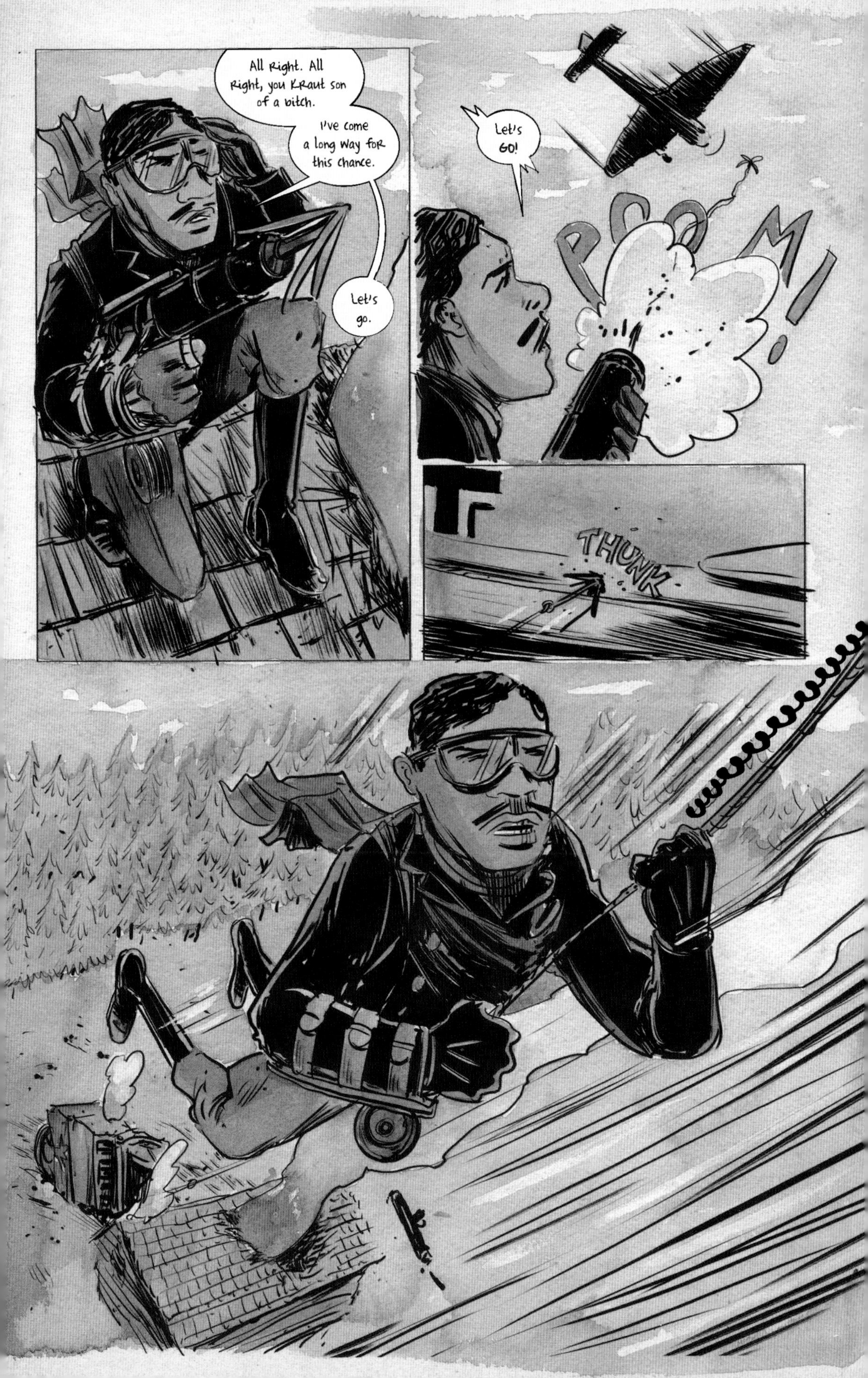
All Right. All Right, you Kraut son of a bitch.
I've come a long way for this chance.
Let's go.
Let's GO!
POOM!
THUNK

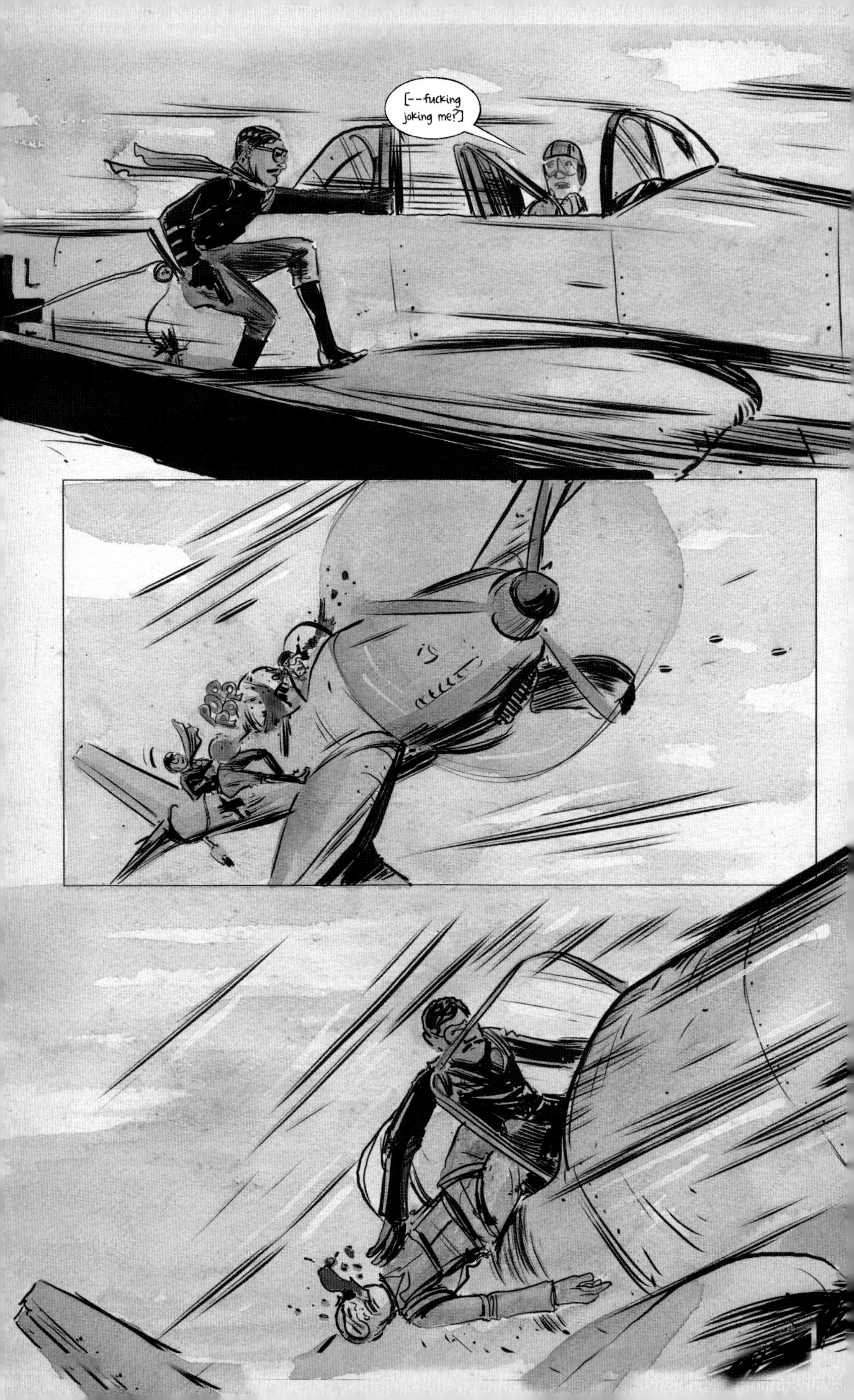
[--fucking joking me?]

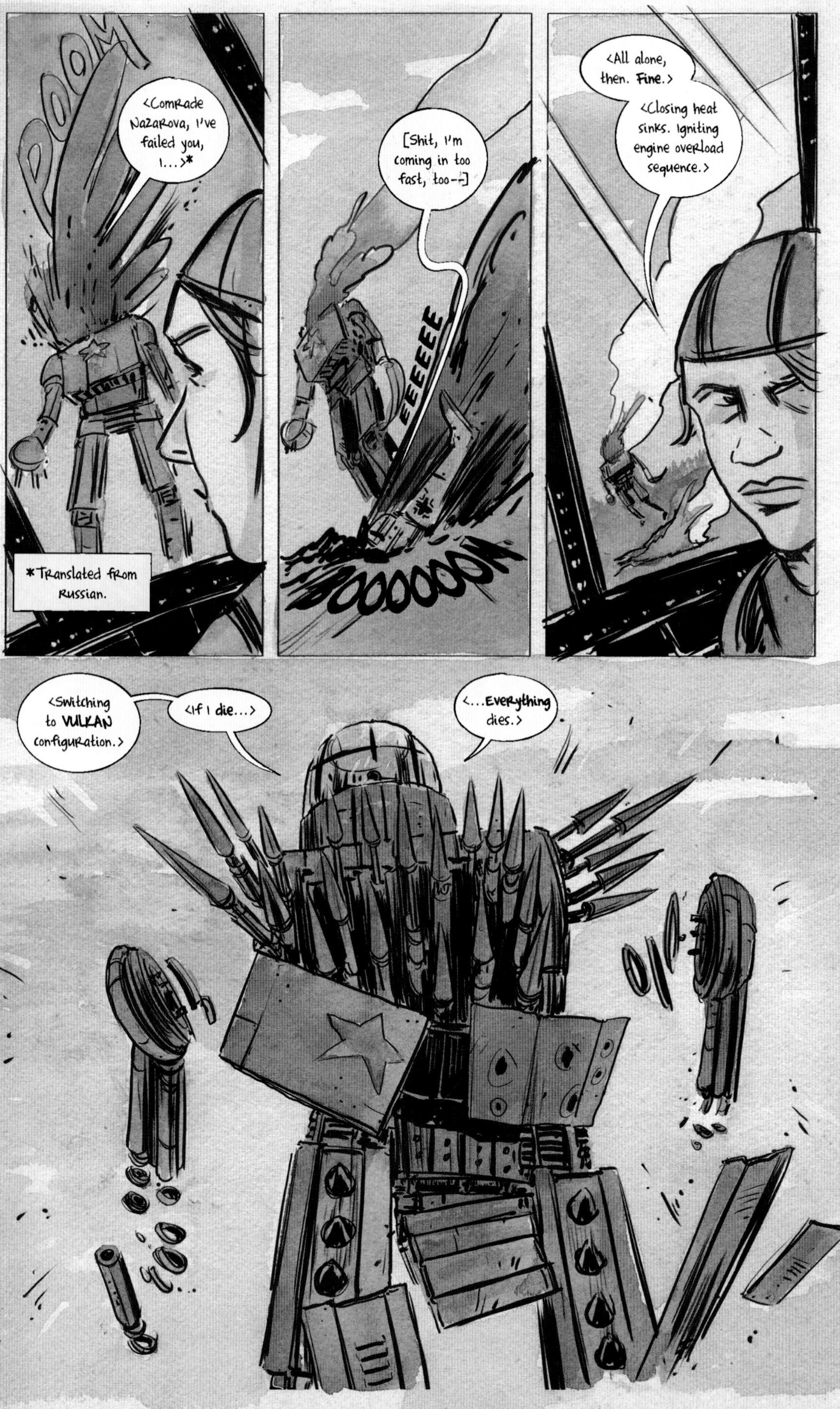
POOOM
<Comrade Nazarova, I've failed you, I...>*
*Translated from Russian.
[Shit, I'm coming in too fast, too--]
EEEEEE
BOOOOOOM
<All alone, then. Fine.>
<Closing heat sinks. Igniting engine overload sequence.>
<Switching to VULKAN configuration.>
<If I die...>
<...Everything dies.>

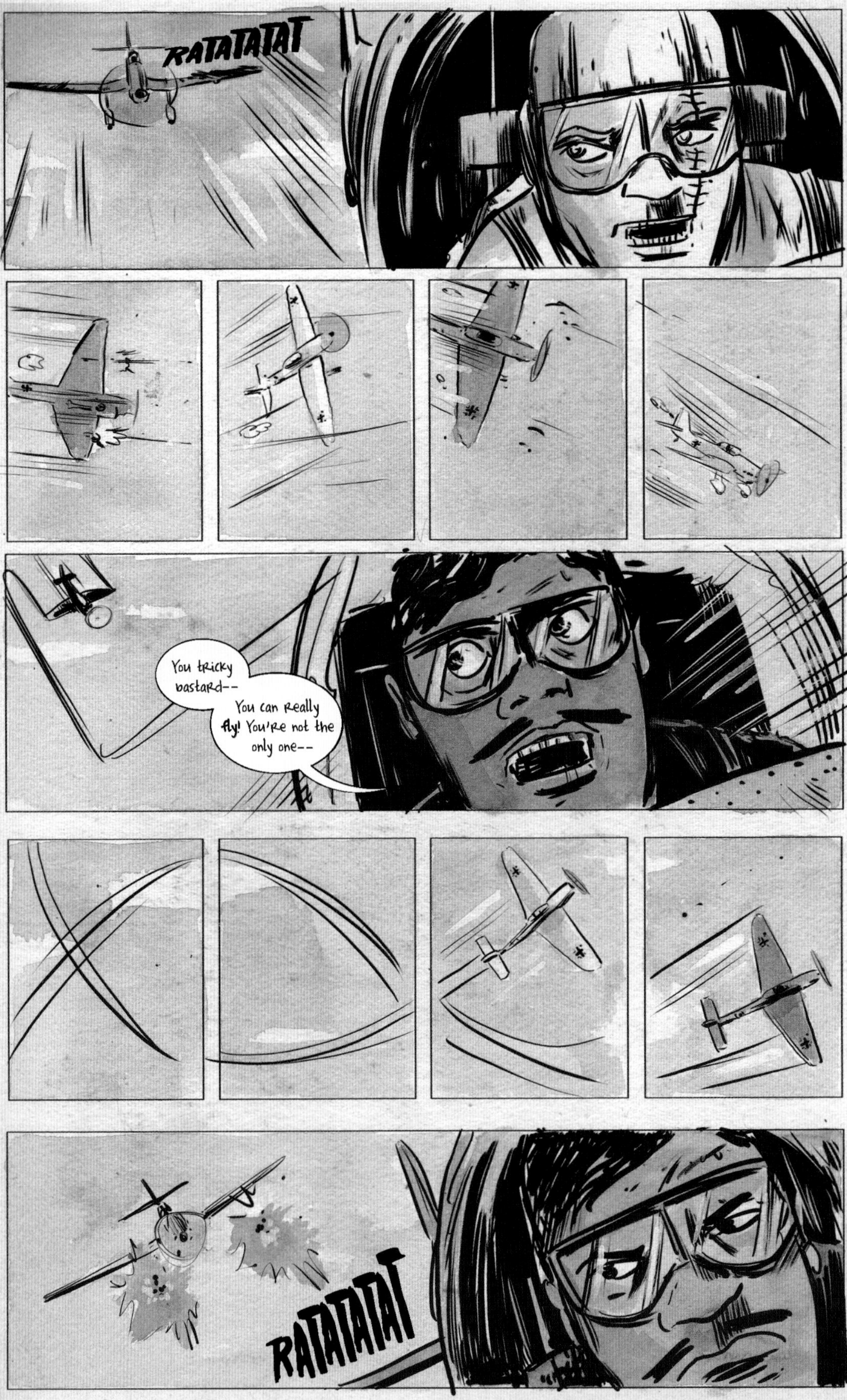
RATATATAT
You tricky bastard--
You can really fly! You're not the only one--
RATATATAT

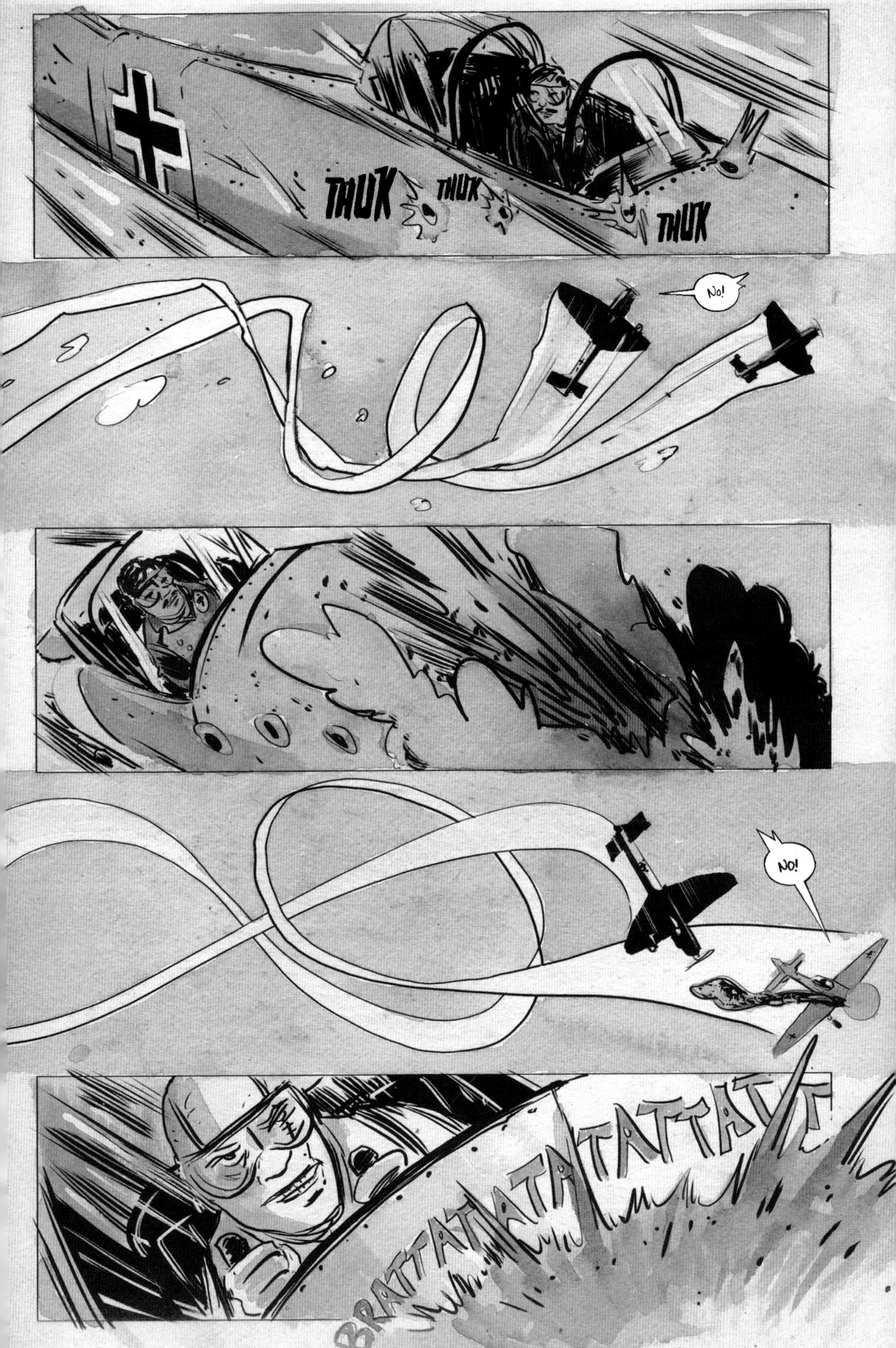
THUK
THUK
THUK
No!
No!
BRATTATTATTATTATTATT

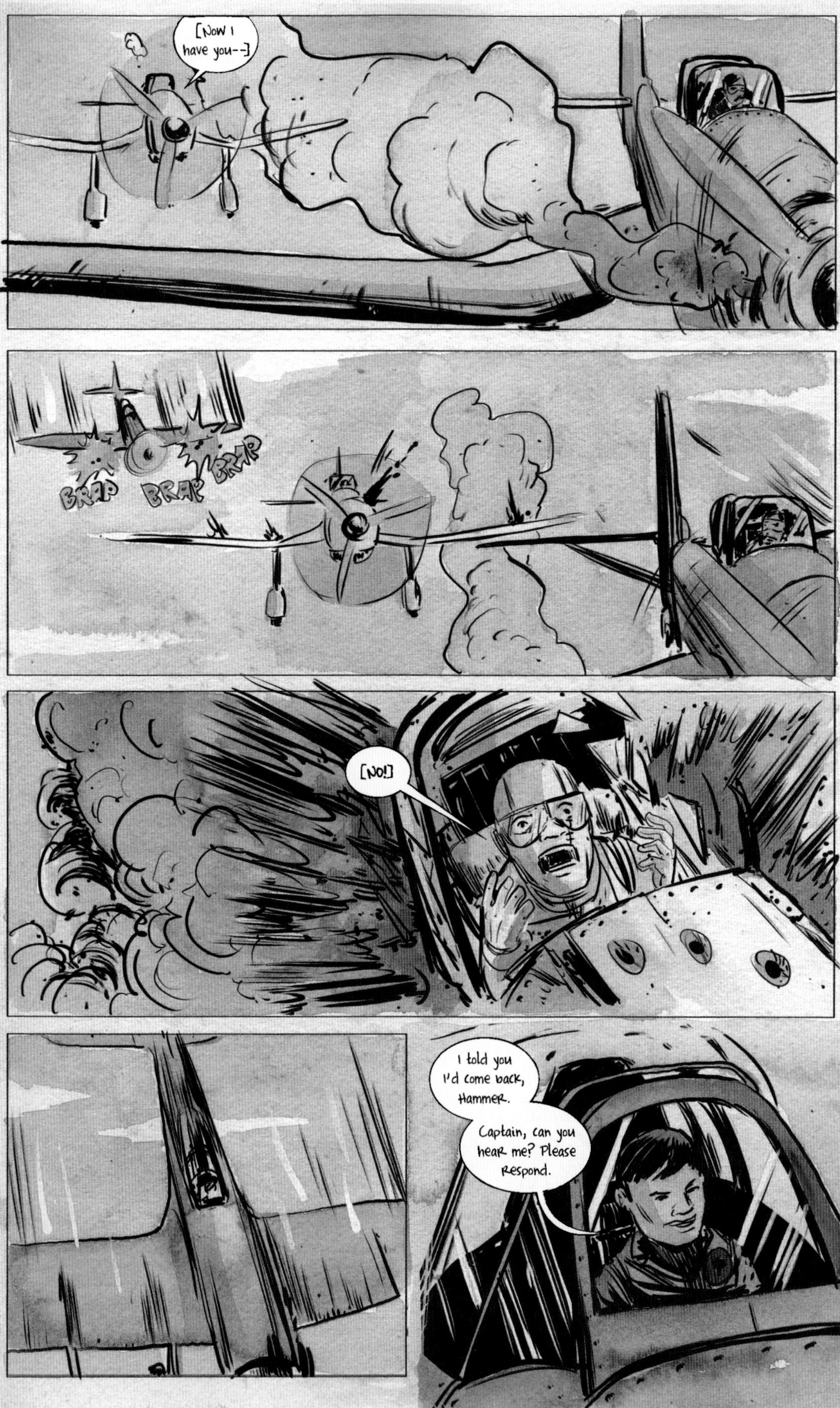
[Now I have you--]
BRAP BRAP BRAP
[NO!]
I told you I'd come back, Hammer.
Captain, can you hear me? Please respond.

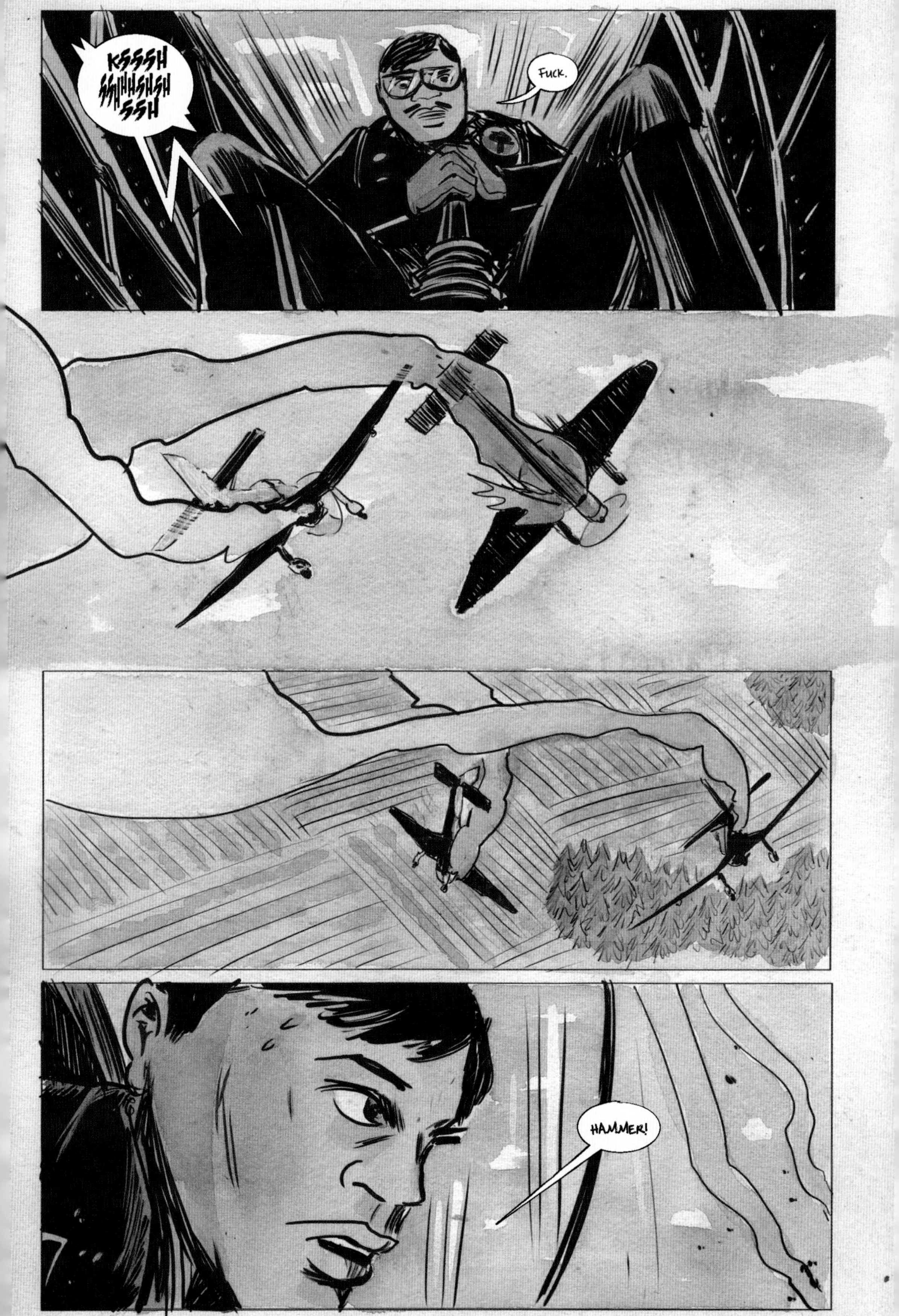
KSSSH SSHHSHSH SSH
FUCK.
HAMMER!

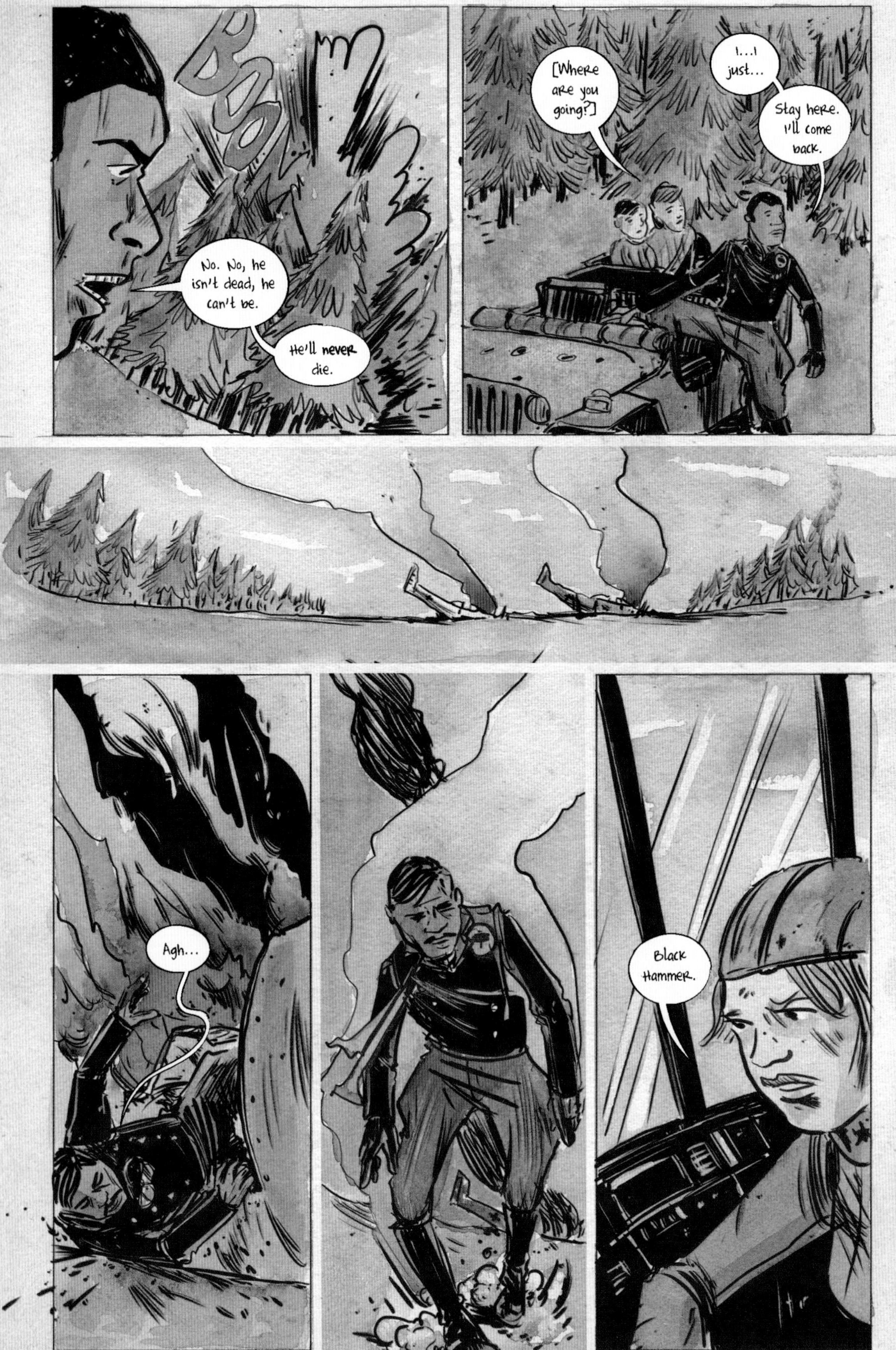
BOOM
No. No, he isn't dead, he can't be.
He'll never die.
[Where are you going?]
I...I just...
Stay here. I'll come back.
Agh...
Black Hammer.

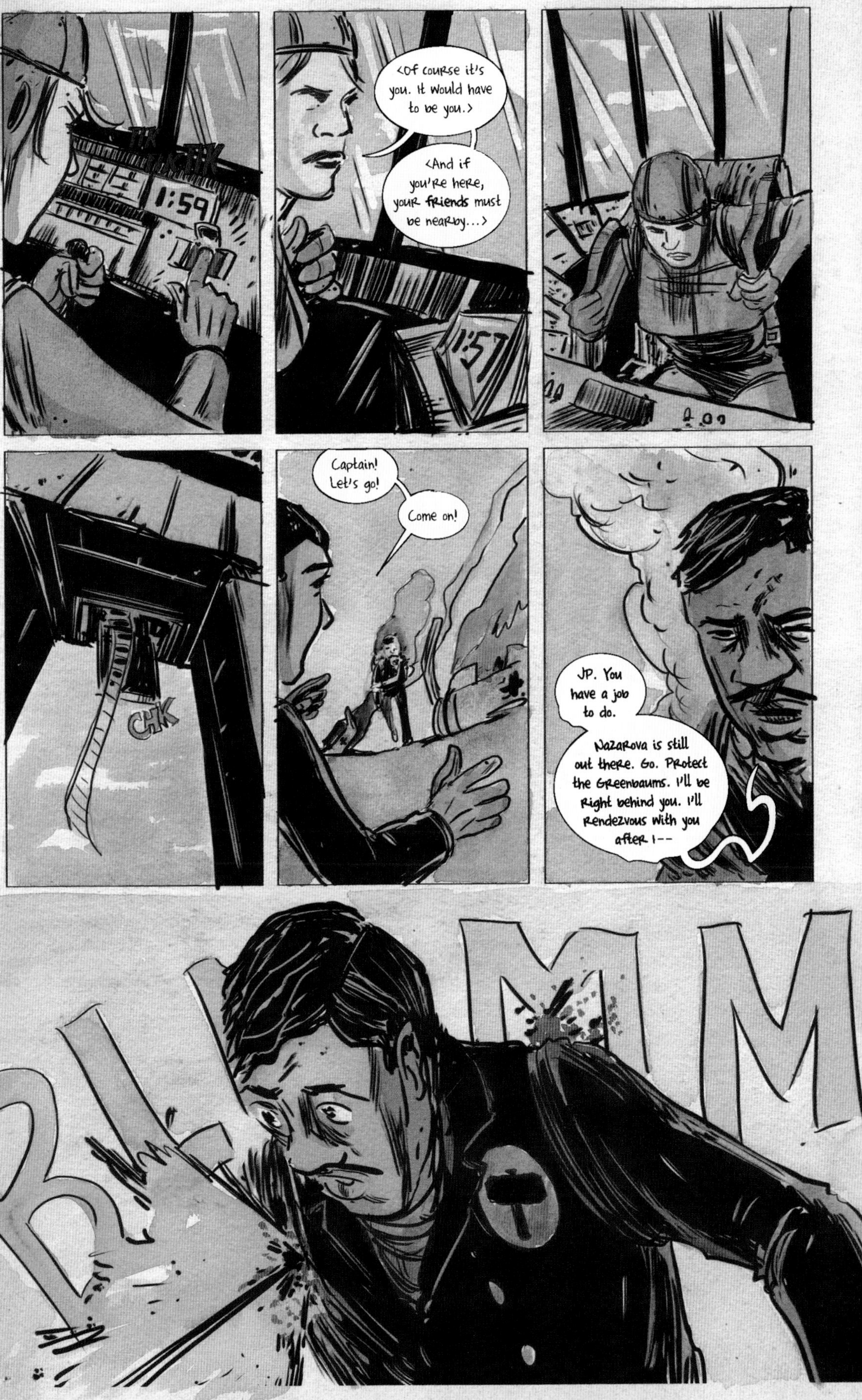
1:59
<Of course it's you. It would have to be you.>
<And if you're here, your **friends** must be nearby...>
1:57
Captain! Let's go!
Come on!
CHK
JP. You have a job to do.
Nazarova is still out there. Go. Protect the Greenbaums. I'll be right behind you. I'll rendezvous with you after I--

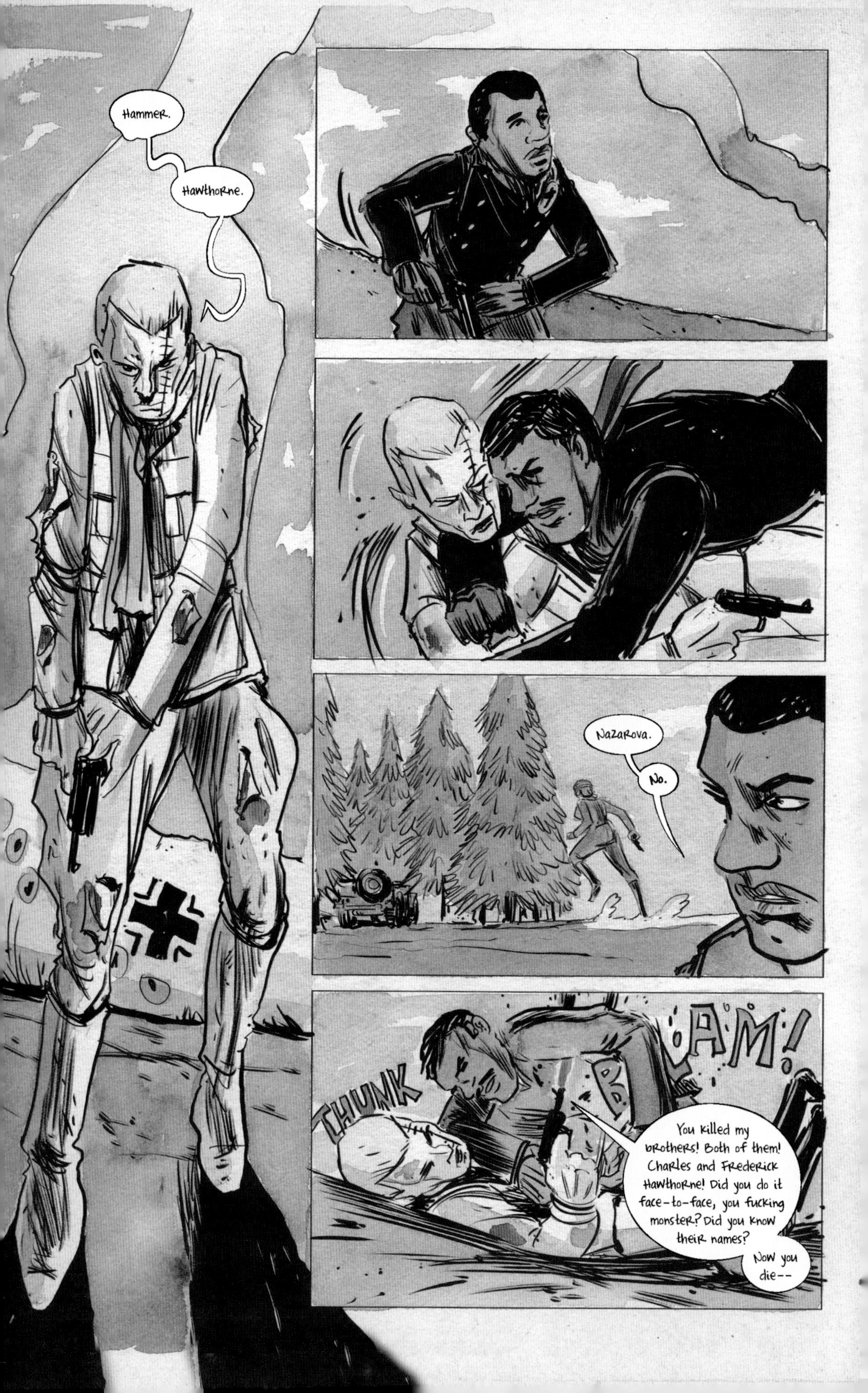
Hammer.
Hawthorne.
Nazarova.
No.
THUNK
BLAM!
You killed my brothers! Both of them! Charles and Frederick Hawthorne! Did you do it face-to-face, you fucking monster? Did you know their names?
Now you die--

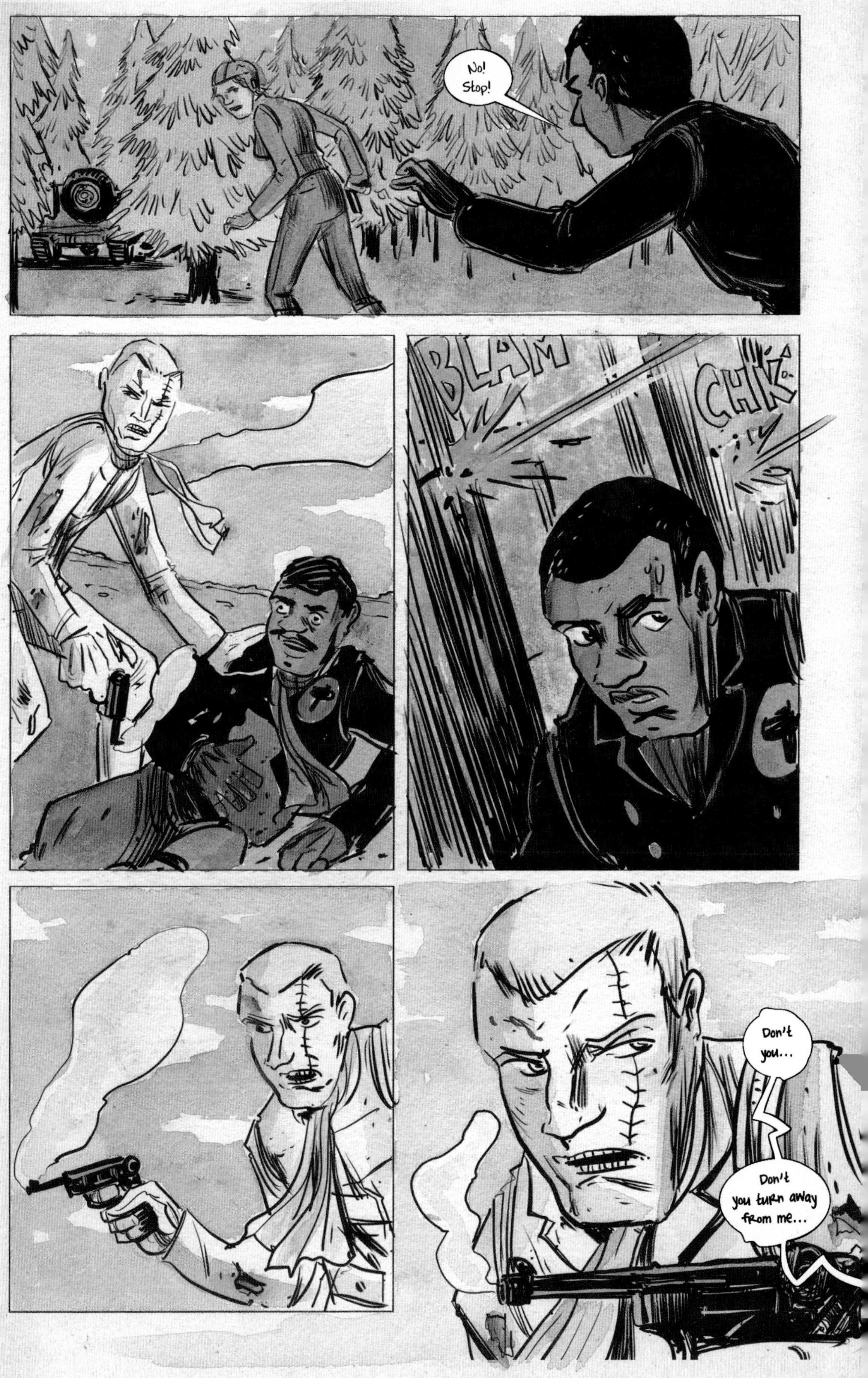
No! Stop!
BLAM
CHK
Don't you...
Don't you turn away from me...

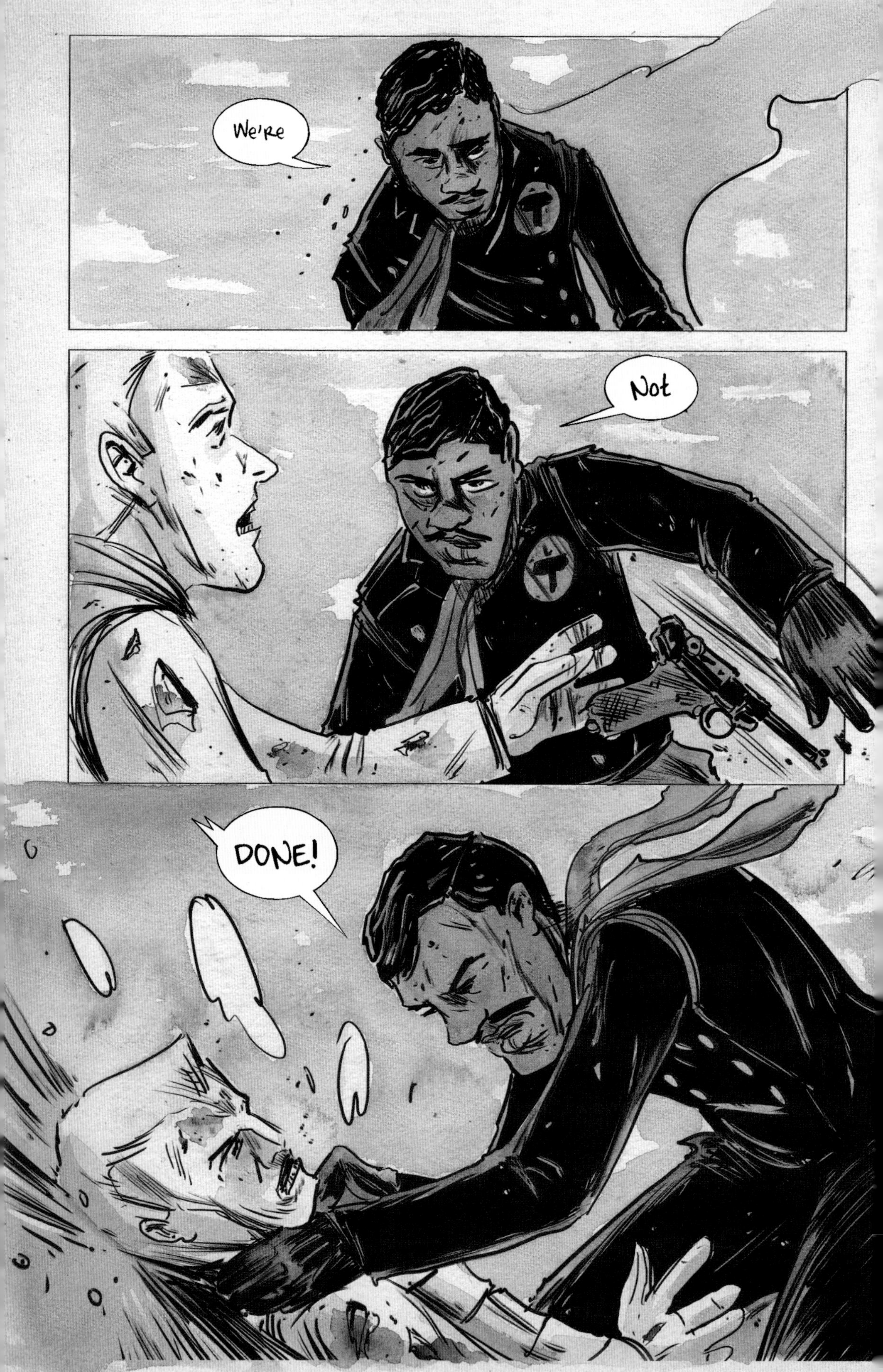
We're
Not
DONE!

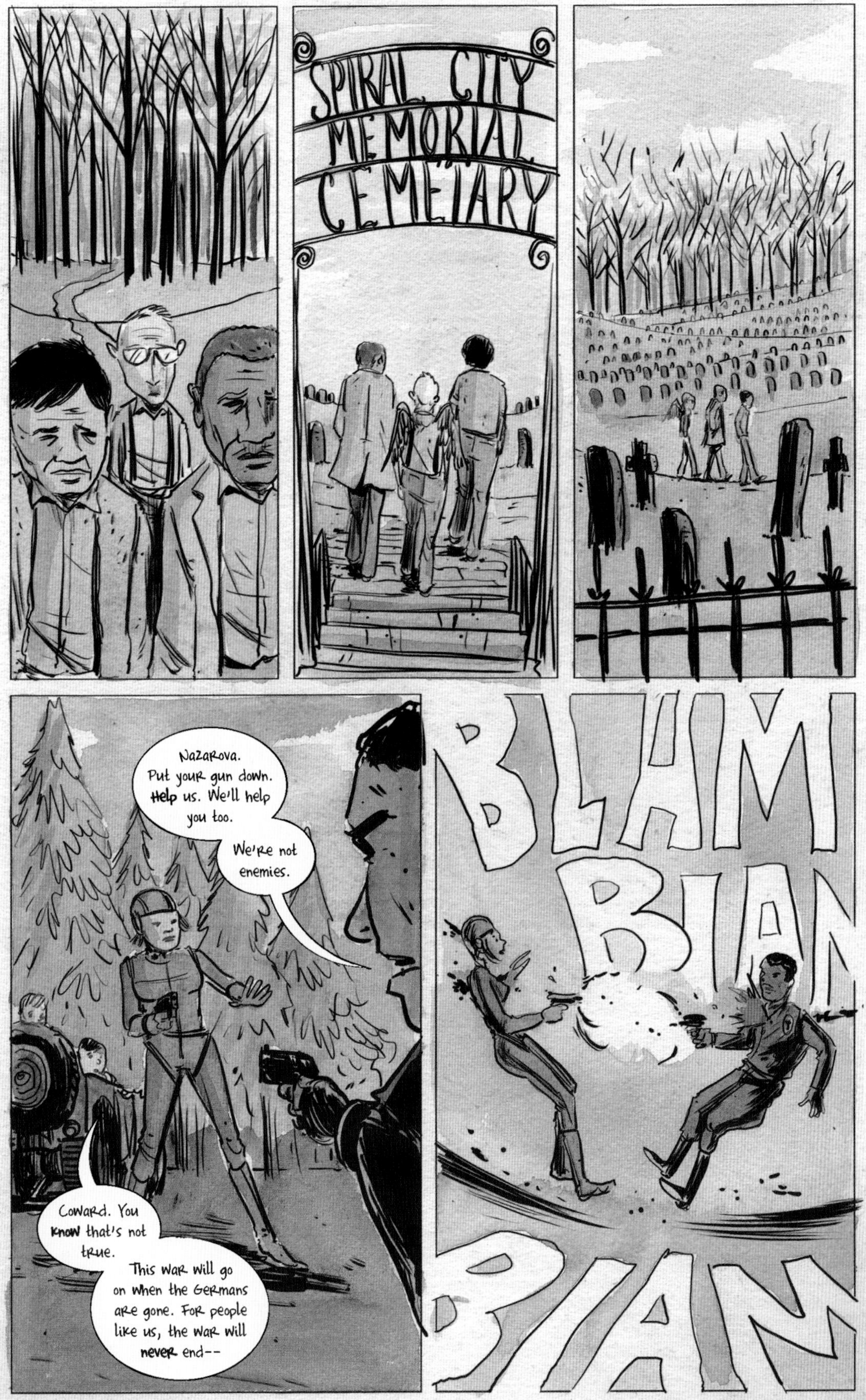
SPIRAL CITY MEMORIAL CEMETARY
Nazarova. Put your gun down. Help us. We'll help you too.
We're not enemies.
Coward. You know that's not true.
This war will go on when the Germans are gone. For people like us, the war will never end--
BLAM! BLAM BLAM

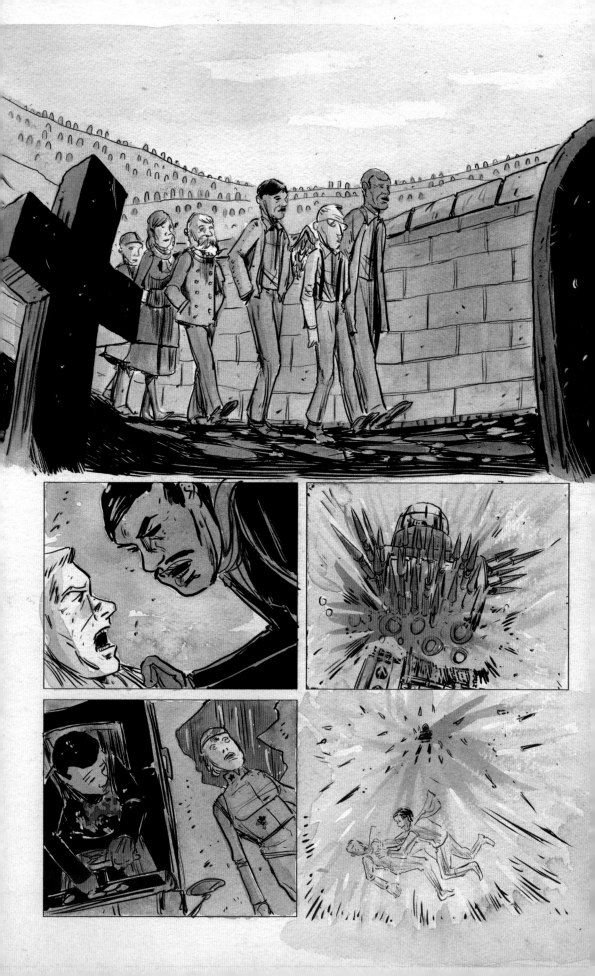

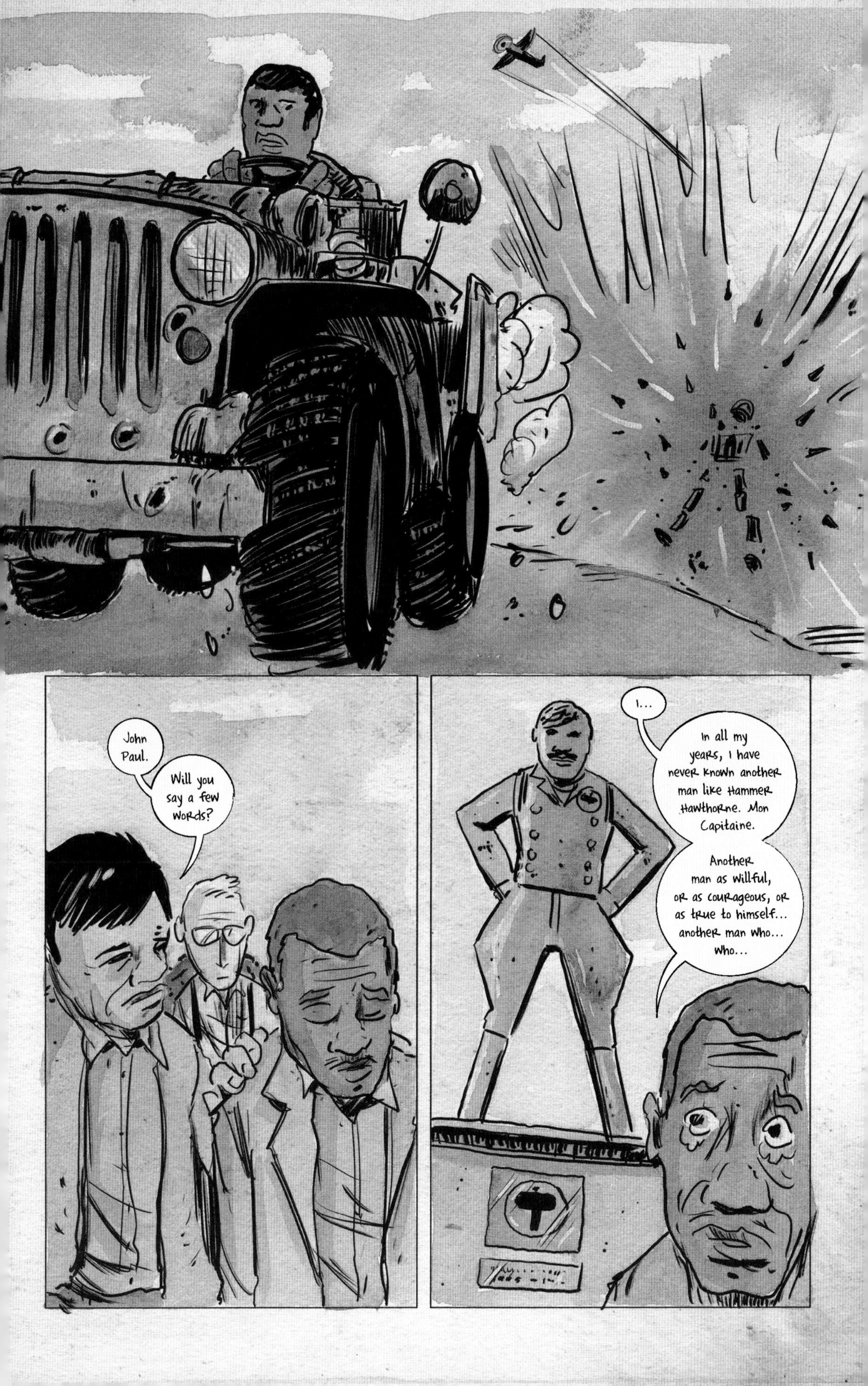
John Paul.
Will you say a few words?
I...
In all my years, I have never known another man like Hammer Hawthorne. Mon Capitaine.
Another man as willful, or as courageous, or as true to himself... another man who... who...

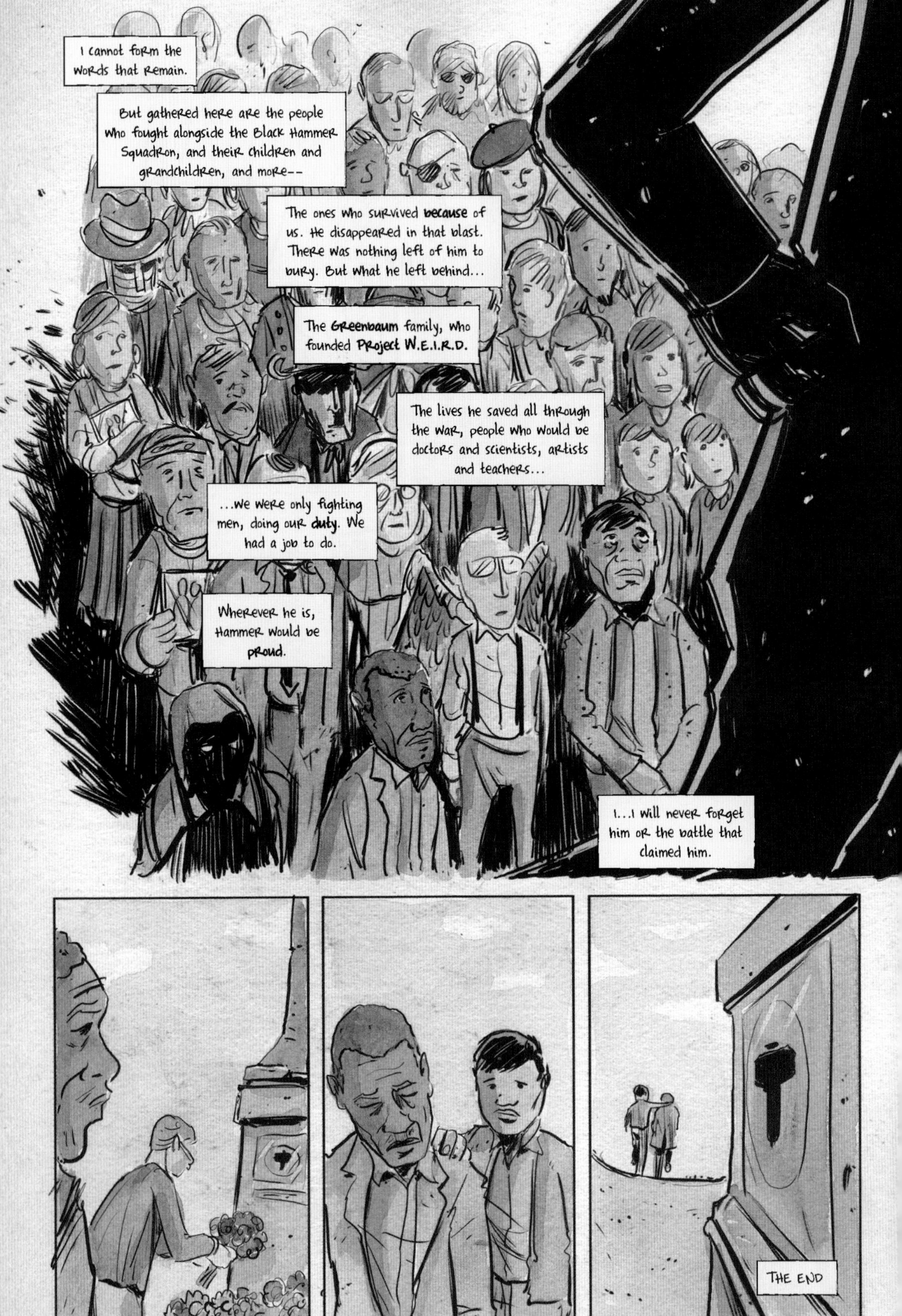
I cannot form the words that remain.
But gathered here are the people who fought alongside the Black Hammer Squadron, and their children and grandchildren, and more--
The ones who survived **because** of us. He disappeared in that blast. There was nothing left of him to bury. But what he left behind...
The **Greenbaum** family, who founded **Project W.E.I.R.D.**
The lives he saved all through the war, people who would be doctors and scientists, artists and teachers...
...We were only fighting men, doing our **duty**. We had a job to do.
Wherever he is, Hammer would be **proud**.
I...I will never forget him or the battle that claimed him.
THE END

BLACK HAMMER '45 SKETCHBOOK

Notes by Matt Kindt

PENCILS | INKS | COLORS

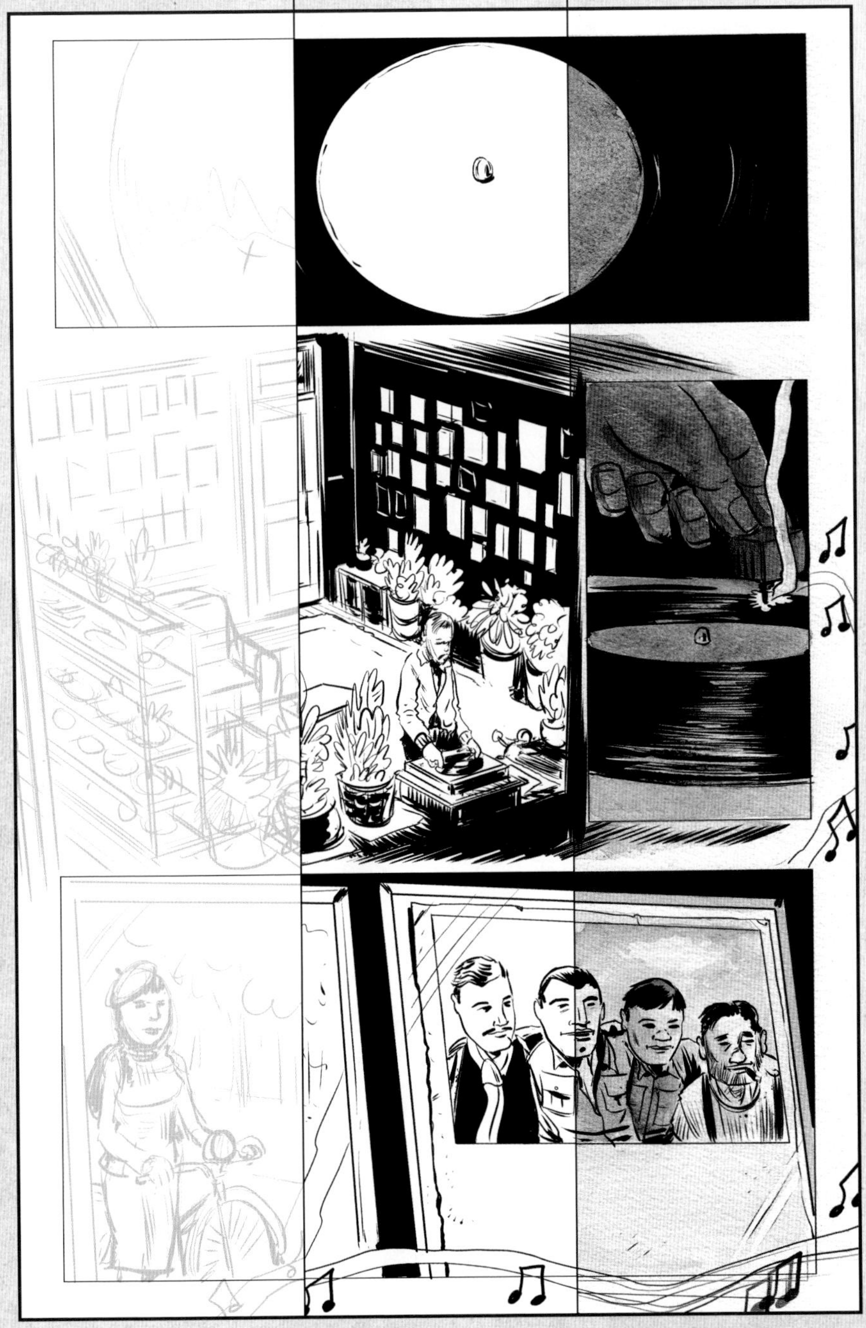

I was really excited to draw a bunch of World War II mech battles and airplanes, and when I got the script . . . it started out with an old guy, records, and a bunch of photos. But this scene really sets the tone, and the old record foreshadows the circular nature of the story really well. Let's just say . . . this wasn't the first page I drew for this issue.

PENCILS | INKS | COLORS

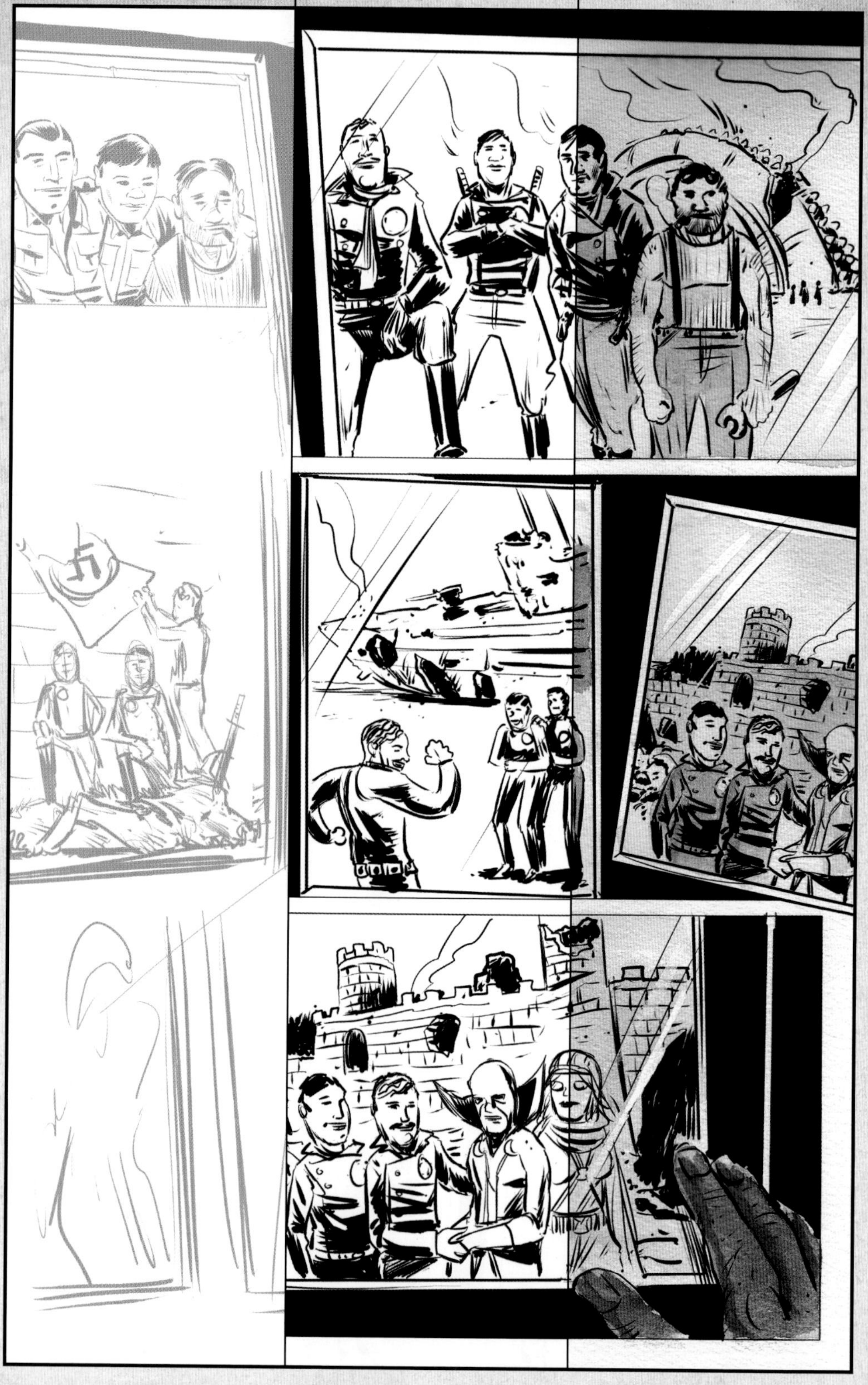

This page also had a lot of heavy lifting on it. All of the characters are present here, and we had to get a feel for their adventures and personalities in a small space and in black and white.

PENCILS | INKS | COLORS

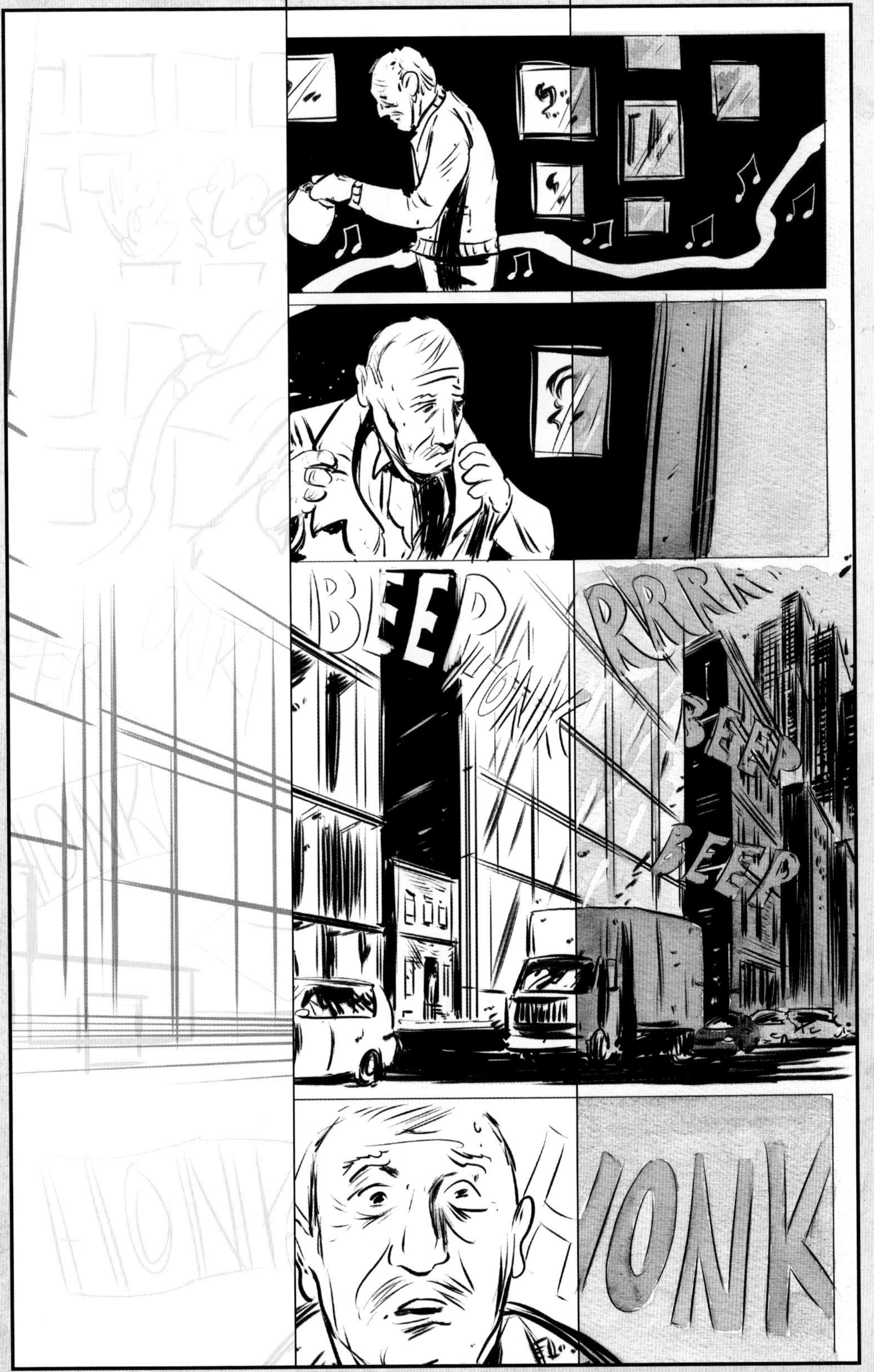
BEEP
HONK
BEEP
BEEP
HONK

This is where those early quiet pages pay off. Sharlene's use of color set all of this up so that the sound effects really pop on this page, and we get the feeling that our hero here is overwhelmed. Comics can't do sound—but it can do a really interesting job of visually representing the emotional impact of sound.

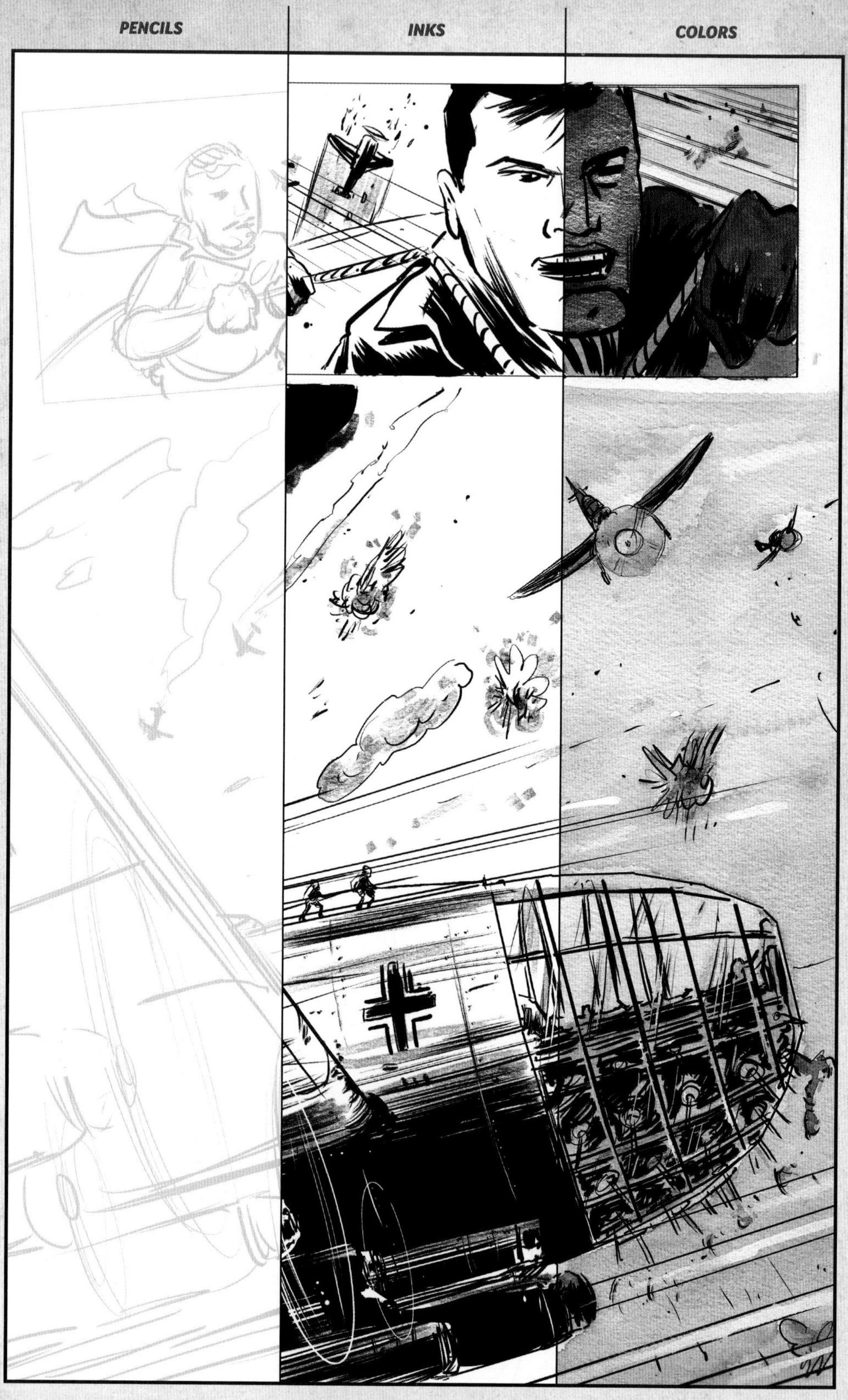
PENCILS
INKS
COLORS

Finally some action! I loved drawing this page and the big airplane. I used to put model planes together when I was a kid just so I could "crash" them and make dioramas with bullet holes and battle damage. Again, Sharlene picked her spots here to keep most of the page cool except for the action focal points.

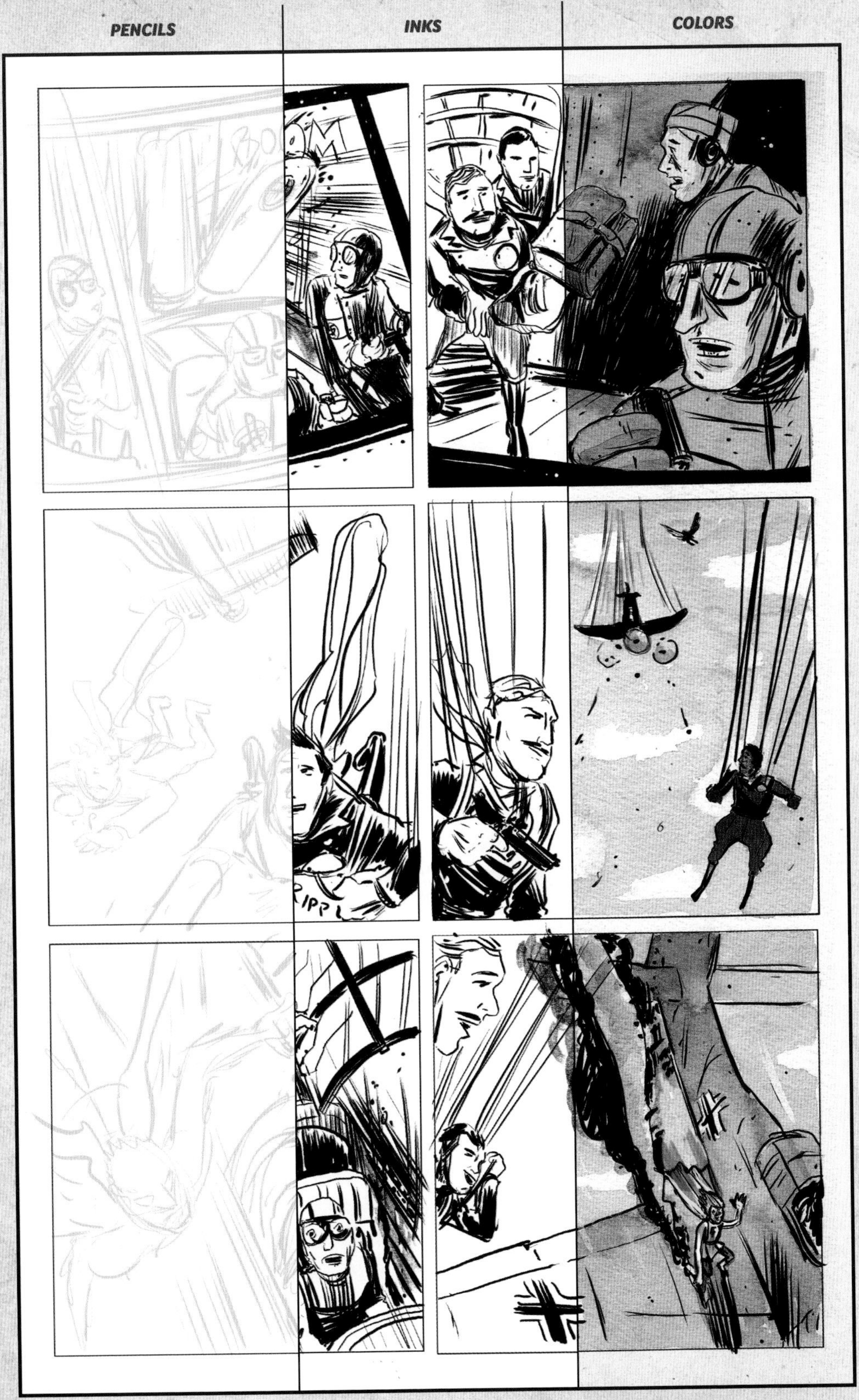
PENCILS
INKS
COLORS

Tough page here with a lot of action going on. I love a classic six-panel grid in the Kirby tradition. Relying on Sharlene's color again to draw attention to the bomb bag in panel 2 and another hero in that final panel that needed to pop.

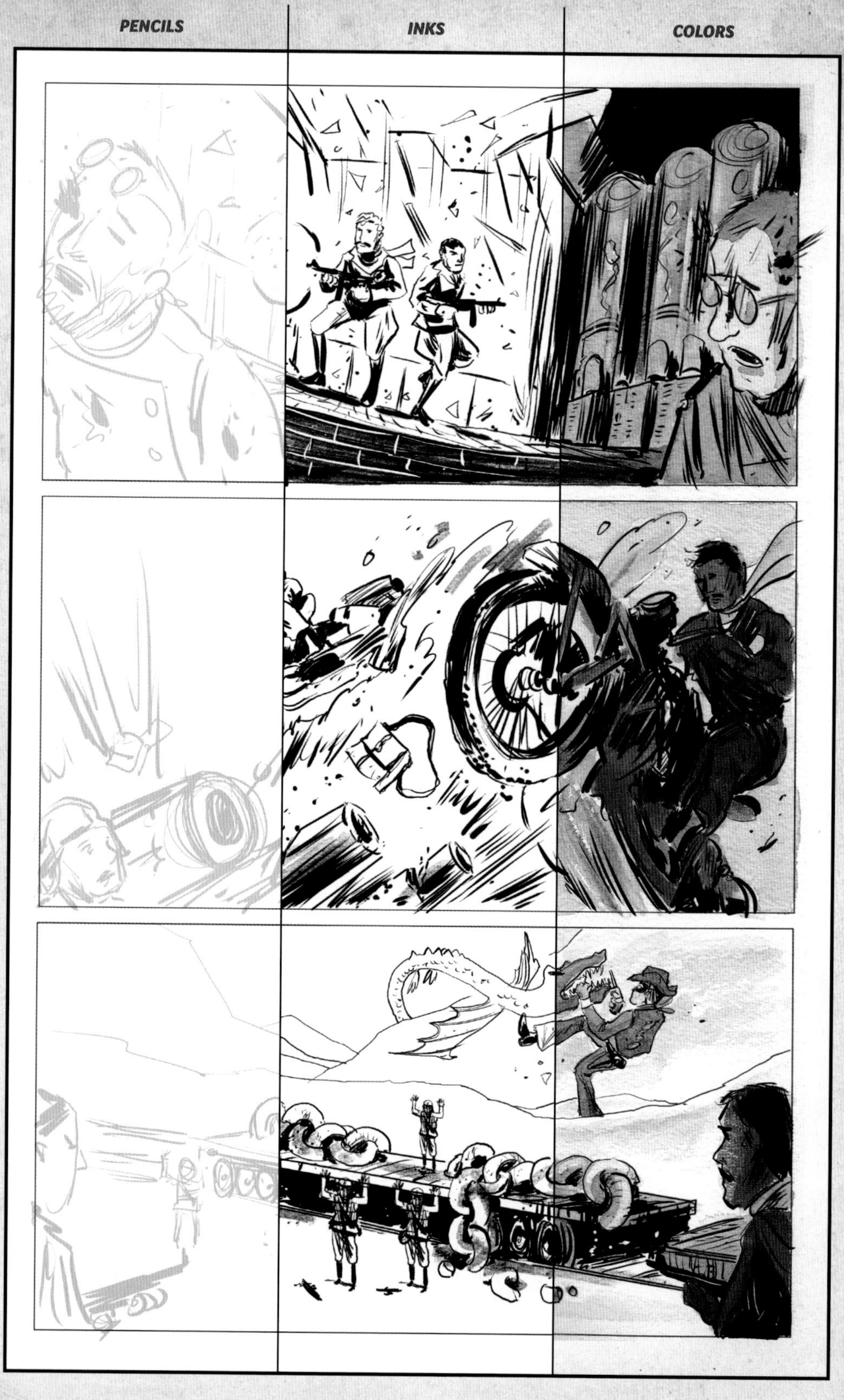
PENCILS
INKS
COLORS

I loved these montage pages. It was a chance for us to change locales and just show the single panel of most intense action. Panel 2 was inspired by *The Great Escape* and panel 3 was really tough—trying to get the sense of scale in the background wasn't easy.

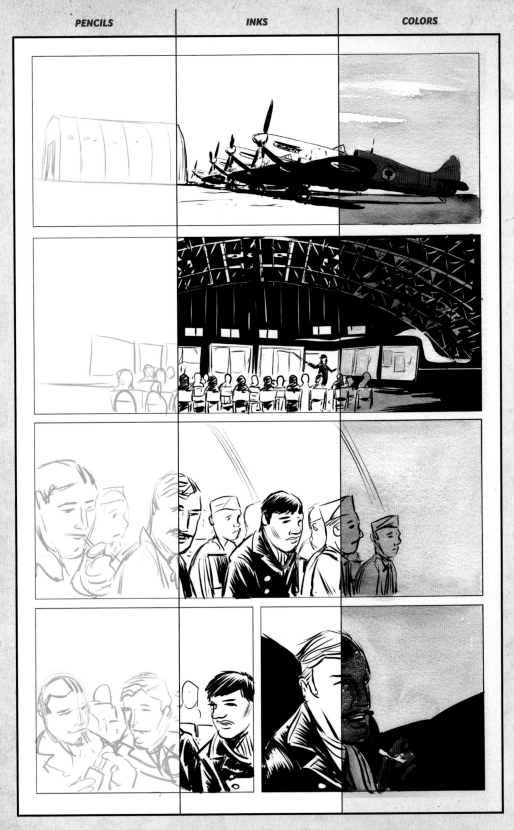

Alex Toth and his inking style was another big inspiration for this page and the entire series. I loved the way he would just block out big swaths of solid black and get the heavy weight of the planes and gear across.

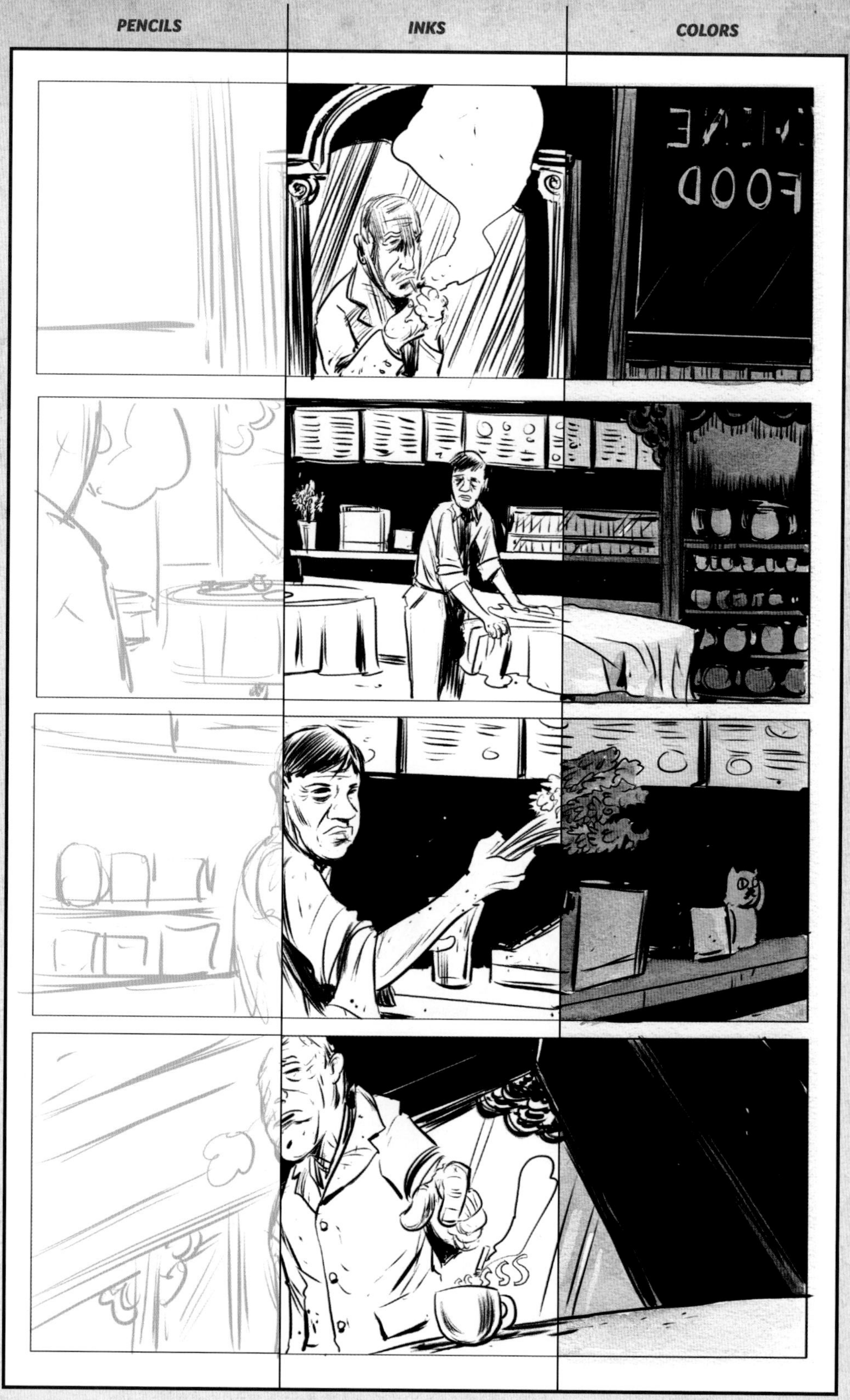
PENCILS
INKS
COLORS

I used a series of four-tier panels here to slow down the rhythm of the story in the present day. Sharlene's use of color here is great. Leeching the color from the characters and shifting it to the background . . . to contrast the colorful versions of these same characters in the flashbacks.

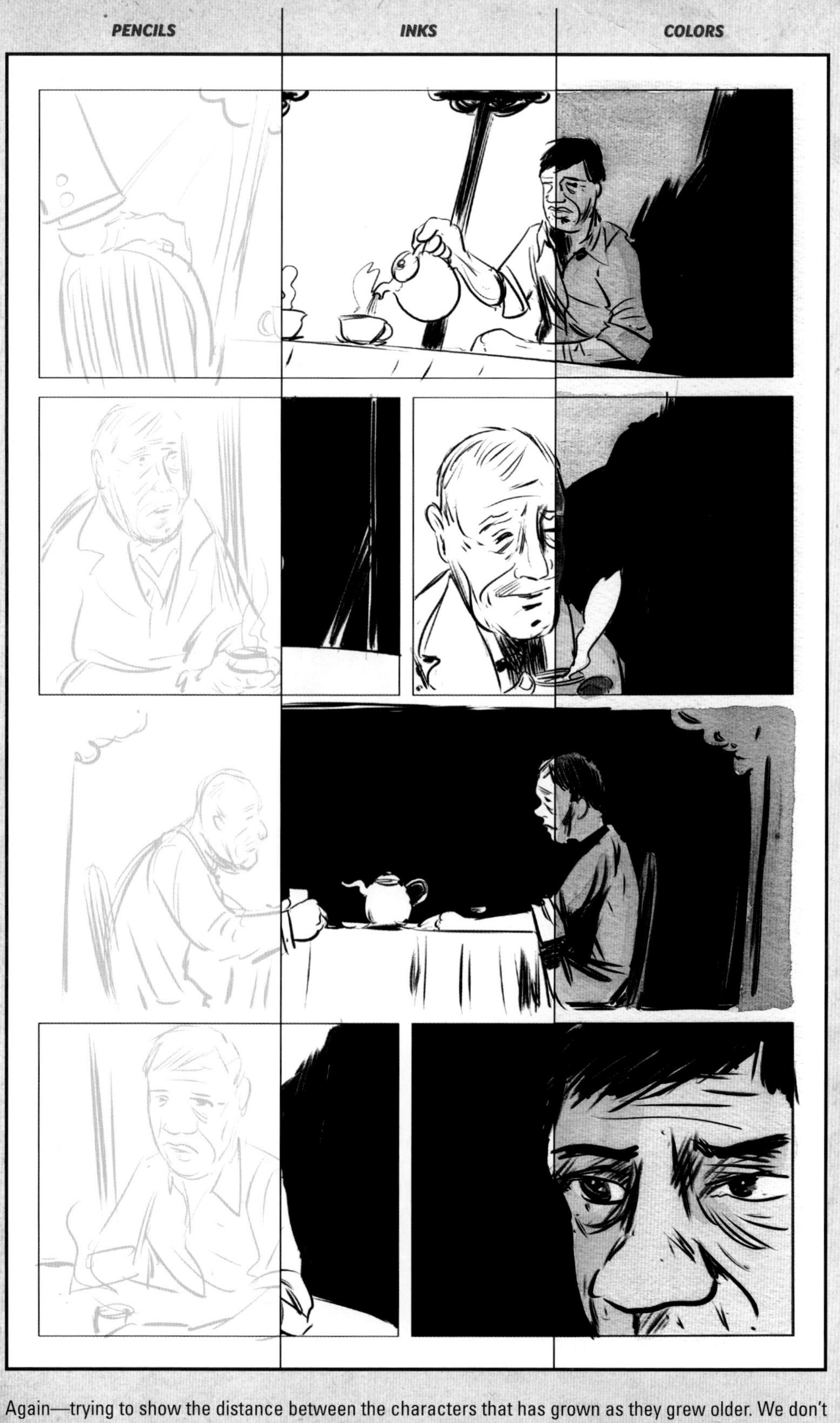
PENCILS
INKS
COLORS

Again—trying to show the distance between the characters that has grown as they grew older. We don't see them in the same shot together—until panel 3—with heavy black and the table distancing them. They are together but there is a lot of history between them.

PENCILS	INKS	COLORS

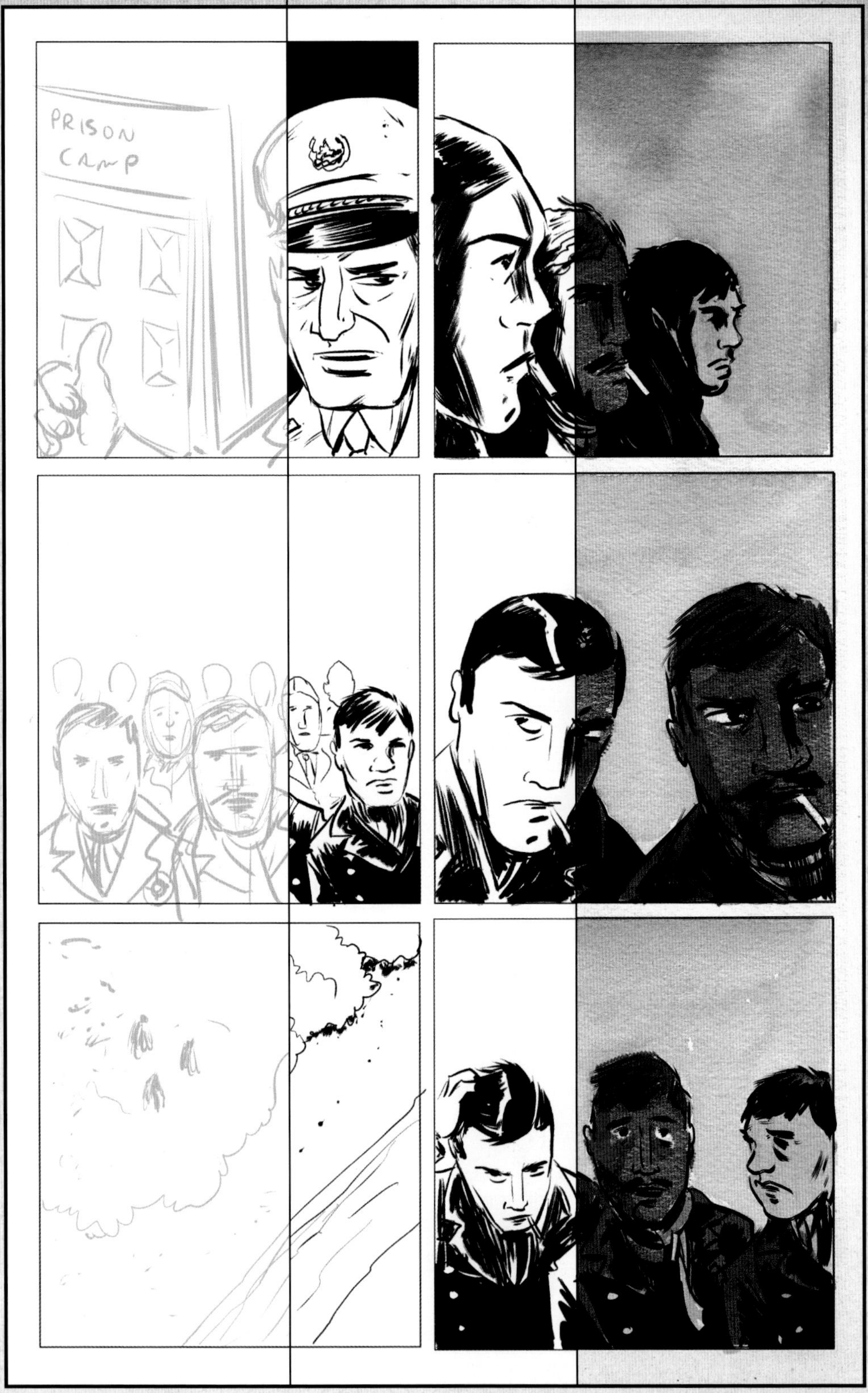
PRISON CAMP

Interesting side note—early on, Jeff and Ray decided to switch the race of the lead heroes. It seems obvious now, but it was such a good idea—it changes everything about the story without being overt. As a result, all the characters had to be re-colored for issue 1 and 2.

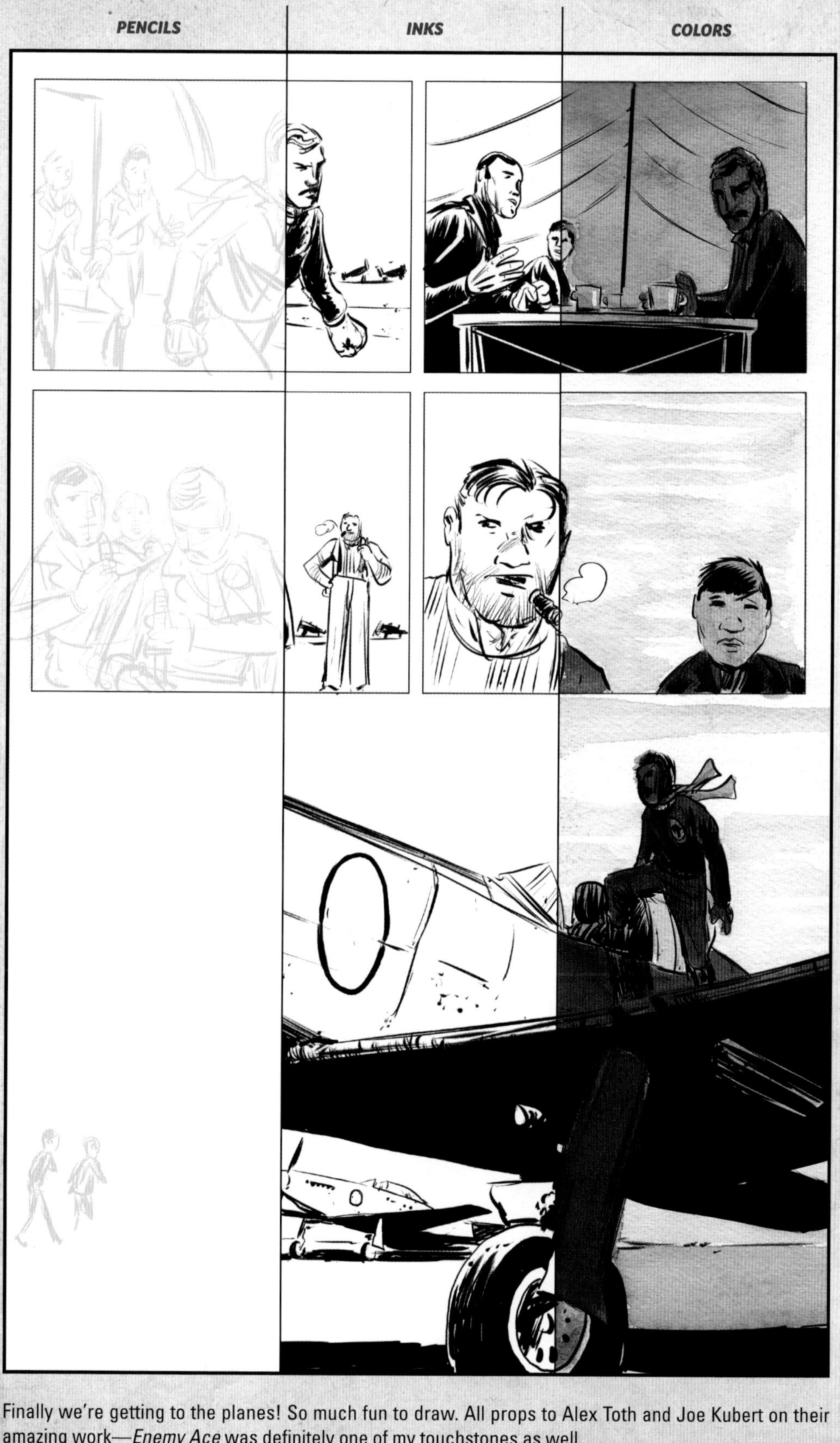
PENCILS
INKS
COLORS

Finally we're getting to the planes! So much fun to draw. All props to Alex Toth and Joe Kubert on their amazing work—*Enemy Ace* was definitely one of my touchstones as well.

PENCILS | INKS | COLORS

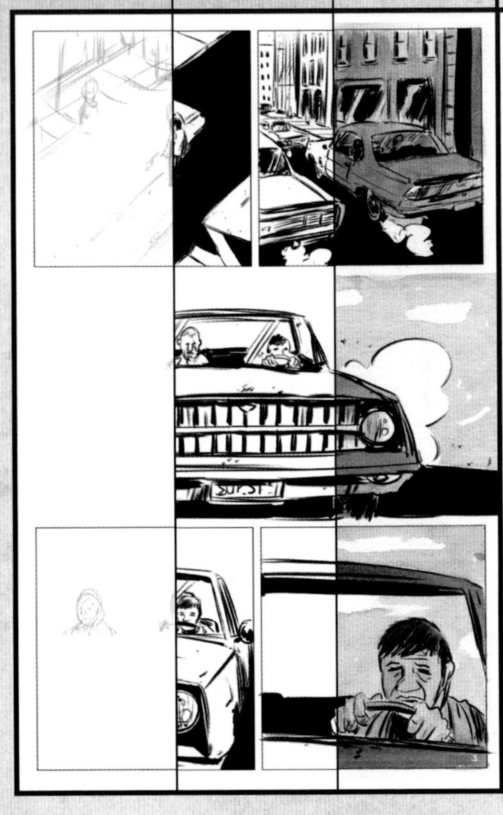

PENCILS | INKS | COLORS

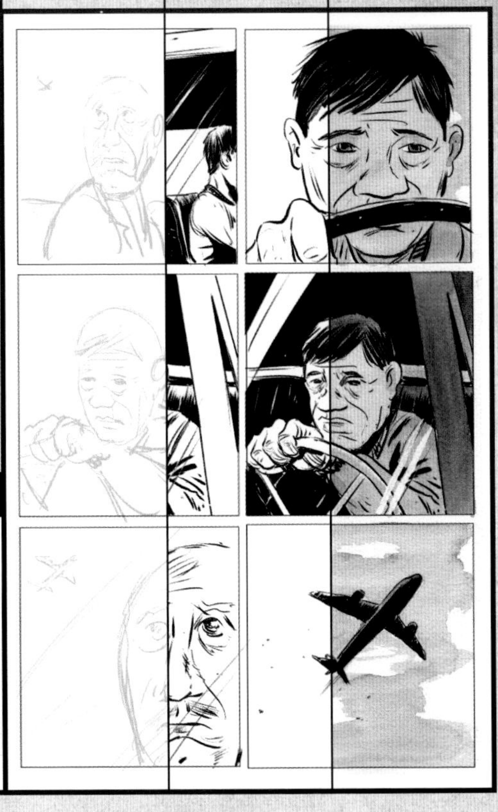

PENCILS | INKS | COLORS

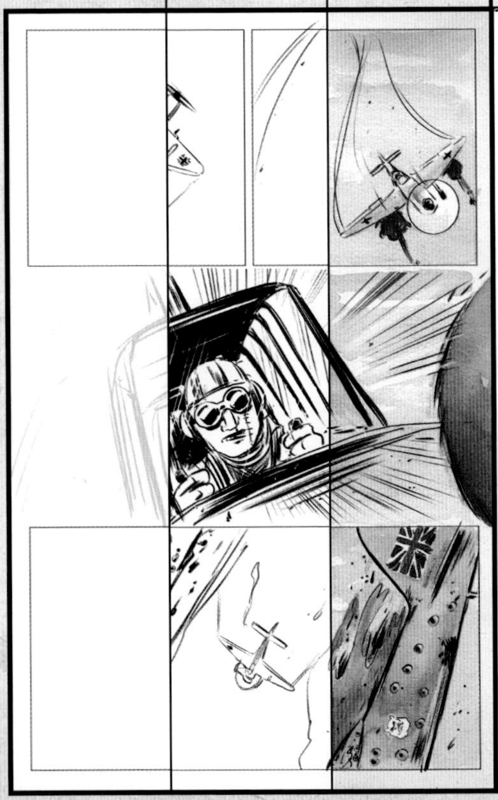

PENCILS | INKS | COLORS

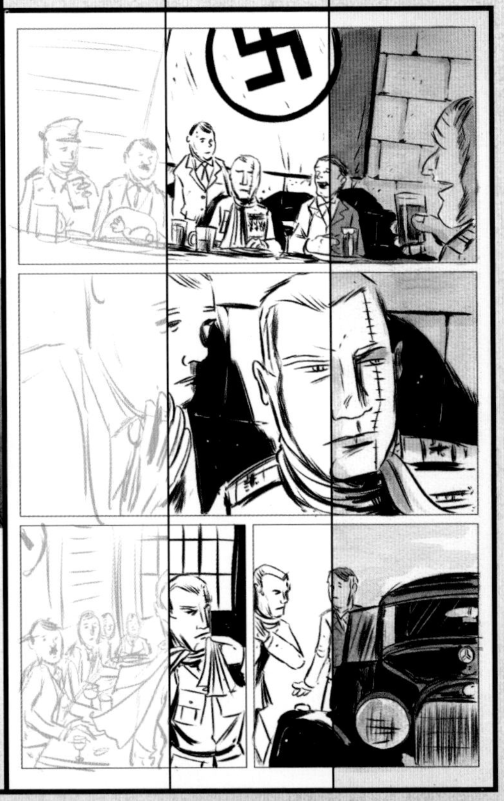

PENCILS	INKS	COLORS	PENCILS	INKS	COLORS

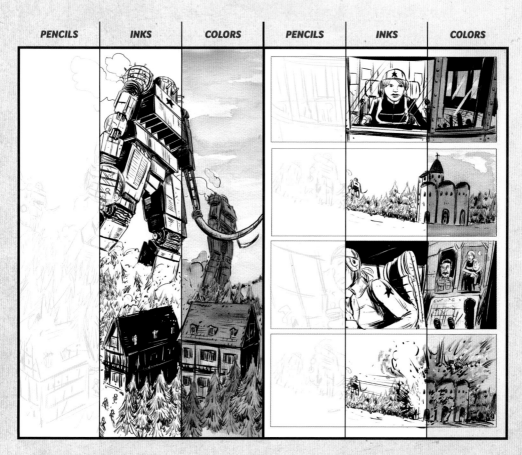

This is the heart of the story—or at least the stuff I was most excited to draw. I've literally **never** drawn a mech before and to design one on top of it . . . was a lot of work. I tried to evoke Russia but also make it something that could exist with World War II technology. The joints are supposed to be working like tank tracks and gears, and the head is inspired by the US bombers with their canopies and guns mounted inside of them.

PENCILS | **INKS** | **COLORS**

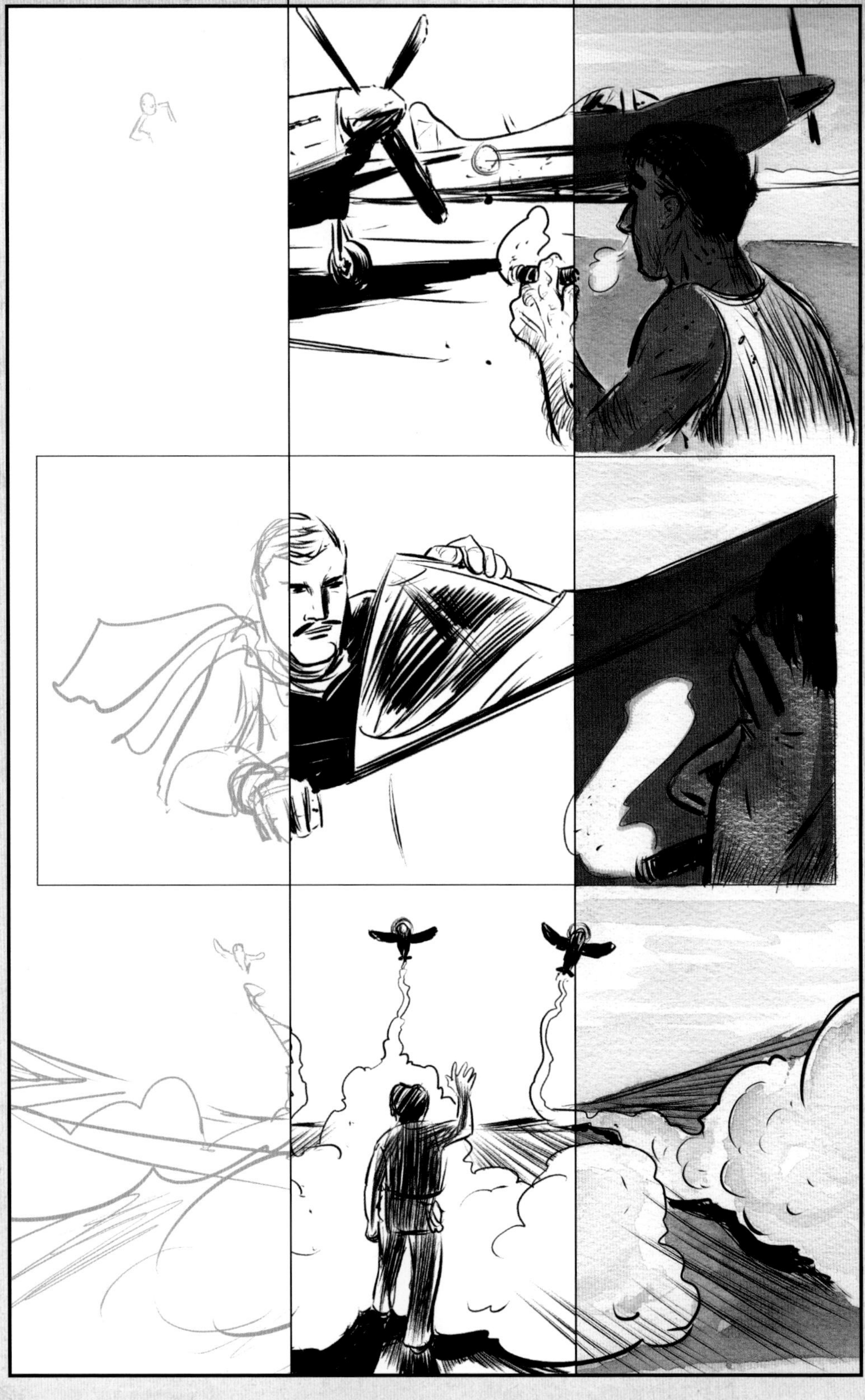

Bending the horizon here in the last panel to give the scene some movement—and keep it from being too static.

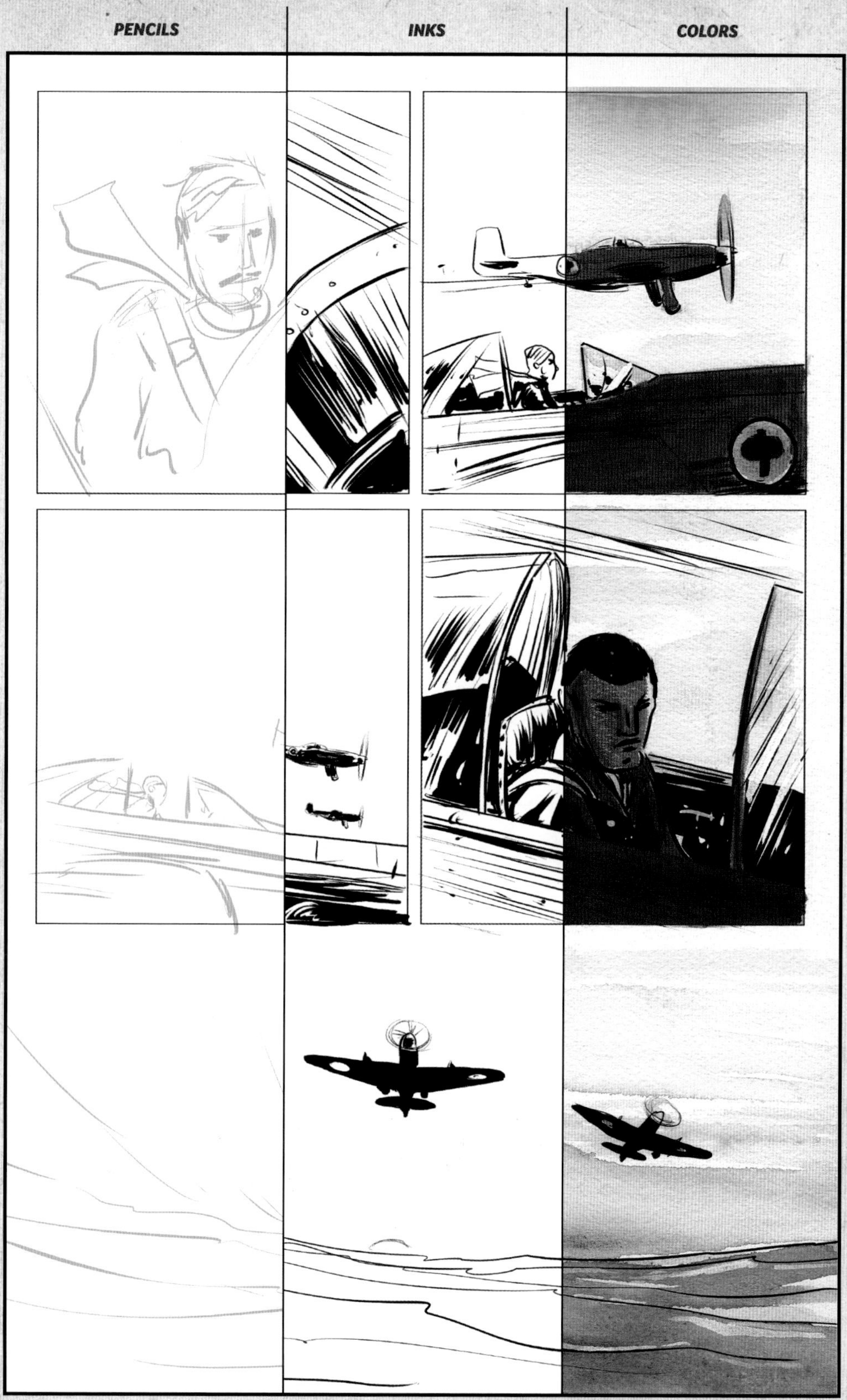
PENCILS
INKS
COLORS

Planes in silhouette is something that Toth and Kubert taught me. But what they didn't have is Sharlene doing the amazing sunsets in the background. I figured this out when I was working with Sharlene on *Dept. H.* The more empty space I can give her, the more magic she can work with watercolor. It's tough as a penciler/inker—the instinct is to fill all of the space with detail. It feels lazy sometimes. But the benefit is that color can do a lot of the heavy lifting if you just let it.

PENCILS | *INKS* | *COLORS*

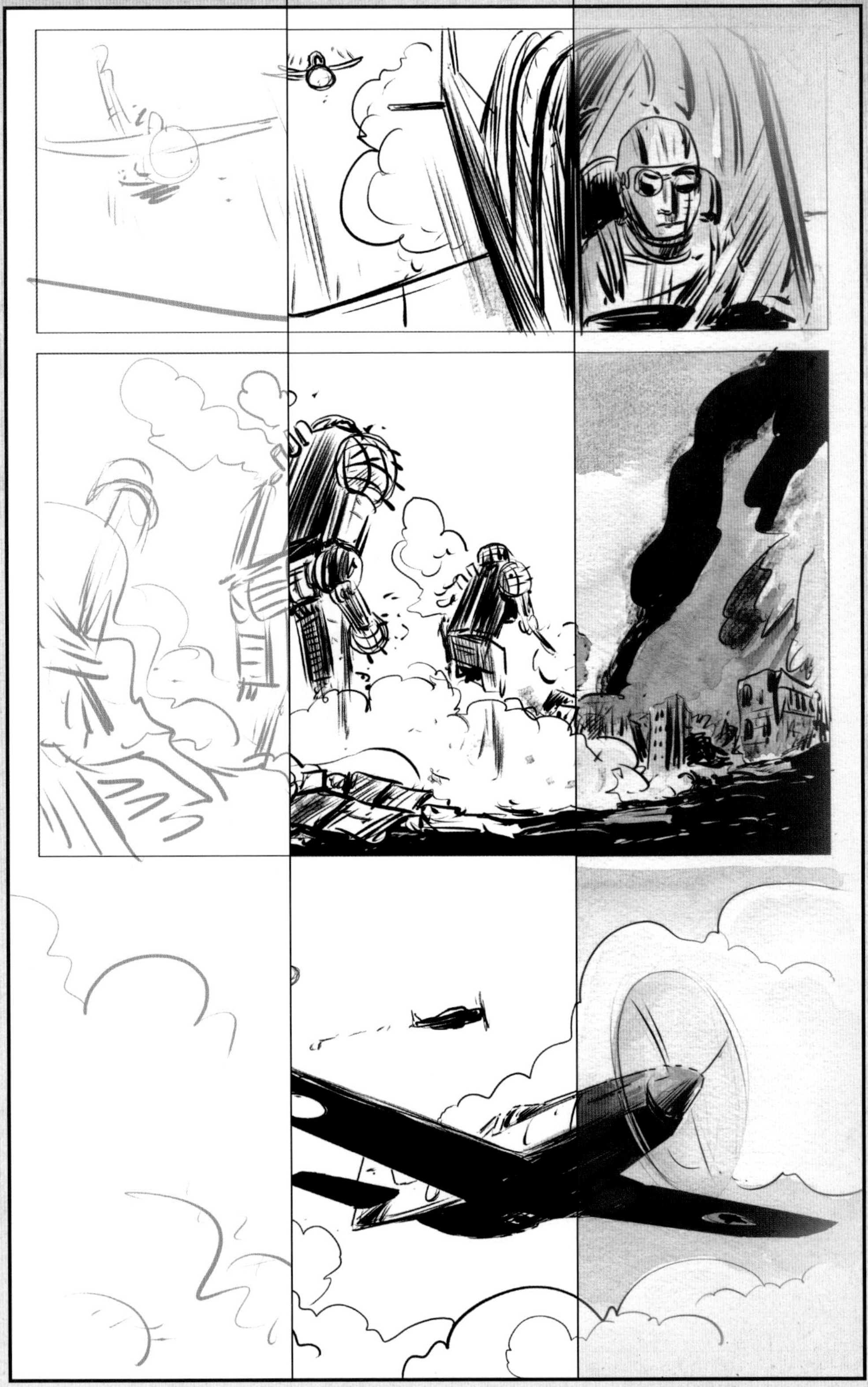

Mechs on the march! And airplanes flying. Some of my favorite pages. The great thing is that while I used a **lot** of reference for the early pages of this issue—I'd never drawn WWII airplanes before—by the end of this issue I could draw them without looking at anything. Practice makes perfect.

PENCILS	INKS	COLORS

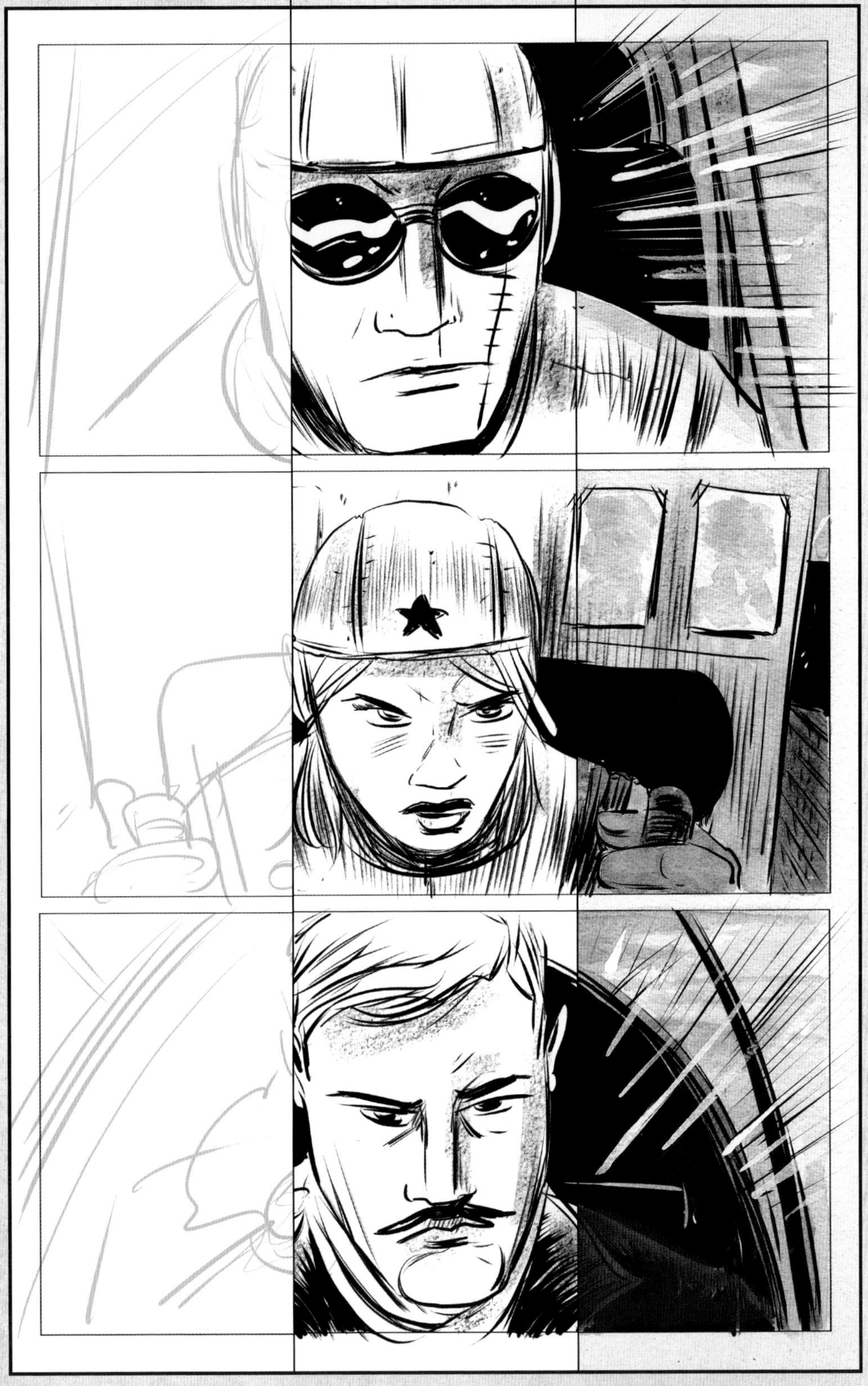

I love this story beat that the guys wrote. Quick shots of each of our main characters . . . all intent and intense . . . flying toward each other. Great way to end the issue.

PENCILS	INKS	COLORS

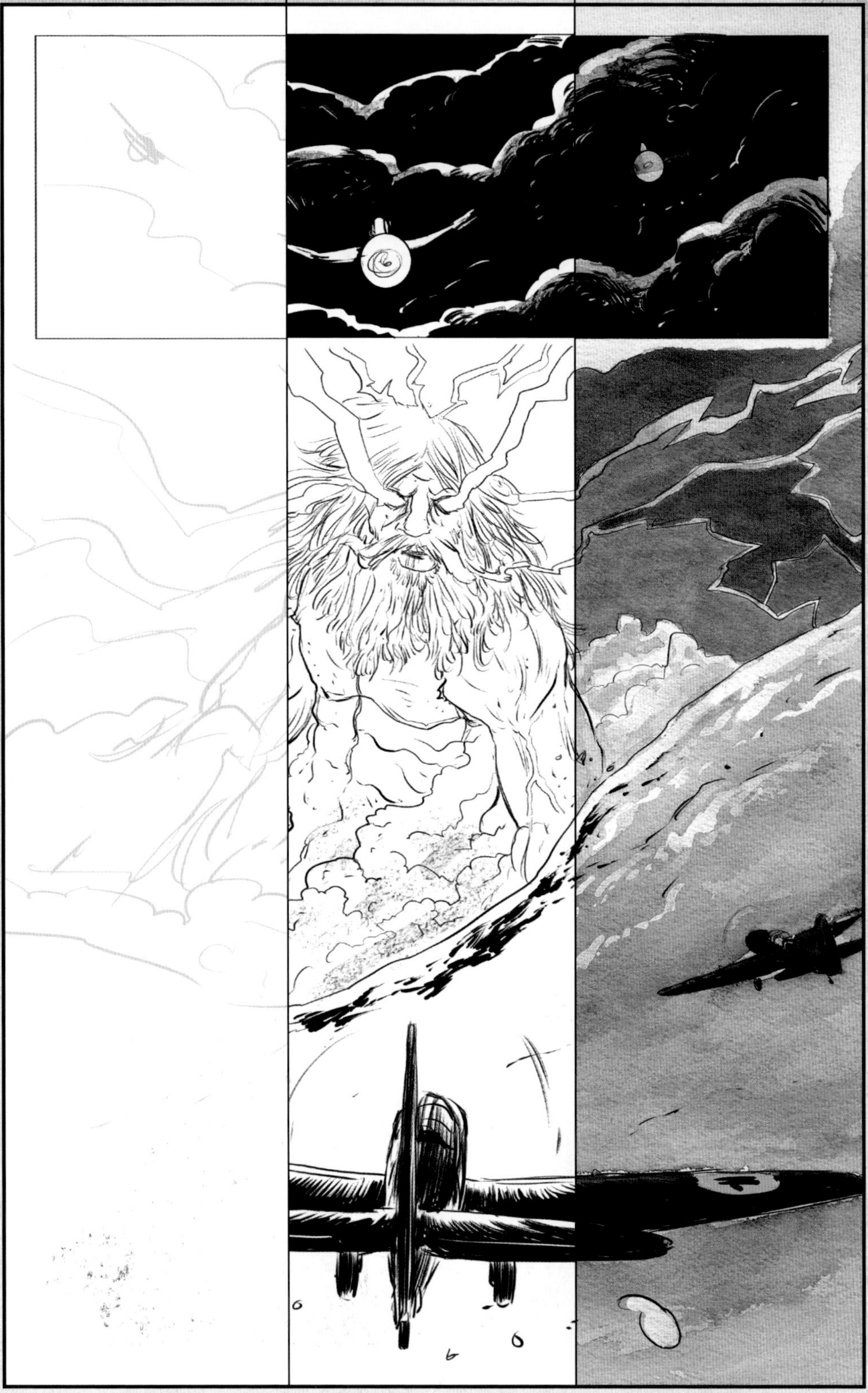

My favorite page of the issue. I felt like the top panel needed to be heavy—solid blacks—which doesn't give Sharlene anything to work with . . . but that heavy panel will be floating above the one below it—